The G[...]
Book Project

Celebrating

365

Days of

Gratitude

2014 Edition

The Gratitude Book Project
San Diego, Calif.
www.TheGratitudeBookProject.com
Support@TheGratitudeBookProject.com

Cover design by Becky Cohen

What Is
The Gratitude Book Project®
and Why Should You Care?

The Gratitude Book Project® started out as a seedling of an idea that quickly grew into a blossom that has become a whole blooming garden! A company mission to guide "would-be writers" to "published authors" turned out to be an ideal partnership with the subject of gratitude. It's a great way to get started in writing while celebrating the art of appreciation.

The first edition, *Celebrating 365 Days of Gratitude*, brought more than 300 people together to share their thoughts and experiences about the power of gratitude in their lives. In keeping with the spirit of expressing appreciation and giving back, net proceeds from national sales were—and continue to be—donated to charitable organizations.

From initial concept to *Amazon #1 Best Seller* in only three short months, The Gratitude Book Project® took on a life of its own. Before the first copy ever rolled off the presses, co-authors and those who missed out on the project were already asking for additional publications dedicated to the people and events in their lives deserving of special recognition—leading to *Celebrating Moms & Motherhood, The Best of Pets, A Celebration of Personal Heroes,* and *My Favorite Christmas Memory.* For The Gratitude Book Project® team, there was no turning back.

Silent or unexpressed gratitude won't hurt—but gratitude out loud and in motion can be a life-changing event. An entire network of like-minded individuals from around the world have come together as part of this project and made it clear that gratitude is alive and well and here to stay!

Readers and co-authors everywhere have made a commitment to themselves and each other to ask and answer a simple yet profound question every day: "What am I thankful for?"

**To find out more about The Gratitude Book Project® and
how you can join in the movement as a supporter or a co-author
visit TheGratitudeBookProject.com.**

The Gratitude Book Project®

is proud to donate its net proceeds
from retail sales to the following organizations:

Women for Women International

who supports women in war-torn regions with financial and
emotional aid, job-skills training, rights education,
and small business assistance so they can rebuild their lives

Feeding America

whose mission is to feed America's hungry
through a nationwide network of member food banks
and engage our country in the fight to end hunger

American Society for the Prevention of Cruelty to Animals (A.S.P.C.A.)

providing effective means for the prevention of cruelty to animals

The Gratitude Book Project® team
thanks you for being a part of supporting these
worthwhile charities.

For more information please contact
Support@TheGratitudeBookProject.com.

Want to be a published author?

Book writing, publishing and consulting services we provide include:

Write Your Book

Write a Book in a Weekend® is an online, virtual course that guides you in writing a "short and powerful" book in two days with pre-formatted templates, how-to information, and expert guidance. Find out more at WriteWithDonna.com.

Publish Your Book

Done for You™ Publishing Services offers everything from editing, proofreading, interior formatting, and cover design, while providing personal connection and top-rate customer service. Find out more at DoneForYouPublishing.com.

Get Answers to Your Book Writing and Publishing Questions

If you're struggling with what to write about or organizing your material, or if you're frustrated because you can't find answers about how the book publishing process works, get a "Big Breakthrough Session" with two-time award-winning author and publishing expert Donna Kozik. More at MyBigBreakthroughSession.com.

Get Started Now
**Download your free book planner at
www.FreeBookPlanner.com**

Get Your
FREE
Gratitude
Journal!

Get your journal at
www.TheGratitudeBookProject.com.

Contents

April

May

June

July

August

September

October

November

December

January

*"Thankfulness is the beginning of gratitude.
Gratitude is the completion of thankfulness.
Thankfulness may consist merely of words.
Gratitude is shown in acts."*

~Henri Frederic Amiel

January 1

Fresh Beginnings

I open my eyes to a new day before me—fresh and unspoiled with mistakes.

A hot shower to rinse off yesterday's dust. A clean breakfast plate to put anything on (and leave anything off) I wish. An open road unwinds in front of me; it is eager to take me wherever I want to go.

A clean pair of jeans. A smile for the next stranger. A blank page in a new journal.

The next thought.

The next feeling.

The next breath.

The next choice.

All are new to me in this very moment. I am grateful for fresh beginnings. There's one every moment of every day!

~ Donna Kozik

Donna Kozik *lives in San Diego and shows people how to Write a Book in a Weekend®. Find her at www.WriteWithDonna.com.*

January 2

Surrender

Iopened my mouth wide. What came out shocked me as much as it did everyone else. It was November 2012, and I was attending a workshop where the participants had to sing in front of the room. As a speaker, there was no fear. As someone who was diagnosed as tone deaf as a child and never took music lessons, there was both fear and dread. So I surrendered. Surrendering didn't mean giving up. Instead I went up to a Higher Power. I got out of the way and allowed it to be done for me. I stayed engaged in the activity but stopped conscious effort. What happened is nothing short of a miracle. The most operatic, hypnotic song emitted from me, mesmerizing the room. The leader encouraged me to explore being a singer. Less than a year later, I recorded my first song—a Sanskrit chant sung hymn-style. It is on my ecstatic meditation CD, *One*. I've been told my voice opens listeners' hearts and quiets their minds. Ironically, that's what I had to do to receive the gift of singing. My gratitude for being chosen to be sung by Spirit is immense. What gift might you receive if you surrendered?

~ Leah Grant

Leah Grant, *founder of Center for Illumination and Creator of Ecstatic Meditation, has been transforming lives for over 15 years as a Master Certified Coach, NLP practitioner, author, and speaker. Learn more at www.LeahGrant.com.*

January 3

Awesome God

Awesome God, Alpha and Omega, we give you thanks and bless Your name. You gave us Shimadoo and now you have taken him away. An Angel blessed and touched us for 15 months, rallying us together. Full of mirth, full of laughter. He chuckled often, and, mouth open, we could count his delicate milk teeth. He gazed into our eyes, read our delight, shared the love he brought, day in day out. His mirth was infectious. He gave us no cause to cringe. He took his tottering steps, kindling in us the awesome future he came to share. Before long, within a span of seven hours, on the fateful 21st of July, all this ceased. There came an unsettling restlessness that won't just go away. Our little Angel had run his course. His little steps faltered to embrace the heavenly lights, oblivious that he had not waved us goodbye. Shimadoo, our bundle of joy, your chuckle, lovely eyebrows, and memory live with us. We were blessed with your presence, little Angel, and we still hold you in our hearts. We'll carry your memory for the rest of our lives. Awesome Shimadoo.

~ *Lucy Irene Vajime*

Lucy Irene Vajime *is a faculty member and life coach in Benue State University, in north-central Nigeria. She is passionate about helping people connect to their inner power.*

January 4

The Backyard

We are blessed with a big old house in a small New England city. We live two blocks up from Main Street and two blocks down from the college campus and across the street from the public library. I love this house and its amazing architecture, but really the best part is our backyard. It's a place in the middle of the city in the middle of our lives where I can breathe. I love the yard in every season. After a blizzard filming our enthusiastic teenager jump off a rear porch roof into a bank of snow. Standing at the window observing the autumn colors weave a blanket of reds and yellows. Turning the compost pile over in the early spring to discover a furnace of hot rich soil ready to go. Watching our grandchildren run free. Sitting at a fire with one of our children, talking, laughing, and making things up about the clouds and the stars as if we were camping. Holding hands with my husband assessing the overwhelming project it can be to live in this life yet so grateful to be doing it together. Sharing it with others. Basking in the blessing of it all.

~ *Megan Paglia-Scheff*

Megan Paglia-Scheff, MS, DDIV, is a Ageless Grace Educator, author, raw foodie, photographer, healer, movement specialist, and educator offering Body Wisdom Coaching. Contact Megan through Facebook, RawYouniverse.com, NakedSophia.com, or MakingMagicEveryday@ gmail.com.

January 5

The Gift of Change!

My gratitude for change is enormous. On one hand I love the adventure, the thrill of something new and exciting, and on another, change challenges me. It stirs up deep wounds, fears, and old patterns I have gathered over my lifetime. As in nature, change is a great teacher. I've learned slowly but surely to embrace change and all that it brings. It is one of my trusty messengers, as my soul gently prods and pushes me to grow and expand. Change is everywhere and teaches many things; if only I have the eyes to see, the ears to hear, and an open heart to feel, recognize, and welcome those profound messages. The mystery I have learned, however, is the deepest part of me never changes; I am infinite. This is the paradox and the gift! Change gives me ongoing strength, inner power, freedom, and trust. I live my life now with a more open, loving heart and am eternally grateful for the connection to my true inner nature. So I welcome change with open arms every day. It is a god-sent gift I embrace.

~ Penelope Elfin

Penelope Elfin's early poor health sparked her journey into inner self-discovery. She works with individuals and groups, and is passionate about supporting others on their own inner personal journey.

January 6

Beyond the Realm

Each day begins and ends with silent acknowledgment and gratitude for the numerous gifts bestowed upon me. A comfortable home, a suitable car, amazing family, fabulous friends, and fulfilling work are high on the mental list along with good health. With a craving for knowledge and understanding of the world beyond what we know, it has been an emotional journey to recently be presented with the outstanding opportunity to have intimate communication with the other side. For those who are already spiritually aware, this may not seem to be such a huge revelation, but I will forever remember the overwhelming impact this occurrence had and will always be in awe of the unconditional love that surrounds us. I am truly grateful to those people who took my hand for this part of my journey. In our unstable world, it is my wish to touch the lives of those less fortunate, less knowledgeable, and less appreciative to help turn greed into gratitude, knowledge into wisdom, and insecurity into love.

~ *Elizabeth Collett*

Elizabeth Collett *is a self-employed dance instructor. She has taught in China, the United States, and Australia. Her instructional DVDs sell worldwide. Learn more at www.LineDance.com.au.*

January 7

Email Marketing to No's

I am grateful for the power of email marketing. I use email marketing to keep in touch with potential clients. This strategy is not only effective, but also relationship-building. While this form of communication is widespread, I don't take this tool for granted. Recently, an ideal client and I carefully conversed about her sales team's needs. We identified the gaps. I sent a proposal and felt sure we were aligned. Then the call came: "No, we decided not to." In my mind, she became the No-Go CEO! While I encourage others not to take "no" personally, I was naturally disappointed. Nevertheless, over the next 18 months, the No-Go CEO opened and read my monthly ezine articles. One day, 45 minutes after emailing my leadership checklist, the steady nurturing paid off. "We need a leadership development program," the No-Go CEO said. We resumed our discussion, this time finalizing a significant contract. The project was won with the culmination of timing, nurturing, and consistent communication. I am grateful to use this powerful system to continually connect to my potential clients. When I hear "no," I am correct to consider it may simply mean "not right now."

~ *Barb Girson*

Barb Girson, *direct-selling expert, sales coach, and speaker/trainer, helps companies, teams, and entrepreneurs gain confidence, get into action, and grow sales. For sales tips and articles, reach Barb at www.MySalesTactics.com.*

January 8

The Body Wise

I am very grateful for the wisdom of my body, and how it speaks through me and to me. Symptoms such as hunger pangs or fatigue are easy to decipher. Noticing early signals, I can take better care of myself. With adequate rest and good, healthy food, I am much happier and my life flows so much more smoothly. Other symptoms, such as tension in my body, may signal when I'm afraid of something, or when I'm out of alignment with my values or who I am at my core. I noticed daily tension in my body years ago while working a job that was no longer right for who I had become. That tension allowed me to ultimately trust it was time to leave that job. Likewise, the sense of expansion I noticed in my body when I visited New Mexico a few years ago, enabled me to trust a move to New Mexico as a next step in my journey at that time. Appreciate and pay attention to the finely tuned "instrument" known as your body. What wisdom is it sharing with you?

~ Nancy Farris

Nancy Farris is an empowerment and creativity coach, author, and consultant living in New Mexico. She is passionate about helping others unleash their true genius. Visit Nancy at www.NancyFarris.com.

January 9

A Cat Called Biggie

I live in the country and shortly after we moved in, the homeless cats started to come. It's like they knew they would be looked after. Big Ears was one of those homeless cats. "Biggie," as he was affectionately called, was special. He followed me everywhere. After his first year with me, he started to show signs of being sick. I tried everything to help him. Unable to take him in the house in case he infected the indoor pets, I made the barn warm and cozy for him and his friends. I installed heat lamps, beds, and blankets. He seemed to know that I was trying my best to help him. But sadly, this past winter, Biggie passed away. I believe that animals are our guardian angels on earth. They come into our lives when we need them, and leave when their job is done. In the midst of the hard work and frequent heartache at the sanctuary, a little cat named Big Ears taught me about unconditional love and that guardian angels really do exist. For that I am truly grateful.

~ *Nancy Galway*

Nancy Galway *is a social worker and writer living in rural Quebec. She shares her passions with her husband, 14 huskies, 10 crazy cats, and a cat sanctuary. Learn more at www.YourCopingCoach.com and www.SnowAngelsSanctuary.com.*

January 10

Live, Laugh, Love!

Who would you *be* if you knew you couldn't fail? How would you live differently, laugh more often, or love unconditionally? When I am not *be*ing myself, I know my friends will help me get out of my own way. They give me the kick in the pants or the loving nudge that challenges me to check out who I am *be*ing. I'm particularly grateful to my friends for speaking up and helping me see opportunities that I am closed off to. They help me remember to *be* who I really am, let go of my blazing independence from time to time, and, have enough foresight to certainly let a gentleman get me a glass of water. Who knew *that* glass of water could lead to love? Thanks to my friends' keen insight to knowing the true me, I have today forever engrained in my heart as the day I got to be on an inspirationally fun first date with the man of my dreams, that to this day feels like we are still on. Who do you want to contact today to show your gratitude for? Remember to live well, laugh often, and love from inside out!

~ *Michelle Wartgow, CPC*

Michelle Wartgow founded Live Your Cause Coaching and has a big goal: to help people get out of their own way—and take action to designing themselves and their businesses from the inside out.

January 11

Reawakening My Creative Pulse

Last year I began to work with a gifted coach about creating the next generation of my company. Much to my surprise, she gave me art assignments to expand my thinking. I began by creating a journal in which to write. I named it "Beaucoup de Possibilities," and filled it with photos and words from magazines that resonated with me. Once completed, I just let the pages fall open and would then write about whatever topic the images prompted. The next journal I created was one in which I painted the pages, providing me with boldly painted surfaces on which I wrote about ideas for my business and life in general. I have gone onto many different artistic projects, both handcrafted and computer-generated. I am grateful for the reawakening of my creative pulse. I once again have a childlike pleasure in creating for the simple fun of it—no grades or scores, just a playground for expression. This creative pulse now beats throughout my life—professionally and personally. My ideas for my business have grown as my art projects have expanded, showing me that creative expression in one area flows joyfully into another.

~ Ann Potts

Ann Potts *specializes in transformative leadership development, leading workshops and offering private coaching on how to be an authentic and courageous leader. Reach her at Ann@ExecutivePerformanceFuel.com.*

January 12

Thanks for Second Chances!

There is a haunting TV ad for a pharmaceutical drug intended to prevent repeat heart attack occurrence. In this ad an empty gurney follows closely behind a person wherever that person goes. The gurney, of course, invokes an image that there might not be a second chance, while the words of the ad underscore the value of the drug for attaining a second chance at life. As I've had heart concerns, I can relate to this ad. Most of us can relate to the value of second chances—more opportunities to get it right—not just in health, but in the fullness of our lives. I like the idea of being human, and I'm grateful for having second chances (and more) in all phases of our lives. We get chances for re-dos. We get chances for relearning. We get chances to forgive and to be forgiven. We get chances to move forward. We get new chances to grow and to give back. I'm so grateful that all we have to do is to say "yes" when that choice shows up for us. The action steps are ours to take, and our re-dos are ours to embrace!

~ *Claire Knowles*

Claire Knowles, *formerly a career HR/labor relations manager, loves to work with leaders and solve people problems. She's a two-time Amazon best-selling author, acclaimed speaker, and consultant. Learn more at www.LightsOnBook.com and www.CanYouSeeThemNow.com.*

January 13

Nearly Narcoleptic

My life is crazy and full of activities; isn't yours, too? Sometimes a week goes by and it feels like a lifetime. I can feel nearly narcoleptic, sleepwaking through it all. Aimlessly in the dark, alone. Thank God for my True Blue Friends (BFFs) who check in on me and leave loving messages. "Hey, haven't heard a peep out of you for three days. What's up? Are you okay?" I am so grateful to be held in their minds and hearts.

~ Ann Bennett

Ann Bennett *is a marketing messenger, and creative muse for entrepreneurs and small business owners. She teaches how to stand out and "market like Madonna." Learn more at www.AnnBennettMarketing.com.*

January 14

High Expectations

Like most kids, I thought my parents were tough. They had strict rules and high expectations; all it seems I ever heard were "No, you can't do that" and "Your grades need to be higher." I just rolled my eyes and complained to my friends about how unfair my parents were. But because of my parents, I graduated as a valedictorian and received a full scholarship to college. When I decided to major in music, my parents thought that was great; they always supported my musical training. Looking back, they had been encouraging me all along, cheering me on at every diving meet, clapping in the audience of every choir concert, and giving me opportunities to try new things. I appreciate that my parents instilled in me a work ethic that motivated me to excel. They knew I could be successful, and their expectations urged me to do better. This assertive prodding was combined with the capacity to ultimately let me pursue my own path in life. The integration of these qualities led me to develop my own high standards and pride in accomplishments, helping form me into who I am today. For this, I am eternally grateful.

~ *Laura Williams*

Laura Williams *is a high school music teacher in San Diego. She tries to give her students the same combination of expectations and encouragement that she received at home.*

January 15

Signs of Life

My bedtime ritual: saying "thank you" for three things that day, a gratitude practice started 18 months ago. But, what does it take to be in a state of appreciation, of thankfulness? Resilience arose as a response. My well of resilience is supported by trust—in the world and in myself. Having an active gratitude practice reinforces my resilience and builds belief/trust in my ability to be resilient. Gratitude practice also takes me out of myself. When I'm lonely it provides an instantaneous connection with the world. When my mom died—and my dad 15 months prior—sparrows and cardinals were a reminder that I was still alive. Daily I was thankful for their songs. I owe my parents my deepest gratitude; they had and passed on this deep reservoir into which I dip. What makes you smile? What are you in awe of? What seemingly small thing are you profoundly grateful for? Give gratitude to yourself for who you are, not only what you've done. Give gratitude to others; everyone wants to be noticed and appreciated. Give gratitude to something in nature. Give...and you will receive expanded spaciousness and joy in your heart, mind, body, and soul.

~ Stephanie Legatos

Stephanie Legatos *is a color and wardrobe consultant, and a career coach. She helps people express their authenticity and passion through their work and their wardrobe. Learn more at www.VisibleYou.biz.*

January 16

Pennies from Heaven

Over the years in my own business, I have noticed a very curious thing. Whenever I am worried about money, as solopreneurs do from time to time, I'll find a penny in the street, sometimes more than one. A few days later, a new client will appear. Those pennies in the street make me smile with anticipation for the new business that is just around the corner. I am very grateful for the good news they bring. But, they are not the only messages I am thankful for. The same mysterious force that drops pennies at my feet also arrives just in time with other information. There was the time I was about to chuck a doctor's appointment again for a mole that was probably nothing. Good thing a little voice said, "You must go today," for you would be reading someone else's entry here if I had chosen not to go. This cosmic messenger service works in all our lives. We just have to pay attention. I'm grateful for these special deliveries and for the expanded awareness that helps me to recognize them when they come. How about you?

~ *Mariette Edwards*

Mariette Edwards *is an executive coach specializing in positioning, packaging, and prepping high achievers to win a job, a promotion, or new business. Learn more at www.DoYourGreatWork.com.*

January 17

Never Give Up!

Never give up! At age 22 the thought of losing my dream of becoming a dancer on the Broadway stage was never something I could have imagined. Several auto accidents and a fall into a sinkhole would change my life forever. Damage to my neck and lower back would squash my dream of becoming a professional dancer. Going through years of therapies, surgeries, and not being able to walk for months at a time, I've learned the true meaning of being "happy to be alive." God has spared my life on numerous occasions and gave me the strength to carry on. He has given me a new calling. I became a fashion stylist so I could help people with their self-esteem issues, and help them feel wonderful about themselves and give back to others in the community. Twenty-five years later, I am grateful that I am still able to walk, for my sister Mary who gives me love and support all these years, and for my friends who never gave up on me and continued to encourage me. I am grateful for my mother and father who always said to me when growing up, "Never give up." Thank you.

~ *Dawn-Marie Mutell*

Dawn-Marie Mutell *is a wardrobe stylist, accessory designer, and philanthropist. Get in touch at www.LetsShopInYourCloset.com.*

January 18

Ahead of Her Time

My great-grandmother (or Great G., as I like to call her) is 98 years old. I've been lucky enough to not only grow up with her in my life, but really be able to get to know her in my adult life. What a remarkable woman she is. A single mother of two daughters, she packed up their life in Kansas and moved out to California, a dream she'd had for years. When the United States became involved in WWII, she found work down in the shipyards as a welder, becoming a true Rosie the Riveter. She saved her money and bought a house in Long Beach, a house that she has resided in for 67 years—and counting. My Great G. is a true example of the American dream, and a woman way ahead of her time. She has shown me that hard work and honesty are what pay off in life. I'm grateful for the time I've had with her. She may not with me much longer, but her legacy will live on and will continue to teach me every day what it means to be a hard worker, an honest person, and a stand-out woman.

~ *Tracy LaMar*

Tracy LaMar *graduated from Cal State Sacramento with a BA in theatre arts. She lives in Southern California, where she is pursuing her dream of opening her own educational theatre company.*

January 19

Incredible Blessings of Faith

Faith is the inner core, the foundation for my grateful journey through life's hills and valleys. Faith is one of God's most incredible gifts, and I have been showered with many over the course of my life.

- Faith that I could have children who would become wonderful adults any one would be proud to call their own.

- Faith that I could build a relationship I wanted to last for the rest of my life.

- Faith that I could once and for all complete the forgiveness cycle and know that it is the best path to personal happiness.

- Faith that I could use my life experiences to help others to make the best career and life decisions possible.

I am so grateful for the faith that has brought me the love of my life, my wonderful and successful children, family, and friends I will cherish forever.

~ Georgia R. Day

Georgia Day *is an author, coach, speaker, and mentor, dedicated to guiding her clients to successful career and life management. Visit her at www.Kamama.net.*

January 20

A Beloved Daughter

She was 14 when I married her father. That was 35 years ago and in spite of a divorce and a death, she is still my beloved daughter. She is as much a part of me as if I'd given birth to her. Clearly, God had a plan when He crossed our paths. I call her Dodi. She calls me Mumster. We celebrate our anniversary every year in gratitude for this gift of being mother and daughter. She called me today as she often does on Friday, the day she volunteers at an animal shelter walking dogs. (It is just like her to love God's critters, especially the vulnerable ones.) She told me that she'd been bitten on the cheek and arm today. She just left the doctor's office and she was fine—punctured and bruised and still high on adrenalin, but otherwise, fine. I began to tear up and felt the depth of our bond. It is remarkable to me that we share such love for each other that we are brought to tears when one or the other suffers. I thank God every day for the gift of my daughter and the joy she brings to my life.

~ *Cathy Raymond*

Cathy Raymond is an author, artist, and public speaker living in Olympia, Washington. To see her art and read about her book go to www. ReclaimingTheSoulOfHumanResources.com.

January 21

I Am Blessed

I am grateful for my awareness of the human energy field, called auras. Over the years, I came to understand my ability. In 1989, my 8-year-old son John suffered abdominal pains accompanied by a high fever, which his pediatrician diagnosed as case of the flu. For several days, John remained bedridden, feverish, and in considerable pain. When he arose to visit the bathroom, I followed him, observing from the door. As he was sitting on the toilet, I "saw" a nasty, intense red, ball-shaped "light" explode from his abdominal area. He then stood up, announced that he felt much better, and wanted to return to bed. "No!" I ordered. "We are taking you to the emergency room now!" I relayed what I saw to my husband and he concurred. Upon arrival at emergency, John's vitals demanded immediate surgery. At the time, we didn't know that he was about an hour away from death. The ER doctor confirmed that John's appendix had ruptured and he had a severe case of peritonitis. If I hadn't acted on what I "saw," John would not have survived, and we would not be blessed with two grandchildren and their father, our son John.

~ *Carolyn White, PhD*

Carolyn White, *PhD, DCH, is a metaphysical educator, energy therapist, Reiki Master, and author of* Think It->Say It->Be It: Use Your Words to Change Your Life. *Learn more at www.ChakraCoach.com.*

January 22

A Lucky Girl

My parents are my heroes. I'm very blessed to have a dad who is always ready to help his family. No matter how hard things may be, he does what he can to make us happy and always has. My mommy has been by my side my whole life. I'm most grateful for her unconditional love. Not a day goes by that I don't thank God for letting me be their daughter. Growing up, my goal in life was to be a mom. While I have become successful in other areas of life, being a mommy is my favorite! I have two gorgeous girls whom I love and cherish. Alison and Kylee are my BFFs, and teach me how to stay young and in love with life. My two girls have an amazing father who I get to call my husband. I am so grateful for our journey together. I love that no matter what we go through, good or bad, we always come out stronger. He is my forever. My parents, my children, and my husband are a huge part of what makes me who I am. I'm extremely grateful for their love.

~ Lisa Marie Benavidez

Lisa Benavidez helps coaches and entrepreneurs plan profitable live events. She believes in making a difference in this world, sharing your gifts, and always growing. Connect with her at www.Facebook.com/ BenavidezLisa.

January 23

Spared

I had an 80-mile ride home after work. Not something I looked forward to every day, but I tried to make the best of it and use that time to listen to some CDs, de-stress, and relax as much as possible. This day, 11 years ago, was a little different. I remember it as if it happened yesterday. I had just passed a small city and traffic was clearing out, but as I came upon an entrance ramp a semi-truck was ready to merge with the highway traffic. It looked like he was driving too fast, and the truck trailer started to sway as he got into the curve. I couldn't stop and let him in front of me, so I changed to the outside lane and accelerated to get out of his way. Had I not done that, I believe he would have fallen on my car and I wouldn't be writing this story. The rear-view mirror was my witness that the driver just barely missed me. The whole truck fell over on its side and broke apart in the median. The next forty miles home I just kept being thankful to God that I was spared!

~ Ingrid Cook

Ingrid Cook *is a Michigan-based Certified Healing Codes Practitioner and NLP life coach. Connect with her at www.Facebook.com/TheIn-gridCook or e-mail MacyBell18@gmail.com.*

January 24

Invaluable Support, Unending Gratitude

Have you ever been sick or injured to a level that required visits to a doctor or hospital? If you have, you know how valuable service and support are when they are given from the heart. It's not just the physical that feeds life. We all interact on many levels and with differing needs at different times. My sharp staff makes it seem simple. The individual caring they show provides opportunity for mutual service. Doctor Wayne True's balanced listening and explaining bespeaks a most generous and genuine professional. His heart "True-ly" inspires. Michelle and Toby, his support team, are interactive listeners who are there to help interpret issues and symptoms. The San Carlos reception staff are specialists attending to patients not unlike extended family, with care, understanding, and patience. Melissa, Amber, Paula, and Sonia are effective because of the interaction of several important factors, not the least of which is the importance of community building during their interactions; they value each other and each of us (patients) as people with our own interests, desires, and needs. Their interactions are an indications of living based on authentic compassion. These are people who bring out gratitude in people who might otherwise feel otherwise.

~ Warren L. Henderson, Jr.

Warren L. Henderson, Jr., *is the owner of Bridges 2 Empowerment life coaching and author of 3dB: Transformational Lessons in Cycles of Success.*

January 25

5, 6, 7, 8!

Most dancers who invest at least 10 hours a week will say that they have been dancing since they could walk. I discovered dance as a passion of mine only a few years ago. After realizing my love for dance, I started taking classes at studios to improve my technique. My passion quickly became an expensive one, but I kept dancing even if it meant only in my garage. However, I was lucky enough to have studio directors see potential in me and I received scholarships. Today, I'm a choreographer and instructor! I am grateful that I came across dance because it not only became a hobby that I love, but a way of life. The fact that I haven't been doing this all my life pushes me to keep up with the ones who have. Dance also pushes me to stay focused and work hard, because I know what it is like to not be able to dance every day due to financial demands. I apply this drive to other important entities in my life such as school and to consistently succeed. Most of all, I am grateful for the colleagues I've met through dance and now consider lifelong friends.

~ *Valerie Juguilon*

Valerie Juguilon *lives in San Diego and loves to dance!*

January 26

Blessings from Strange Places

One of the things I enjoy doing at night is reading posts on Facebook from my iPhone. I will often see the exact quote or comment that I need to read at that moment. I guess this could be considered a "virtual fortune cookie"! Well, one night I was on Facebook and came across a video from Dr. David Schiller. There was a link to a video where he explained his process and linked to his website. I felt that this was the exact message I needed to hear, especially when I discovered his area of expertise and that his office was only 25 minutes from my house. Long story short, in three months, Dr. Schiller has helped me increase my health and reduce my weight more than I've been able to accomplish in 10 years of trying on my own. The icing on the cake came when my primary health physician, who had been having me come in quarterly, said to me, "Wow, keep doing what you're doing. I'll see you in a year!" Thank you, Dr. Schiller. I am so grateful for you! You've given me a new lease on life and I love feeling so vital and energized!

~ *D'vorah Lansky*

D'vorah Lansky, *MEd, is the bestselling author of* Book Marketing Made Easy. *She works with authors across the globe in developing their online presence and their celebrity author status. Learn more at www.BecomeACelebrityAuthor.com.*

January 27

Those Who Mentor

I have a deep thankfulness for the many wise and trusted relationships—mentors in my life's journey. It has created an opportunity for demonstrating right and wrong actions, observing the good and bad actions, and confirming the correct course in moving forward with dreams, ambitions, career and connections. My many mentors: grandparents who shared Depression survival skills; parents who demonstrated love, caring, and kindness; sisters for showing me better paths to take; dear friends who listened and gave trusted advice; my spouse for command presence and outspokenness in what you believe in; and key "at the top of their game" career professionals for taking me under their wing to demonstrate integrity, caring, knowledge, and risk versus hazard expertise only they can share, having walked the path before me. Through my mentors, dear friendships were created, informal communication enhanced, and many molding and directing (teachable) moments have been shared by them having trusted in me. How wonderful! As Ralph Waldo Emerson said: "Trust men and they will be true to you; treat them greatly and they will show themselves great."

~ *Nancy Moorhouse*

Nancy Moorhouse, CSP, ARM, has a safety consultancy, Jointly Achieving Success, Trust and Accountability, to educate and teach what mentors taught her. She can be reached at Nancy@JASTAGroup.com.

January 28

Everywhere I Turn

Growing up I remember being told to "stop, look, and listen." At the time that wise parental guidance was to keep me safe when crossing the street. I still follow that advice today but as I have grown older, and hopefully wiser, those three words have taken on a whole new meaning. Now when I stop, look, and listen, I pay attention to the ordinary things that surround me and often find something to be grateful for. As I write this, I glance over to my cat, who reminds me that stress can magically melt away with one luxurious stretch, a long yawn, and cozy nap in the warm sunshine. This is sage advice on stress relief from a cat, for which I am grateful! As you stop, look, and listen today, where can you find something within the ordinary to be grateful for? I believe you won't have to look very far.

~ Susan Boras

Susan Boras enables business leaders to remove their blind spots so they can shine, love what they do, and still have a life! You can reach Susan at Susan@SquareHoleCoaching.com.

January 29

Grateful for the "Bumps"!

I am grateful for those pivotal "bumps in the road" of my life that helped me to step into my power, took me on a spiritual growth journey, and brought me to where I am today. I am healthier, happier, and more at peace than I have ever been before. Yes, we can find gratitude in the "bumps." It all started with my decision to quit my big corporate job on the spot to start my own business and then—BAM—one year later I get diagnosed with MS. Talk about a curve ball! I made a decision: Worry and stress were no longer options! My thoughts were my weapon for positive change. I saw the perfection in my timing of quitting corporate and how it gave me the time to take care of my own spiritual, emotional, and physical well-being. Everything happens for a reason. We all have a choice at how we respond to what life throws our way. And I am grateful for that choice. It was a pivotal moment where I chose to step into my power, focus on the positive and my bigger vision, and see that the "bump" was actually a blessing.

~ Maria Lesetz

Maria Lesetz, CEO of Lovin' Life, is living her purpose and passion by teaching women how to reclaim their power, thrive through adversity, and create success from the inside out. Get in touch at www.LovinLifeNow.com.

January 30

Sensitive, Chubby Italian Girl

Growing up I was a a highly sensitive, chubby girl, and my family didn't know how to deal with it. The best they could offer were a hug and some homemade meatballs, because those always cheered me up. But my family is the best and I am so incredibly grateful to have been part of such a loving, warm, and funny bunch! Pockets of my mind and heart are filled with memories of celebrations, laughter, good times, and, as always, pasta! Food was celebration, food was passion, and food eventually became a way for me to soothe my emotions, lending to a lifelong weight problem. Yet I would not be the woman I am today had it not been for my upbringing. If it wasn't for that weight problem, I wouldn't have found a solution. I thank the Universe every day for my struggles, because it has pointed me in the direction of how I am to serve and help others. My heart is filled with nothing but gratitude for my past and my Italian family!

~ *Maryann Candito*

Maryann Candito *is the founder of Synergy Weight Release™ and author of* I'm Losing It! 7 Simple Steps to Jump Off the Diet Roller Coaster, Release the Weight and Heal Your Relationship with Food for Good. *Learn more at www.SynergyWeightRelease.com.*

January 31

Growing Where Least Expected

Several years ago, I underwent emergency surgery for a life-threatening issue. I was told another week could have meant my death. I was "temporarily" repaired, and another surgery was required to put everything in place. The stresses associated with this were amplified six weeks later when I learned my marriage was ending. There were many moments of "why me?" and "why now?" But in all of this, I was blessed by the generosity of others: people cutting my grass or shoveling my walks because I couldn't; those bringing food; the resilience of my children in helping me heal; friends and coworkers visiting me, giving me a chance to talk, whether happy or sad. I came to realize how fortunate I was, in spite of the turmoil and dismantling of what I thought was essential to happiness. The actions and generosity of others, especially by those not close to me, were exceptionally humbling. As a result, I began to give more of my own time and efforts because of what was done for me. In doing so, I am more content with where I am in life and more grateful for what I have been given, both in talents and friendships.

~ *Donald Capan*

Donald Capan *works as a caseworker and educator. He is active as an assistant scoutmaster. He enjoys Civil War reenacting, fishing, gaming, and camping with his kids.*

February

*"Gratitude is a quality similar to electricity:
it must be produced and discharged and used
up in order to exist at all."*

~ William Faulkner

February 1

The Capacity to Trust

Faith is the priceless capacity to trust. I heavily rely on it whenever I board a plane. Although it seems impossible to me that such a massive object can fly, I trust it will get me safely to my destination. When we have absolute assurance of something, we don't need faith. It's the things for which we have limited knowledge or experience that faith is required. I know very little about planes, but I've experienced flying enough that, even though there's risk, I still choose to trust. I'm especially grateful for a capacity to trust in the Creator and His promise of spending eternity in a body that's non-perishable. I'm slightly past middle age (okay, more than slightly), so the prospect of having endless energy without earthly limits brings joyful anticipation every time I think of it. I may have limited knowledge and experience of my Creator but, based on what I do know and have experienced, I completely trust Him. This gives me peace in the present, too. Whether I live long or die tomorrow, I will have won the race and received the prize. I'm truly grateful for the capacity to trust.

~ Valerie Edwards

Valerie Edwards *is a businesswoman and inspirational writer and speaker. Valerie can be reached at Valerie@ValerieEdwards.com.*

February 2

Glad to Be Alive

I knew exactly what was going to happen the moment the back wheels of the brand-new, ruby red company car grazed the central reservation of the M4. It was 1992, 8:00 a.m., and I was on my way to London for my first day in my new job as a national sales trainer, and I'd already been driving three hours though the dark, foggy, drizzly January morning. I remember thinking, "I know my physics" as I took my hands off the steering wheel and raised them in a surrender position. Resigned to the inevitable ricochet that followed, I prayed it wouldn't hurt. The car spun, making a double figure-eight across the three lanes of rush-hour traffic. I still remember seeing the guy's face in the middle lane as I faced him head on, his eyes resembling something from a *Tom & Jerry* cartoon. Suddenly, I was on the hard shoulder. I took hold of the wheel and came to a perfect stop, albeit the wrong way round. Not a bump, not a scratch—just the pungent smell of burning rubber and the wonderful feeling that I was still needed.

~ *Ellen Watts*

Ellen Watts *founded her own training company, ElleRich Ltd (www.ellerich.co.uk) in 1996. Her book,* Cosmic Ordering Made Easier *was released on February 2, 2013 and is now available from www.Ellen-Unlimited.com.*

February 3

Rainy Days

While I love sunshine and hot summer days, there's nothing more enjoyable than the occasional rainy day. There's something about the rain that has always brought about a sense of cozy contentment. As a child growing up in Southern California, I loved it when it rained. I would ask my mom if I could put on my red raincoat and matching rain boots so I could walk around outside and splash through puddles. I recall the sour smell of the petunias in the garden, the droplets clinging to their colorful displays. I loved breathing in the heavy, rich scent of the newly dampened earth. The freshness in the air was so exciting and exhilarating. Even today, the rain brings back many of these same memories. And when I'm in bed, there's nothing more delightful than the hypnotic pitter patter of rain drops hitting the roof and window panes. A few minutes of listening to that beautiful sound quickly hastens me to a peaceful slumber. And, should the rain linger into the daylight hours, it still brings me joy. There's nothing more relaxing than sitting in my office, enjoying a hot cup of tea while listening to the rain.

~ Tara Kachaturoff

Tara Kachaturoff *is an online business manager and the creator, producer, and host of Michigan Entrepreneur TV. A native of Southern California, she currently resides in Birmingham, Michigan.*

February 4

Loving Is Soaring

Love has been the most transformational and valuable piece of knowledge I have ever discovered in my life! I have so much gratitude for the ever-expanding, undefinable treasure that Love is. Love is the healer, the peace-giver, the motivation to change. Love corrects all wrongs, giving you the strength to move on. Love is the power behind your growth; it's the fuel that we all need the most! Love is the sleeping giant you forget is there, protecting, encouraging, and ridding you of fear. Love is the hope for what cannot be seen, the motivator to accomplish your dreams. Love is the solitude that exists in all storms and, if you're willing, will wrap you in its arms. Love is infinite and eternally kind; it's waiting patiently for you to find. Love is you and it's me; Love is the gift that sets us free. Embrace your Love for you, then share your love with others, too. This is where peace soars like a dove, when each of us embraces and gives our love.

~ JoAnna Ashley

JoAnna Ashley *is an inspiring and encouraging coach, leader, and speaker. She founded the "GABE: Fast Track for Mind-Set Transformation and Healing System" and is the owner of www.Healing4Bodies.com.*

February 5

To Mom With Love

I find myself in an odd place, wanting to extend gratitude to my mother—a woman who was so wrapped up in herself she had little time for me when she was alive, and no patience. We had love, yes. Kindness, no. But now as I look back I see the gift she gave me—the reason, I think, that we came together in this lifetime. My mother had an intense interest in and appreciation of the occult. She visited psychics long before it was popular, hid astrology books under the bed so my father wouldn't see them, and gave me Tarot cards when I was a preteen because she thought I was a witch. Eventually, I would do an in-depth study of Tarot cards, which led me to pursue my study of metaphysics and Universal Law. I am now a minister of Spiritual Science, thanks to my mother's belief in the non-physical world. Without my connection to other realms and my ability to work with energy, I don't know how I would have survived all the challenges in my life. Thank you, Mom. See you on the other side.

~ *Rev. Susan Bassik*

Rev. Susan Bassik *utilizes akashic records, channeled guidance, Reiki, and Soul Memory Discovery as healing tools. She is the originator of the internationally acclaimed "Awaken the Healer Within" audio. Learn more at www.AkashicHealings.com.*

February 6

College Students

Every year when I start a new semester teaching at a local community college, I wonder what the term will bring. I begin by telling my students they all have As and what they do with them over the next 15 weeks is up to them. They can nurture them throughout the semester or they can let them wither and die. My intention is always the same: let this class be one that nourishes both the minds and spirits of my students. As I write this, I am looking at a room filled with bowed heads, as my students take their final exam. I am peaceful, knowing it has been a fabulous semester. This group, above all others, has truly grown. They will leave my classroom with the poise and resolve of those who have mastered something new. They will go into the world with confidence. They leave here more polished and professional than they were just 15 weeks ago. They've learned that learning can be fun and laughter is definitely a part of the classroom experience. What am I grateful for? The endless joy that teaching brings and the opportunity to watch minds open and grow.

~ Angela I. Schutz

Angela I. Schutz, founder of Driven to Succeed Consulting LLC, is a published author, professional speaker, and career coach dedicated to helping others empower their lives. Reach her at www.DrivenToSucceed.net.

February 7

Meine Frau

I'm married, actually remarried, to a German woman named Christine. She came into my life when my 6-year-old son and I lost his mother in an accident. What I love about Christine is that she is not a worrier and tells it like it is. I've taken many risks in my business since I met her and faced some very large financial ups and downs. But all the while that I was concerned, Christine was reassuring and helped me make peace with any worst-case scenarios (which never happened, by the way). We now have a 2-year-old son, in addition to my 14-year-old son, and are living in Germany for a few years so that her parents can support her with our newest addition to the family. I think the biggest gift that Christine has given me is the ability to make peace with the answer to the question: "What's the worst that could happen?" And I've found that once I've made peace with that, then whatever happens is okay and often much better than I had supposed. Thank you, Christine, for being in my life for me and for our two sons.

~ *Rob Goyette*

Rob Goyette *is an internet entrepreneur and coach. He currently lives in Gorlitz, Germany. You can learn about Rob's latest project by going to www.RobGoyette.com.*

February 8

Angels with Tails

When I lost my perfect, pure-bred dog in a horrible accident, I didn't think I would survive the pain. Distraught and in shock, I decided to just visit a dog from a rescue seeking comfort for my broken heart. She placed her little paws on my knee and jumped up on my lap, as if she belonged there. When we arrived home, I looked at the stinky, straggly, skinny little dog with an under-bite and crooked teeth, and I thought that she must be all I deserved, since I didn't protect my other perfect dog from being hit by a car. Through my bitter tears, I doted on Hailey, and I pledged to try to love her as I had my other dogs. She was in shock, too; I wonder what she had endured to be so battered physically and emotionally. I watched her fears subside and the shock wear off. Slowly, my tears turned into gratitude, as I realized that this imperfect mess no one else wanted had blossomed into the cutest, sweetest dog in the whole world. She is *perfect*! Rescuing a dog was about more than saving her life, it was a great gift in my life.

~ *Kellie Rae Nicholson*

*Author, speaker, life coach, and business consultant **Kellie Nicholson** conducts personal growth workshops in the Los Angeles area and online via her website, www.FindYourExcellence.com.*

February 9

Legal Secretary Love

Gratitude is love, and as a legal secretary who loved what she was doing, how could I communicate that love? By sharing information with my co-workers and empowering them to do the best they could, I realized that my strength was in training. As a legal secretary for many years, I love working with other secretaries and law office support staff on how they could best perform their duties and survive life in a law firm. Dealing with difficult employers, clients, opposing counsel, and even other co-workers is so important when working in an environment that is not conducive to sharing and empowering each other. Technical knowledge is paramount when the rights of the client are involved. The stress of working in this environment is tremendous, and taking care of ourselves is necessary. It takes a special person to work in a support position in a law firm, and most of us do it because we want to be of assistance to our clients and the attorneys we work with. Many do it without recognition. By learning to love ourselves and take pride in what we do, we can continue to provide the excellent service our clients deserve.

~ Deanna A. Pepe

Deanna A. Pepe *has been a legal secretary, trainer, and law office manager for more than 35 years. She provides training for support staff. Her website is www.DeannaPepe.com.*

February 10

I Live To Sew

I love to sew, and have been sewing since I was 12 years old. My dad wanted me to learn and I'll always be grateful. I make and create dolls that make people smile and quilts that keep people warm. When I'm busy creating a quilt, I know how it will make the person who will receive it feel. Making quilts for our veterans gives me great pleasure in knowing I'm giving back to one of our nation's heroes. They protect and serve our country, and when they come home they are presented with a quilt from a quilt group. I like to meet the person who will receive one of my quilts, I love to design it with that person in mind. All this is made possible because my dad insisted I learn how to sew; it didn't take me long to realize he was shaping my future. I thank my dad for believing in me, because sewing has been my passion my whole life. It makes others happy, which makes me very happy indeed.

~ Theresa Nielsen

Theresa Nielsen, *sewer, quilter, writer, and animal companion to her flock, loves to write and make quilts to make others smile.*

February 11

My Perfect Partner

As I reflect on my life for a special moment of gratitude I believe I am most grateful for my supportive and loving wife. She is the answer to my dream of getting married and raising a family. She helped us learn to become a loving couple and guided us as we started our family-building journey. She made even the smallest apartment feel like home and found new ways to have fun while we traveled on our new journey as a couple. She listened to my crazy ideas, sometimes challenging my assumptions, but supported my decisions including those that weren't that good. When we faced a challenge, she was there to pull me through my low spots and soared with me to celebrate the wins. She taught me the importance of taking time to get away and truly relax, even if it is a rarity. A couple of years ago we started what we hope will be the last chapter in our life. We moved to be closer to the grandchildren and to spend more time enjoying ourselves. I cannot imagine a future without this fantastic woman who means so much to me.

~ Don Craig

Don Craig is the founder of Discover Your Desire Now, LLC. He works with individuals to establish a clear vision and use their strengths to take action to realize their dreams.

February 12

Because He Loves Me

Because He loves me I was created—created to join the home of a lovely couple named George and Isabella Matheka as their first-born daughter. Because He loves me, He gave me not one, not two, but three great younger brothers, Robert, David, and Stephen. Because He loves me, He helped me grow in a comfortable home in the presence of a loving family. Because He loves me, I went to school for many years, in more than one country, and got to learn a whole lot. Because He loves me, He chose a life partner, James, for me whom I have known and loved for 16 years. Because He loves me, He blessed me with a baby girl called Amy, and then four years later He blessed me with another baby girl called Joy. Because He loves me, I have a fulfilling job to do each day that has helped me to discover my true purpose. Because He loves me, I am blessed with a healthy body that challenges me daily. Because He loves me, I have been on earth 44 amazing years. For all of this I am truly grateful. He is my Creator and God.

~ *Rita Matheka-Njenga*

Rita Matheka-Njenga *is an entrepreneur, author, and success mentor for high-achieving women. She teaches them how to get organized and focused so that they can achieve their goals and dreams. She lives and works in Nairobi, Kenya.*

February 13

A Treasured Photograph

One of my treasured photographs is also a reminder of miracles. It's a simple picture of a flower growing amid rocks in a shallow stream. While I love the image's message of beauty and growth in an unlikely place, the photographer is the real story. She is the miracle. Today is her 32nd birthday. She's "Mom" to two daughters and married to a great husband. But that's not the miracle. She's an honors college graduate and extraordinary glass artist. And she had just climbed a mountain when she took the picture. Why is all of that remarkable? Her probabilities were much different. Born three months premature, she suffered hemorrhages in her eyes and brain. Her prognosis was pretty bleak. The picture the doctors painted included learning disabilities, leg braces to walk, and, without surgery, blindness. What made the outcome so different? Medical miracles? Perseverance? Absolutely! But it was also more. It was unwavering faith in another possible outcome. This has been and remains a personal quest. The photographer is my daughter. For the last 32 years we have lived and grown in the stream of God's possibilities. I am grateful that He chose her as my daughter, as our miracle.

~ Kathi C. Laughman

Kathi Laughman is an author, inspirational speaker, and certified life coach. Her mission is to inspire, facilitate, and invest in the success of others. Learn more at www.MackenzieCircle.com.

February 14

Radical Love

Today let's be grateful for love, not just romantic love. Rather, the kind of love which is actually deeper than loving another in romantic union. This love inspires us to step into our most magnificent selves. It opens us up to something extraordinary; it goes beyond our intellect and expands our awareness and our connection to the Divine all loving force that exists within each of us. This kind of love deepens our abilities to give and receive love to and from others. It is the most challenging and significant love of all: It is the love we give to ourselves; it is self-love.

Learning to practice self-love in all of our endeavors requires a radical shift in our inner dialogue as well as our outward behaviors. The practice of self-love necessitates that we continually ask ourselves: "Is this an act of self love?", "How would love behave now?", and "What would love do, think, or say next?" Ultimately, this process is reflected outwardly toward everyone around us, and back at us, from every direction. It overflows with an abundance of rich, juicy, blissful love and joy into our entire world. This is radical self-love.

~ *Lori Ann Spagna*

Lori Spagna is a best-selling author with over 20 years of experience assisting others to improve their lives by tapping into their true power via the Universal Source of Love. Visit www.LoriSpagna.com to learn more.

February 15

Love and Blessings

My favorite time of the day is when the tasks are done and I can sit at my prayer table to count my blessings. Called synchronicity, called Holy Spirit work, and myriad names in between! I woke up the day after I had retired (offered at age 50) in what I would describe as the prime of my life wondering who I was. You see, when this happens, everything you were known for, every title you ever received, becomes superfluous; all the descriptors leave with your work title! Slowly and carefully I began to pick up the pieces of "who God intended me to be". It became very clear to me that if I always did what I had always done, I would always get what I always got! It became my mantra. Try new things, Shelley. If you reach a T-junction in life, simply choose another path, Shelley. I start each journal entry every day in this way: "Beloved, thank you for my precious, abundant, love-filled life, all that I have and all that I am." Watch how the blessings come, one after another after another. Be obedient and the blessings flow.

~ Shelley Bent

Shelley Bent is a free spirit whose purpose is to "help people to help themselves heal and grow." Twenty-seven of her 34 years in corporate South Africa were spent in training and development. Learn more at www.Facebook.com/Shelley.Bent.50.

February 16

Counting Your Blessings

As I travel through life, I reflect on one "special thing" that has made a wonderful difference in my life. The knowledge of being grateful. To overcome the trials and tribulations I have experienced and the ability to grow from each one. I'd like to share the loss at a young age of 8: the loss of my brother, only 18 at the time of his passing. I was grateful that I could share his laughter, his smile, and his passion for life. My mother's grief was heart-wrenching. I prayed that God would heal her grief. Shortly there after my mother was diagnosed with breast cancer. After surgery and treatment, her survival rate was five years. My "gratitude" for the time spent laughing, sharing, comforting, soothing her pain until she took her breath was a very special gift. The meaning of gratitude comes with the ability to grow from the trails in one's life. Today my "gratitude for life" is a gift of giving and the knowledge to share and treasure.

~ *Jacqueline Carter*

Jacqueline Carter dedicates this in loving memory of her mother, Marcell, and her brother, Earl. For all the joy and happiness they brought to her life. By sharing this piece, she hopes to touch someone and make a difference. Life: a gift of gratitude—to celebrate.

February 17

Grateful for Creativity

Mystic Angel Creations was founded in 2001, as an outlet for my creativity and as a vehicle to teach others the art of handcrafted jewelry. In 2012, my daughter, Jennifer Craft, joined the business as my business partner. Over the years, I have realized how fortunate I am to have a God-given talent that enables me to make part of my living doing something that I love to do. In this business, I have come into contact with numerous customers, many who repeatedly add to their jewelry collections by purchasing our designs. One of the lines that we produce is for Dia De Los Muertos, or Day of the Dead, which is also recognized as All Saints Day. One of the customers who purchased some of the pendants told me that she was going to celebrate her mother's life by having a special memorial service for her. She was going to give the pendants that I had made to her mother's sisters and keep one for herself and her young daughter. Coming into contact with customers such as this young woman are a reminder to me that the care and detail I take in my work really do matter, and I will always be grateful for appreciative customers.

~ Sandy Forrest-Hartman

Sandy Forrest-Hartman *has two different careers: one as a long-time paralegal who has worked in the legal profession for almost 30 years and one as a handcrafted jewelry artist. She opened her company, Mystic Angel Creations, in 2001.*

February 18

Nothing to Be Sorry For

Mother and I spent years without getting along. I convinced myself she didn't know it; only I did. Starting as a sullen pre-teen, and growing into a stiff-necked young adult, I resolved to leave home. As soon as I could, I moved away.

Our relationship had started fine: I was her first-born daughter, and she loved me. She read me endless stories, never saying no when I'd pound the book, insisting, "Again!" But then, when we moved overseas, she was forced to homeschool me. I hated her strict rules, her tireless drilling. She tried to be understanding—when I'd mess up, saying I was sorry, she'd respond matter-of-factly, "There's nothing to be sorry for." I hated that. And then I had my daughter. Mother traveled a long distance just to help. The evening before she was leaving for home, we sat together on the brocade couch she'd handed down to me.

Holding my daughter, I suddenly realized Mother had held me just like this, heart bursting with big love. My own heart nearly stopped, realizing the pain I'd surely caused her. "Mother," I said, "I'm sorry for the years we missed—I get it now."

"Oh, honey," she replied, "there's nothing to be sorry for."

~ *Elizabeth Sutherland*

Elizabeth Sutherland *is an author, writer, project, and life work coach. Connect with her at TakeNoteWords.com and TakeNoteCoaching.com.*

February 19

Sick, Tired, and Grateful

Being diagnosed with a chronic illness is not something most people would feel grateful for, so it is surprising that it's one of the things I appreciate most in my life. I was diagnosed with fibromyalgia in 1998 and suffer daily from chronic pain and fatigue. So, why do I feel grateful for being burdened with a painful illness? Most people would react with disbelief, anger, and resentment (and believe me, there are many days I do feel that way). Ultimately, I'm grateful because I have chosen to triumph and succeed in spite of my illness. Foremost, I never would have dreamed of having my own business before fibromyalgia. Now, I can't imagine living any other way. I've been able to build a career around my illness, which provides me the freedom to work when I want and where I want, spend more time with my children and family, and have time to rest when I need it most. Having fibromyalgia has taught me to appreciate all the blessings in my life—the stuff that really matters. It has taught me resilience, patience, and strength in ways I never could've imagined. For these lessons and so many more, I am eternally grateful.

~ *Cindy Earl*

Cindy Earl, *founder of ClaimYourSpotlight.com, helps entrepreneurs grow their businesses using authentic relationship marketing and simple, proven strategies to attract more clients and "walk the red carpet" to business success.*

February 20

Tough, Tender Love

I was a single parent with four boys and no place to go after my divorce. My mother offered us a room in her home for the short time of eight weeks. I did not understand why she offered such little time for me to pull myself back together again. I found myself uncertain, determined, and yet strongwilled. In my intense state of mind, I decided to "show her" what I was made of. I would get a job, find an apartment, and move us out even sooner than she expected. When I moved out in just six weeks, my mother cheerfully embraced me, giving me the biggest, tightest, most powerful hug ever. She said to me, "I knew you would step up and step out, and make it happen. You did it!" Noticing the tear in my eye, she continued, "Getting off your pity party is where you found your power. You were given a chance and you created possibility. You took the challenge head-on and you found your strength. I am so proud of you!" I felt proud of me, too, and that day her tough love taught me to believe—in me! Thank you, Mom!

~ Cheryl Hall

Cheryl Hall is a coach, speaker, and author. Coaching possibility, purpose, and excellence is her passion. You can find Cheryl at AuthorOfMyLife.com.

February 21

My Mother, the Bride

Ring. Ring. My mother's answering machine kicks on. "Eight-fifteen on a Friday night and you're gone? If you're on a date, make sure he brings you home at a decent hour!" Click. Mom had been widowed for nearly 20 years and showed no interest in dating or remarrying. My message was banter—or so I thought!

The next morning Mom calls. "You'll never guess where I was last night!" She had indeed been out with a man—someone she dated long before Dad. I wasn't sure I wanted to hear this! A few weeks before, Mom and Marvin met again at a local dance hall. He, too, had lost his longtime spouse. Marvin asked Mom to dance. She said no. What? Playing hard to get at the age of 74? This was too much! But the image engraved in my mind is how beautiful and happy Mom looked in her wedding gown at her second wedding. The way she glowed brings tears to my eyes. Mom and Dad had been married 38 years when Alzheimer's took him away forever. Mom and Marvin had been married 370 days when cancer over-took his frail body. Yet, my mother the bride lives happily ever after with the memories of two wonderful husbands.

~ Peggy Lee Hanson

Peggy Lee Hanson mentors those who experience life-changing situations and guides them through their journey using proven strategies. You can reach Peggy at MyDreamArchitect.com.

February 22

Quilts of Love

My mother was a quilter. It was her passion, and over the years she created hundreds of beautiful quilts that she only gave away. I have always liked the quote "Our lives are like quilts—bits and pieces, joy and sorrow, stitched with love." We lost our mom earlier this year, and that quote really sums up her life and her legacy. When I think of the word *gratitude*, my family and friends instantly come to mind. I thank God for all these special people every day. I love to think of how each person in my life is similar to one of my mom's quilt squares. A single piece of fabric is nice by itself, but when you sew them all together, you end up with something more beautiful than when you started. My husband, children, and sister are the center pieces, and it expands from there. Every single person I know holds a special place in my life and for that I am so grateful. We are all sewn together in a beautiful way. I can only hope that I can add to others' quilts, as all of these people have contributed to mine.

~ *Peggy McGinnis*

Peggy McGinnis *is a customer care expert. She educates businesses and coaches on how to provide exceptional service and to love their customers for long-term retention. Find out more at www.SpeedScription.com.*

February 23

A Treasure Beyond Measure

"Agrateful heart knows many joys" is a saying that has inspired me daily for many years. From appreciation of the tiniest things in Nature all the way to experiencing huge miracles, my heart overflows with joy. My grateful heart is by choice. For me, choice is a treasure beyond measure. This day, this moment, I get to choose! I choose my thoughts, beliefs, dreams, actions-reactions, attitude, gratitude, and everything else that creates me. Shall I smile or frown, wear bright or brown, be snippy or sweet, learn or lose, eat cherries or chocolate or both? Choice is endless and powerful. Thrilling indeed! Balance is also choice. If I am out of balance, it is ultimately because of choices I have made. However, I can choose to have the Courage (yes, with a capital C!) to make necessary adjustments to love and care for myself. Other factors and people do play a part in life, yet I am forever grateful for this beautiful gift, my treasure of choice. Choosing to live in love versus fear and realizing that receiving love *is* giving, makes a delightful difference. Today and always, may your heart know many joys.

~ *Dequa S*

Dequa S *loves sharing encouragement and inspiring others to receive TLC. Nature, flying, energy medicine, and her granddaughters are a few passions. Connect with Dequa S via www.Essentials4U.moxxor.com or Dequa508@gmail.com.*

February 24

Grateful For Birthdays

We are all quick to find our own flaws and imperfections, like the things we would like to change about ourselves. It doesn't have to be a physical change; sometimes we don't even like our own name. Would you change that? One thing most people are happy with, though, is their birthday. It's the one special day set aside to celebrate our life and the day we entered the world. As time and years go by, we come to realize who appreciates us and values our uniqueness, along with our accomplishments. It's the one day when the phone rings off the hook, and our inbox puts a smile on our face from all our admirers. Growing up as an only child, this day was truly my own. But, my sister-in-law and her son share this day as their birthday, too. We used to always try to celebrate together because of how special it is. Now, it is not always possible to celebrate together. Even though we share this day as our birthday, we marvel at the differences, similarities, and uniqueness in each of us. We are truly grateful to share this commonality, all within the same family.

~ Barbara Rae Zak

Barbara Rae Zak, *is owner/author of www.GoalForTheGreen.com. Barbara has successfully integrated her daily work with developmentally disabled adults into her passion for writing and blogging.*

February 25

Make Your Day Count

My mom gave me advice when I was a little girl, and I have used that advice every day. She told me to make my day count by learning something each day. She turned me into a lifelong learner. I've learned amazing things and little things, things I share and some gems of knowledge that I like to keep to myself. Sometimes I say that I know a lot of things, but not enough to be dangerous! I've tried to pass on the love of learning to others, just as my mom passed this on to me. I'm just dazzling at a dinner party and great at playing Trivial Pursuit. Thanks, Mom. I am truly grateful.

~ Cat Traywick

Cat Traywick *is a life success coach who works with clients all over the world to make life or career changes. Cat's website is CCTCoaching. com.*

February 26

Honed by Gratitude's Journey

D iamonds are the fascination of nearly every woman, the obsession and downfall of many a man. The hardest mineral on Earth, diamonds are sought after in the depths of caves and displayed in windows of high-society shops. In the rough, diamonds are an unkempt stone—an unlikely star. Only after they've been cut, polished, and set, do they become brilliant, reflecting their inner beauty and fire. I wear diamonds on nearly every finger as a reminder of my life's journey: the loss of my father as a child, later my mother; having cancer; suffering pain; the darkness of depression; crossing death's threshold—then rising again to write, teach, love, and laugh. We are all diamonds in the rough with the potential of becoming sparkling gems. We can shatter beneath the pressure of tragedy, loss, illness, abuse, pain, hardship, or crime. We can crumble, having been broken, beaten, or bruised. Or we can allow those abrasions to chip away the darkness, exposing our many shimmering facets. Set properly—let's call this mindset: intention, perception, disposition—we discover we have not lost pieces of ourselves. We have not been fractured. We've become more valuable. Treasured. Shine on, sparkling diamond. Shine on.

~ *Rev. Jamie L. Saloff, C.M.*

Rev. Jamie L. Saloff, *"The Author's Prophet," is a self-publishing specialist helping authors write more, sell more, and be more. She's also a Lily Dale–trained intuitive and healer. Learn more at www.Saloff.com.*

February 27

Another Adventure, Mamie?

When people ask me why I have such an optimistic attitude about almost everything in life, I always say, "I got it from my mom."

In all of our lives, calamity or disasters or just plain scary things happen. It's a part of life. Yet we still have choices about how we respond.

A quick example: One summer I was at our lake cottage in the boat, with all four young kids, my sister, and my mom, Mamie.

A huge storm came up without much notice: hard rain, thunder, and lightning. We were far enough away from our cottage to be very concerned.

Instead of everyone panicking, my mom kept telling the kids what an adventure we were having as my sister and I navigated our way to an unknown neighbor's dock for rescue. I don't believe the children were ever scared (although I remember my sister and I being pretty nervous!) because Mamie had convinced them easily that we were having an adventure.

It wasn't drama; it wasn't a catastrophe. It was simply an adventure.

~ Kim Kirmmse Toth

Kim Kirmmse Toth *is a business coach helping women over 50 create their own financial security by designing and sustaining successful online businesses.*

February 28

Amazing, Exciting New Technology

I am grateful for the Internet. It continues to surprise and delight me.

My mental horizons get a daily stretch and workout with Google, YouTube, teleseminars, and webinars. Dictionaries and recipe books still have their place, but are seldom first port of call.

My emotional and spiritual roots are nourished through e-mail contact with family and friends. I still cherish letters I get from friends. The fact that they are not a daily occurrence makes them special, but it's wonderful to be able to exchange instant e-mails with people it would take an hour's drive to be with—friends and colleagues interstate and on the other side of the world.

The Kindle has transformed reading, one of my favorite activities. It's so easy to download a new book! Even better, I can sample before I buy. I still enjoy holding and reading "real" books, but the Kindle is easier to read in bed! I can sample and read books that otherwise would have been overlooked or on my wish list for years.

Most interesting of all, perhaps, social media like Facebook and LinkedIn have given me a new perspective on how human interconnectedness can work in practice.

What's next?

~ *Justus H. Lewis, PhD*

Justus Lewis, PhD, from Melbourne, Australia, teaches and practices the EMF Balancing Technique® and other life-transforming processes that invite human happiness. Reach her at Transformasia.com.au or EMFMelb.com.

March

*"Hem your blessings with thankfulness
so they don't unravel."*

~ Author Unknown

March 1

Mother and Friend

Once past childhood, and following my stint in the Air Force, I saw my mother's life from a new perspective. And she no longer thought of me as someone needing her parental teaching and protection. We discovered several common interests. And good sport that she was, Mother entertained many of my new interests. I cherish memories of the adventures we shared. One summer we began driving into the northwest states, and for two weeks decided, each morning when we awoke, which narrow, old highway to travel that day. Though neither of us could swim, I twice talked her into sailing on tall ships in the Caribbean. And we spent one entire summer searching out the best pie in town. It was more fun than chore when we moved cross-country together, where we created a shared home, spending her last years together. I miss those days spent in loving communication with her. She taught me to share my heart with an "I love you" to friends and family. I'm so grateful for those years we spent as friends. And on quiet mornings, and late at night, I still hear her whisper, "I'm here. I love you."

~ Suzanne Gochenouer

Suzanne Gochenouer *is grateful for books, peace, and the healing energy of love. She coaches writers, as well anyone seeking a joy-filled life, and blogs at TransformationalEditor.com and PeacemakersPath.com.*

March 2

A Strong and Powerful Woman

My mother, Andrea, is an amazing woman. She probably doesn't know she is, but I certainly do. My parents divorced when I was 5 years old and my mom was 24. She worked full-time to take care of my little brother, Josh, and me, while simultaneously putting herself through nursing school. She graduated magna cum laude and managed to single-handedly provide for her family. This was definitely no small feat. I am grateful for all of her hard work and the many sacrifices she made over the years.

I am also so very grateful to my mother for instilling within me a can-do, no-excuses attitude. I have always believed that I can do anything or be anything that I desire if I set my mind to it and work hard. My mom taught me this, not only through her words, but through her actions. My mission in life is to do the same for my three daughters, Maya, Alexa, and Reyna. I am grateful that I come from a long line of strong and empowered women, and I'm even more grateful for the opportunity to contribute to this legacy. I thank God every day for my mother and my daughters.

~ Tiffany deSilva

Tiffany deSilva, MSW, *helps women balance it all! Conquer chaos and overwhelm. Achieve success in business and life! Find her at OrderAndBalance.com and OrderAndBalanceForSuccess.com.*

March 3

Grateful for My Freedom

No longer do I live under your power. I am free, free to love me free to speak for me. I am free to worship my life. I am free from the boundaries that you placed on me. You will no longer hurt me. You will no longer hold me down with the shame you placed inside my head. I AM FREE. I am saying yes to my freedom, to walk with my head up high. I'm saying yes to my freedom, to love me and to be in love with me. I'm saying yes to my freedom, to touch me, to hug me.

~ S.D. Nelson

*As a former victim of sexual abuse, **S.D. Nelson** gives honor to God for the courage and strength to stand up and say no more bondage, pain, and fear.*

March 4

Miracles Happen Every Day

I am truly grateful for my daughter, Gabrielle, who brings so much joy and laughter to my life every day. She is the miracle I prayed for when I was just 11 years old. I knew, even then, that I wanted to be a mother. On February 17, 1999, my dream came true when I was 35.

I know every mother understands that special feeling you get the moment the doctor places your newborn in your arms, and you finally get to kiss your baby. You count every tiny toe and finger. You know you are holding a miracle!

I believe that miracles happen every day, from the smallest seed of grass growing to someone surviving death. Just look in the mirror. As you become more grateful for the miracles around you, you will notice more.

I try to keep this miracle of my daughter every moment we are together. Now she is a teenager, and is full of unique opinions and ideas. She has learned that all her dreams can come true as long as she believes in herself.

It's amazing, but no matter what happens in my busy day, every time I look at my daughter, I smile. I look at those big, brown eyes, and I know that miracles happen every day and that God has truly blessed me!

~ Margo Dewey

Margo Dewey, *a professional television and newspaper journalist for 20 years, is the CEO of In-Focus TV Productions Inc. She is currently writing a series of adventure fantasy novels for children.*

March 5

What I Am Grateful For...

I am grateful that even though my apartment is in foreclosure, my trust in God has not failed. I know I will have the money to pay off my mortgage, be debt free, and purchase a second home—in cash!

I am grateful that my love and confidence in myself have not diminished. I am grateful that despite the fact that my job will end in a few days, God is opening doors and bringing opportunities my way that I never imagined possible.

I am grateful for the love and support of family and friends.

I am grateful that even though my best friend, Marguerite, and my dad, Carl, are no longer here on earth with me, they left me with their spirits, which bless me daily.

I am grateful that God hears me and answers my prayers for me and for family, friends, and strangers.

I am grateful that my mistakes are forgiven and I will overcome all obstacles.

I am blessed; I will accomplish my dreams; I am in God's favor!

To God go the Victory!

~ Demethress Gordon

Demethress Gordon is a native New Yorker, living on the Upper West Side. Her dream is to fulfill her destiny and master her God-given talents as a writer.

March 6

A Nurse's Gratitude

I am grateful for becoming exactly what I never wanted to be: a nurse. Let me give you the backstory here. I was born the second eldest in a family of six. My mother died when I was 9, and my father drank. I had a lot of responsibility at a young age, and I spent much of my younger life strongly resisting anything having to do with the role of caretaker. I did not see much power in that! I entered nursing, intending to use it as a stepping-stone to what I perceived as a more powerful role. But life came along, as it often does, and I remained in nursing, in direct patient care. And what a gift that has been! To be of service and to work so intimately with people, in settings where we are all the same, stripped naked (sometimes literally!) of the masks we wear in our daily lives. To help support others through experiences of transformation, and to see up close and personal the amazing power of the human spirit. To learn that true power often happens in less visible ways. That is truly something to be grateful for.

~ Betsy Burke

Betsy Burke is a nurse trained in both traditional and alternative therapies. She currently resides in Southern Maine, where she supports both children and adults in matters pertaining to health.

March 7

My Mother's Wisdom

"We are here today not for ourselves but to serve others, that is our purpose. Life is about us using our gifts to help others and when we do that we are filled which leads to happiness."

She proceeds to say "When I am working at the barber shop, I will get someone who sits in the chair, we will talk and they will leave better than they came. That is what we are to do: lift people up and let God work through us to help others. Every time that happens I realize why God has kept me alive, it is not for me, it is for others.

It is my purpose to still do His work for Him and help lift others up. I may die tomorrow but for today I am here and you are here, so do all you can, be all you can, serve all you can and believe. That is purpose."

I am so grateful for my mother, Linda Santore, and her wisdom. She has taught me so much and I hope today she taught you something! Know today you are here for a purpose, now go out there and live it.

~ Darleen Santore

Darleen Santore *is a motivational speaker, Peak Performance Coach and transformational expert who empowers people to make a choice and take a chance to create life change. Take action at www.TheDealCoach.com.*

March 8

Socks Are the Solution

Seeing socks on the floor makes me smile.

There are socks everywhere in my house. On the floor in most rooms, strewn across the couch, dangling off light fixtures—it seems that anywhere you look, a sock will catch your eye.

I didn't always feel this way. When Josh and I moved in together, I started an anti-sock-on-the-floor campaign. It went like this: Leave your socks on the floor, and they end up in the trash. After a few days of cold feet, all socks were miraculously picked up!

But now, when I see socks on the floor? I just love those socks.

Those little socks are a symbol of fun. I picture the moment my 2-year-old fell to the ground in a fit of giggles and pulled off her socks with delight. I visualize my 5-year-old whipping off her socks in anticipation for a pedicure.

I work at home, so those moments when I stumble across a sock during my day makes me smile. I anticipate the moment someone will rip off a sock in my office, gleefully exclaiming: "Pink toes!"

Loving socks on the floor is one milestone in my quest to let it be.

~ Jill Shaul

Jill Shaul *is a mom, personal growth coach, martial artist, knitter, marketing professional, and much, much more. Follow her on Twitter @JillShaul or on her blog, www.JillShaul.wordpress.com.*

March 9

Why Work From Home?

Thinking about my life as a wife, mom, and business owner, my family is my motivation to work hard. The decision to work from home has enabled me to juggle all three dimensions with balance, a sense of sanity, and success. For this choice, I am grateful.

During my corporate phase, I experienced countless examples of job stressors: heavy travel, dreaded meetings, inflexible deadlines, plus an income ceiling.

The conclusion to build a home business, with an emphasis on helping people grow their businesses, has eradicated these issues in one stroke, and my career satisfaction has grown exponentially. Working from home, sometimes in yoga pants, with a 16-step commute, gives me the flexibility to set a schedule on my terms, as opposed to my employer's terms.

I am also grateful for my favorite time-saving tools (for example: Apple products, Keynote, Keynote remote, Gmail, Freshbooks, Expensify, and Freeconferencing). I appreciate having the ability to achieve structure, spontaneity, and family time.

The rewards I gain from helping others to grow sales are only enhanced by my freedom to do so from home. For professional success on my own terms, I am grateful.

Is it easy? *No!*

Is it worth it? *Absolutely!*

~ *Barb Girson*

Barb Girson, *direct-selling expert, sales coach, and speaker/trainer, helps companies, teams, and entrepreneurs gain confidence, get into action, and grow sales. For sales tips and articles, reach Barb at www.MySalesTactics.com.*

March 10

Breakfast?

Breakfast? As I sit sipping coffee on a crisp autumn morning, the sun crests the nearby range of hills. Scattered clouds catch the color and distribute it across my vision. My eyes mist at the beauty. A hummingbird comes to feed. It, too, is adorned with beautifully blended colors. It sees me watching and hovers near my face. Is it saying "thank you" for the sweet nectar in the feeder? I reach to protect my eyes from its long beak. It frightens the bird away. Morning is a time for feeding, it seems. I see Black Buck deer in the pasture. They are not deer at all, but more like one would imagine a unicorn. They are not so brightly colored as the hummingbird and sky, but quite dramatic with contrasts of black, brown, and white. Their twisted straight antlers are unique, their movements graceful. One catches my scent, raises his head. His eyes pierce me. I stay motionless. Reassured, he bows to eat, and I sip coffee. I marvel at the beauty about my doorstep, and pause to say "thank you" for eyes to see this beauty, for eyes taken for granted, for eyes that have served me these many years.

~ Sue Taylor

Sue Taylor, *certified Law of Attraction coach, teaches people to use natural laws to clarify their life purpose, their dream, in order to live authentically and by design. Learn more at LiveByDesignCoaching.com.*

March 11

Grateful for the Choice

I lost everything: my home, my job, my money, my car, and even a few people. I lost my identity, my title, and my ability to whip out a checkbook whenever I wanted. Everything I had worked so hard to get was gone.

This was when meditation came into my life. It was the thing that calmed and centered me.

I was able to see my beliefs were creating the patterns in my life. "Why does this keep happening?" was a frequent refrain—until I realized these awful experiences were lessons.

When I didn't get it the first few times, the Universe said, "Okay, Deborah. Are you going to get it this time?" It took me losing everything to finally see it was all about me—how I felt about myself, and what I believed was possible or not possible for me.

When I finally let go of everything, I found me. I finally got that if I wanted something different, I could make different choices.

I am grateful for everything that happens in my life, positive or negative, for they are blessings. They continue to awaken me to my true nature and to understanding how I create my life.

~ Deborah O'Rell

Deborah O'Rell, *as creator and founder of LetGoandGrow.com, is proof that if you live fearlessly and follow your passion, the money will follow. Be the love you seek.*

March 12

Gratitude for Divine Providence

Throughout my life, the people I need in the moment appear. Sometimes they have been on the fringe of my life and move to center stage. Other times they stay forever, but more often they move on to assist others. For these people, I am grateful.

I've noticed I pull wisdom beyond my own, especially in crisis (both mine and others'). I have spoken with others without thinking about it, and later they have told me that what I said made a huge difference. I never remember what I said. I am grateful to the Source from which this wisdom comes.

Experiencing these two phenomena gives me the confidence to meet each life challenge. I know the people and knowledge I need at any given time are available to me. I know the Source and the Sustainer of the universe is present with me when my human frailty is most evident. For that assurance I am eternally grateful.

~ Sue Taylor

Sue Taylor, certified Law of Attraction coach, teaches people to use natural laws to clarify their life purpose, their dream, in order to live authentically and by design. Learn more at LiveByDesignCoaching.com.

March 13

Grateful for the Negative

I spent most of my career feeling frustrated and unappreciated at work. I had many reasons: The work was boring, the environment demeaning, the leadership nonexistent. I wanted to change things—to make work a better place for everyone.

I quit my job and went back to school to learn how to fix organizations. But no one wants to be told they are broken and need to be fixed, so my post-grad efforts to build a business fixing "broken" organizations never really got off the ground. When I stepped back to re-assess my approach, I discovered some important reasons to be grateful to my former employers.

They paid me well, which gave me the freedom to explore new opportunities without having to worry about money. They taught me how to be a good leader—mostly by negative example—but learning from bad examples is actually a very effective way to learn. And they motivated me to go back to school and begin a new chapter in my life.

To be truly grateful for the amazing life I have now, I have to acknowledge the part my former employers played in helping me get here. They were my inspiration!

~ *Kathy Scheiern*

Kathy Scheiern *helps people struggling to change their lives get back on track to achieving their hopes and dreams. Get in touch at www.YourBigBreakthroughCoach.com.*

March 14

Always Have Faith

There is much of my mom that is a mystery to me. But there are some things that she taught me without realizing it. As missionaries in Africa, my parents chose to send us to boarding school. This was not always easy for us, or her. I realize now that she taught me the value of doing whatever was necessary to fulfill your calling in life, even when it is hard. Her complete belief, passion, and faith for her calling have been an example I have recalled on many occasions when it felt like I'd lost my own.

Without knowing it, her example taught me to find a way to be resourceful and have courage, no matter what life threw my way; to have a foundation of fortitude; and to never let go of my faith. Her decisions taught me to be independent and to consider the whole picture before making a choice.

Through her actions, my mom showed me what it meant to hold a vision of a better world. She showed me how even the smallest contribution can make a big difference.

Thank you, Mom, for your unwavering faith and constant prayers for me.

~ *Teresa C. Lea*

Teresa C. Lea *shows people how to heal, reclaim their lives, and step into a place of personal power. You can reach her at InTouchInLife.com.*

March 15

Joy Is Like a Boomerang

Each time I visit my favorite deli, I'm greeted by Melissa, the super-sweet manager who strives to give me the best experience possible. She lights up when I come in, goes out of her way to welcome me, and is one of the reasons I love being a customer. So I sent the owner an e-mail with feedback about how Melissa enhances my lunchtime visits.

The next time I came in, I felt like a celebrity. Melissa ran right over to me, hugged me, and said, "Come with me!" She led me into the back room, where a printed-out version of my e-mail was hanging on the wall—with the supervisor's words plastered at the top of the page in black marker: "GREAT JOB!" Melissa exclaimed to her co-workers as she pointed at me: "She's the one who sent the e-mail!" Then after another hug, she quietly said, with such depth in her eyes: "You don't know this, but you made my day."

And what she didn't know was that by seeing and feeling her joy, she made my day.

Joy is like a boomerang: Dish it out, it comes back to you.

How will you spread joy today?

~ Michelle Joy Stimpson

Michelle Joy Stimpson is the premier life coach for positive change and joyful living at LifeShine®, working with women who feel stuck and who are ready to make important changes. Find out more at www.LifeShineCoaching.com.

March 16

My Life Purpose Journey

Life experiences inspire us to take action. For me it was surviving breast cancer and a post-operative hemorrhage. I realized God had spared my life for a reason. So I became the Gratitude Queen, volunteering and giving back in ways I felt mattered. However, as my fifth anniversary as a survivor approached, there was an intense yearning to know and live my life purpose. Was I on the right path? Thus, my journey to discovering my life purpose began.

The Universe orchestrated events so that a conference I'd planned to attend was cancelled. This freed me up to attend a life purpose training that I'd known about for months and yet had not acted upon. There my life purpose clearly came into focus. Now I live my life purpose as a spiritual teacher and counselor, and joyously share my deep inner wisdom with love and heart with the individuals I am blessed to serve. Each morning my journal entry begins with "Thank you God for this day." Then I ask that I be led make conscious decisions that support and honor my life purpose journey.

~ *Cecelia Dawe-Gillis*

Cecelia Dawe-Gillis, MS, CPC, *of www.PalmPurpose.com is a retired Navy Nurse Corps Captain whose spiritual journey led her to becoming a life purpose coach who helps others live their life purpose.*

March 17

How to Stay Married

I was singing and he was playing trumpet. We began as high school sweethearts. Today we're Baby Boomer lovers. Many people ask us how we've done it. How have we weathered the storms that inevitably happen in a marriage? How have we stayed married, let alone be crazy in love? The answer is both simple and complicated. It's simple, because we both decided at the beginning that this was a lifelong commitment. It's complicated, because when you're young and in love you have no idea what commitment really means.

In our situation it meant holding him close during a near bankruptcy instead of being angry at him for the mistakes that cost us our home and our bank account. A few years later commitment meant that he would forgive my dangerous flirtations with another and ask what he could do to satisfy my needs. With our children commitment meant, instead of finger-pointing and blaming, we prayed together for our precious, rebellious teenagers who were kicked out of private school and caused us both to lose our teaching jobs.

What am I grateful for? The God-given decision to be committed to each other "until death do us part."

~ Cherie Mason

Cherie Mason *started both of her businesses, Cheryl Mason Interiors (design) and GEMCA Productions (acting and modeling), after turning 50. Her passion is to help others follow their dreams.*

March 18

Magical Memories

Thanks, Dad, for introducing me to the world of card tricks and magic. I have fond memories of sitting with you and learning how to set them up. I loved the tricks, and I loved the thrill of delighting kids with ESP and magic. Over the years, as I made a way for myself in the teaching profession, the magic wanderlust inside of me grew and blossomed into a hobby that is still an important part of me today, some 45 years later.

At first, I was the "magic sub," very popular with kids and teachers because I always got the work done—and I always found time for a quick magic trick or puzzle.

Throughout my 30-year career as a science teacher and as a science department head, I found ways to weave magic into my lessons and mentoring sessions. I hosted a Public Access TV show last year called *Show Me the Science: The Magic of Science and the Science of Magic.* This year I developed two magic toolkits for teachers that will help teachers to motivate and captivate students of all ages.

Thanks, Dad—for the gift of magic!

~ *Peter Suchmann*

Peter Suchmann *(aka "Presto Pete") is a retired educator and owner of Magic Moments with Class. Find him at www.MagicMomentsWith Class.com or e-mail Contact-Pete@MagicMomentsWithClass.com.*

March 19

Watching My Mother

After 16 years of teaching in public elementary school, I've spent countless moments in my classroom thinking about all the things that I have learned from my mom. My mother's influence on my life is evident each and every day in my classroom. When I watched her care for people at the nursing home, I learned compassion. When I watched her play the piano week after week at our church, I learned to have the heart of a servant, to use my gifts to glorify God. When I watched her greet everyone with a smile at our school, where she was the secretary, I learned the importance of making people feel valued and welcome. When I helped her prepare our meals after a long day at work, I learned the importance of time with family. When we visited her aging siblings, I learned about responsibility, love, and respect for those who once cared for us. I am grateful for the opportunities to observe my mother and learn from her Christian example. I know that her influence flows through me and on to my students every single day.

~ *Laurie K. Wells*

Laurie K. Wells is a teacher and lives in Tyler, Texas. She loves to bike, camp, and read good books. Reach Laurie at Laurie.Katheryn@yahoo. com.

March 20

Lessons in Nature

Metaphors are everywhere, especially in nature. Words alone can be powerful, but when I actually get to see and experience a lesson, the message really hits home. Fog is one of my most favorite elements of nature. Fog represents mystery, uncertainty, faith, and trust. We need all of these in our lives—yes, even uncertainty. If everything was predictable, we would be very bored.

Trees are full of endless lessons. Like trees, we need deep roots to ground us, solid centers to stabilize us, and outstretched arms to open ourselves up to receive and to provide refuge. Daring to be the top of the tree will yield the highest view, but will also make us more susceptible to strong winds. As long as our center stays strong and roots are deep, we can weather anything.

Storms are also great teachers. Lightning and thunder may seem scary, but usually there is nothing to fear. Many of the things we worry about are never really a threat, either. Life may be stormy on the outside, but I can remain calm and safe on the inside. Storms in life provide contrast so we can better appreciate the sunny days.

Live, love, and learn!

~ Angela Howell

Angela Howell *is passionate about helping others find truth, beauty, and vision. She is writing a book titled* Finding the Gift: Daily Meditations in Nature. *Contact Angela at www.ShutterCreekPhoto.com.*

March 21

Lost and Found Moments

My life has been a series of lost and found moments. Being lost so many times has made me unafraid to speak to strangers. Every time I have reached out for directions they have always done their best to help me. Being lost has brought me into parts of the world I would have never, ever gone or even known about. After I got over being angry and frustrated with my GPS or at the fact that I was late, I realized I would have missed some very beautiful places near and far from my home. Being lost in this journey has done more to cause me to go deeper inside of myself than being found ever did. However, the joys of being found, missed, or discovered are also cherished highlights.

Perhaps being lost and found is how we make the most profound discoveries about life, and about ourselves and others. May this day be sprinkled with lost and found in the dark moments, causing us to expand our universe and to press in, dig deeper, until the Light shines through!

~ *Theresa McMorrow Jordan*

Theresa McMorrow Jordan *is the mother of Jeff and Seth, and has a lifetime vision and mission to see the Earth become more like Heaven. She is a published songwriter and author of the soon-to-be-published* Get Crowned.

March 22

Thank You, Divine Mother

I am grateful for the loving presence of Divine Mother in my life. Known by many names, Her gifts of light, healing, and peace fill every cell of my being. Her re-emergence upon this beautiful planet marks a time of great shifts. I am grateful to ride the waves of Her loving energy.

I am Grateful for the bold strength I feel within when I invoke Her divine presence.

I am Grateful for all the ways Her light radiates into the core of my being, holding me up and allowing me to be one of the beacons, sharing Her wisdom and light.

I stand in the center of a beautiful meadow, circled with sacred, healing light. My arms stretch up to the sky, expressing my gratitude to the Universe, feeling my heart full as I imagine Her sweet loving energy enter my crown chakra, and gently flow this liquid light down into the deepest wisdom area's my heart.

Anchoring the blessing of Her energy into my heart. I open my heart, like a full blooming rose, and radiate this energy, truth, and blessing forth to the entire planet. This is my shared blessing to you. Right here, right now!

~ DaKara Kies

DaKara Kies *is a gifted intuitive healer who specializes in clearing core issues and energy blocks that hold you back from stepping into your true purpose, power, and passion. Learn more at HPTHealing.com.*

March 23

Take Time to Reflect

It is easy to get caught up in cacophony of daily life and miss the opportunity to appreciate the beauty that surrounds you. That first breath that you take in the morning after you awake is a reminder that you are alive and vital, and that today is going to be the day you make a difference.

Two of the things I love to witness are the sunrise and sunset that bracket each end of the day. Many days the skies are an expression of variegated hues painting a unique picture that will never be repeated. Taking a moment to witness a sunrise or a sunset is a great way to step out of the turmoil of daily life and to experience a few minutes of peace.

The next time you're able, take a minute, stop, and just look at the skies as the sun sets or rises, and reflect on what you do have and what you can do. Take the time to find peace with yourself. In the crimson beauty that spreads across the horizon, take time to reflect on what your day can be or what your day has become.

~ Dan Weigold

Dan Weigold is a career and leadership development coach. He works with people who face the issue of AD/HD who desire to develop ways to increase their success and happiness.

March 24

The Gift of Imperfection

Perfection is such an illusion. Not one of us can obtain it, yet we try daily. We are not consciously thinking about it; it's subconscious, which is even more frightening. What is it about imperfection that we find so distasteful? We all have experienced failures and disappointments, which clearly is nothing new. What is it about not being right that causes us to cringe and want to hide from the world? Where did that come from?

Today let's be grateful for our imperfections. We were custom-designed (flaws and all) by God the creator, so who are we to alter his most prized creation? Rick Warren once said, "We are all intentionally flawed to make us unique." That truly is the way God wanted it. Our best contribution to the world comes from sharing our pain and imperfections with others. We give them permission to do the same. Looking back, it has been those imperfect situations that we have fought through, and came out better and stronger on the other side of, that really truly count. Now that is what I call *perfection*.

~ *Dana M. Rosser*

Dana M. Rosser is dedicated to educating people on how to support loved ones and their challenge with obesity. You can reach her at www.FacingObesity.com.

March 25

My Mother's Gift

When my mom was pregnant with me, my sister, Linda, then only 2, was dying of leukemia. It was a struggle for her to care for her dying child, a grieving husband, and the child she held inside her womb.

As the weeks passed, she grew weary and heavy with the grief she felt she could no longer carry. In her tender words: "I went to my knees in fervent prayer and asked God to help me. Then a miracle happened. I could actually feel the weight of the pain I felt being lifted from my shoulders, and a comfort unlike I had ever experienced. I knew that I was not alone, that I would have the strength to go on."

Linda died two weeks after I was born. Mom said it was the "arms of God" that carried her through as He took one angel home and sent another.

I now have four wonderful sons of my own. I am so grateful for my mother's courage and faith, and the message of hope she has given to me and our family: "We are never alone, even in the darkest hours." Thank you, Mom.

~ Christine Marie Jones

Christine Marie Jones mentors bodywork professionals to take their business to the next level. You can find her at twitter.com/ MentorChristine.

March 26

My Grateful Journey

My gratitude is for the direction my spirituality and business have taken me, and how I have incorporated both career and personal growth.

If you enjoy your work you never have to work again. This is now my motto, and I give thanks every day for this opportunity.

I recall asking the Universe with total sincerity if it was possible to help guide or coach people and make a living at the same time, after assisting a friend through a difficult time.

Guess what? It wasn't long before this opportunity became a reality. I stumbled across a coaching course that fit the bill quite nicely, and that was the beginning of the rest of my career and life.

There have been challenges along the way, as such big changes often bring. As much as I wanted this, I was in a place of resistance that I needed to overcome.

With the support and belief of family and friends, I have come out the other end, and, yes, my dream has become a reality.

Although I continue to learn and grow, I am so grateful that I have found this path and am so excited for what the future will bring.

~ *Deb Leonard*

Deb Leonard *lives with her husband, Bill, and children, William and Gemma, in Australia. She is the founder of Choices 4 You and a Law of Attraction coach. Learn more at www.Choices4You.com.au.*

March 27

Thank You, My Angel

I look through the window and see my beautiful little girl happily playing in the morning sunshine. She is collecting mini beasts, from the garden, and every few minutes she brings them before me to inspect. I praise her for her triumphant find, and off she skips to continue her mission.

What she doesn't realize is that every time I look at her it is with a heart full of gratitude, as six years ago she saved my life.

Four days after she was born I was rushed to the hospital, having multiple seizures, and diagnosed with a large meningioma brain tumor. It was the natural water loss after birth that had caused the tumor to destabilize, trigger the fits, and prompt the emergency team to do a head scan.

Unknowingly, I had been living with the tumor for several years, and without the pregnancy it would have continued to remain undetected.

Sophie had not only saved my life but every day thereafter she was my inspiration to get well and make a full recovery.

Life is the most precious gift you have.

Don't take it for granted; be grateful for every single day.

~ Debra Jayne Gotch

Debra Jayne Gotch, is the author of Embracing Life-My New Normal, a personal story inspiring brain tumor survivors to overcome fear and find happiness. Learn more at www.My-New-Normal.com.

March 28

A New Beginning

Gratitude for the gifts of life is easy. My "gift" was two lay-offs in one year—a cosmic comet aimed at my head and my heart. I didn't recognize the gift at first and rushed off to apply for a new job. This was what I knew. On each interview, I found that my well of enthusiasm and passion had run dry. A few years back, I had begun planning what I would do when I retired. What would it be like if I just started to do this now instead of waiting?

I began writing a book, *Career Savvy: Keeping and Transforming Your Job*, a project that had kept slipping behind more immediate goals. Based on my coaching work, I knew this book could help a lot of people who only knew how to manage their career when the economy was strong. At the same time, I realized that the wave of layoffs could represent an opportunity for me. I started a company, Kalm Kreative, Inc., to offer marketing, writing, and speaking services to downsized companies. With each passing day, I realize that, without the layoffs, fear would have kept me from realizing my dream.

~ Denise P. Kalm

Denise P. Kalm, BCC, *is a coach, writer, and entrepreneur. Denise is a popular speaker at conferences and is available to speak to your group. Learn more at www.DPKCoaching.com.*

March 29

I Just Managed

As a young girl growing up in West Africa, I admired and loved my father for his supportiveness. He was a school-teacher who taught us kids to value education, strive for life's best, and always express our needs.

As I grew older, it started to bother me that my dad didn't let my mother have a voice, or support her life's goals. Instead Mama experienced ongoing hardship because of his infidelity (which was condoned by our culture). Mama's dream was to be the first among her mother's children to ever graduate from high school, continue on to college, and become a professional woman. But she became pregnant with me when she was in 11th grade, married my dad, and had six more children. She never completed her schooling or lived the lifestyle she had envisioned for herself. I wondered many times how she felt all those years. Finally, after my dad died, I had the courage to ask her. She replied, "I just managed. The struggle was worth it because the cause was noble." In that moment I realized the valuable lifelong lesson she taught me by the way she lived her life. I love you, Mama!

~ *Winifred Q. Giddings*

Winifred Q. Giddings, *international life coach, equips modern-day professional women to reclaim their ability to dream and discover their truth. Find her at PerceptionMattersCoaching.com.*

March 30

So Grateful to Know

I am so grateful to know that every single being has at least a little positive thinking—that every single being has the same fundamental nature: They each want to be happy. True happiness is their nature; it is the nature of their thinking. They never need to be taught this; they just naturally, always, want to be happy.

I am so grateful to know that whatever we think grows, so that whenever we have positive thinking it grows. When we have more positive thinking it grows even more, and at the same time it deletes negative thinking. This is the law of nature.

I am so grateful to know the first teaching of the Buddha, the Four Noble Truths, which contains all wisdom of the enlightened ones regarding suffering and its cause, and true happiness and its cause. From that I know the cause of my suffering is my own negative thinking and negative karma, which is also the condition for others' suffering. And I know the cause of my happiness is my own positive thinking and positive karma, which is also the condition for all others' happiness.

Amazing! Amazing! What a victory! I celebrate with boundless elation!

~ *Devatara Holman*

Devatara Holman, MS, MA, Lac, *is a physician of Oriental Medicine, Upasika Bodhisattva Dharma Teacher in the Dzogchen Lineage of Tibetan Buddhism, Qigong Master, and healer. Read more on her work at www.MarinOrientalMedicine.com.*

March 31

The Gift of "Special"

As parents we know that every child is special. Their laughter, smiles, kisses, and hugs can make all the bad in the world disappear. I was given the gift of an extra-special child, whose continued childlike innocence has allowed me to enjoy that incredible innocence so much longer than most do. The excitement of Christmas and Santa Claus, Easter and the promise of candy delivered by the Easter Bunny still a bright gleam in his eyes. People will tell me I must have the patience of a saint. That is not at all true; if anything, quite the opposite, but my gift has helped me to quell the agitation I feel when my patience is at its end. It has taught me to look at other parents with empathy when their patience is tried in public, and it has taught me to embrace the uniqueness in all extra-special children. My amazing gift has taught me many things and revealed many things about myself I may never have known. Have I over the years wished things were different? Sure. Would I change it if I could? Not a chance. I am grateful for "special."

~ Sheryl Marshall

Sheryl Marshall is a hobby writer and poet, as well as the mother of a very handsome, extra-special, young man.

April

"*Praise the bridge that carried you over.*"

~ George Colman

April 1

Hairpins, Cows, and Laughter

This April Fools' Day, I am grateful for the gift of laughter and a proper perspective on life. My mother taught me that. She was always sharing jokes and funny stories with us growing up. No matter what was going on, she would often be the first to laugh at herself for doing dumb things or taking herself too seriously. Sometimes when we were traveling across country on a month's vacation with the five of us children in a small car (think Volkswagen Bug in the ' 60s), Mom would get a little testy in the front passenger seat. Picture this: There's a flailing baby on her lap as she's trying to make cucumber and tomato sandwiches using the open glove compartment as a table. Hungry, squabbling kids in the back seat are vying to get theirs first. All this commotion escalates through hairpin turns in the mountains, traveling at much higher speeds than she thinks safe, until she finally comments on my dad's driving. Whew! It's no wonder... But at that, the backseat chorus sings out, "Mom, don't have a cow!" Why not live this day lighthearted? Don't stress and "have a cow"! Unwrap your gift of laughter instead.

~ Lois Gallo

*A minister's daughter retired from the financial profession, now turned author, speaker, coach, and artist, **Lois Gallo** continues to inspire people to embrace life every day. Visit www.LivingWithHeartAndPower. com for more inspiration.*

April 2

Thoughts of Spring

Spring is my favorite time of year. Summer is nice, when school is out. Autumn is great, especially on Halloween. And it's hard to find anything more pleasurable than sharing a cup of cocoa under the winter Christmas tree.

But spring—just thinking about it makes my eyes go misty. The snow turns to slush, the slush turns to streams, and the streams trickle down the side of the road and into the drains, taking with them every last memory of the cold, harsh winter. Then the birds start singing. No birds have sung for four months, but now the forest is alive with song.

Then the flowers start sprouting, and the butterflies arrive. And the overcoats are hung in the back of the closet, waiting for when it gets chilly again.

I sometimes wonder if, when I grow older, I will still take the time to enjoy sitting in a tree to read a good book, or run through the fields without a care in the world, or just lie down in the grass and listen to the sounds of spring. I hope so.

~ *Mark Prusakowski*

Mark Prusakowski *is a 13-year-old middle school student who enjoys designing games and reading. He is a contributor to Kudoskids.com and has a blog (FunBrainPlayground.org).*

April 3

Retirement with a Purpose

Gratitude for retirement may be assumed for most people, but in my case it was an opportunity to embark on the journey to my life's purpose. As an avid photographer, I dreamed of my talents being used to serve others.

With my focus on this goal, opportunities appeared before me. In January 2012 I was invited to join a dedicated group of physicians, nurses, and support staff on a medical mission to Calapan in the Philippines. I was to be the photographer, documenting the entire mission. The mission was self-funded by each volunteer. The common thread among the group was the willingness to serve and to offer solutions to Philippine residents who had never before received medical care.

The mission was coordinated by the Catholic Diocese in Calapan. A large clinic was created from a church hall, and two local hospitals offered the use of their operating rooms. In less than five days, the mission team treated over 1,300 residents and performed over 70 life-changing operations. I was privileged to photograph many of the operations in the hospitals as well as the clinic. It feels like my camera has grown wings! For this I am extremely and grateful.

~ *Diane Watson*

Diane Watson *is an aspiring author and an award-winning photographer from Atlanta, Georgia. Since retiring, her photographic mission has focused on serving the less fortunate of the world.*

April 4

Be Quick, Sincere, Heartfelt

Gratitude and thankfulness are your recognition that some-one kind showed love and concern for you.

Your recognition of their kindness means far more to them in return, no matter what it cost them in time or money.

Do it quickly, sincerely, often, and without fail, and tell them what it meant to you. No doubt they will say "Glad to do it" or "Don't mention it," but in their heart they will rejoice and love you even more.

"Like apples of gold in settings of silver is a word spoken in the right circumstance."

~ Proverbs 25:11

~ Don Smith

Don Smith is the founder and director of Village Empowerment, teaching villages in the poorest areas of Africa and the Philippines life skills and to be self-sustaining. For more information go to www.VillageEmpowerment.org.

April 5

Bittersweet

O f all the things I get to do, serving at the homeless shelter is one of my favorites. It gets me out of myself, and reminds me that life isn't all about me and that a small sacrifice translates into hope-filled moments for hopeless people. I get a deep sense that I was in the presence of something sacred.

I listened to their stories and offered my new friends a cup of encouragement in Jesus' name, knowing that typically not everything was okay, but in that moment of time it was. We talked about the bitter and the sweet—how nothing is wasted. Not even the bad stuff.

I think I'm catching on and getting closer to something God wanted to show me all along. I cannot take away their homelessness or another person's pain. But I can be there, and I can feed them, and I can listen to their stories. No matter how small, we can make a difference in someone's life. That is sacred.

The harder I look, the more thankful I am for what I learn and become, and what God teaches me. For this time, and every time, I am thankful.

~ Donna Buice

Donna Buice *is the creator of Inspired Living, created to encourage and inspire women to live a life of passion, purpose, and fulfillment. She can be contacted at www.Twitter.com/DonnaBuice.*

April 6

Where Is My Gratitude?

D o you sometimes ask yourself, "Why don't I feel grateful all the time? What does it take for to me feel grateful for all the amazing and exquisite people, things, and opportunities in my life?" Gratitude isn't easy when you've been focusing and listening to the outside (ego/programming/materialism) of you and ignoring the inside (soul/spirit/heart) of you. If the inside of you is not engaged there is no way for you to feel authentic and permanent gratitude. With all the chaos in today's world keeping us in a continuous whirlwind, it's so challenging to find the time to go within, and to know and listen to the inner you. True? Actually, there is time, so start now with these few simple tips:

- Start noting the good in everybody and everything.
- If you say or think something unpleasant, nasty or in anger, cancel it and follow it up with forgiving yourself and the word "love."
- Surround yourself with positive, happy, and grateful people.
- Look, be open, and find the silver lining lesson.
- Don't give up. Be committed.

Remember: When you are feeling (inside) gratefulness, then your world (outside) will be grateful too!

Namaste with Unity "Love" Consciousness

~ *Wendy Baudín*

Wendy Baudín, MPA, SLC, *is a Self-Love Sherpa, "Your Self-Love Transformation Journey" mentor, spiritual life coach, speaker, and author. Learn more at www.WendyBaudin.com and www.Facebook.com/ WendyBaudinWisdomGuide.*

April 7

Changing Seasons

I magine the beauty that is delivered to us each day of the year as the seasons change. I am grateful for the variety.

Every day a new scene is presented, and throughout the day the lighting is automatically adjusted. The changes can be subtle from day to day. Sometimes the changes are sudden and dramatic, like when a storm cloud rapidly blows in, delivering snow or a heavy downpour. Sometimes a sudden drop in temperature causes condensation or frost patterns on the windows. On cold and rainy days I yearn for the hot and dry days. On the hot, dry days I recall the snowy, winter days and the crunch of crisp snow under my feet.

I enjoy feeling the warm sun on my face or the wind pushing against my body. I enjoy hearing the rain, wind, and thunder, and smelling the fragrant blossoms.

I appreciate every nuance of fall's kaleidoscope of colors, and spring's multitude of green hues, from budding trees and emerging plants stretching for the warm spring sun.

Thanks for the changing seasons.

~ Doug Jarvie

Doug Jarvie *graduated in honors physics, taught electronics, and designed and programmed energy management systems. Executive responsibilities led Doug to mentoring and coaching others about personal energy and expectation management.*

April 8

God Is So Good

"God is so good.

God is so good.

God is so good.

He's so good to me."

I've sung this song in Sunday school for years. Its simple words and tune are a constant reminder of all that we have to be thankful for. In fact, my favorite holiday has always been Thanksgiving. Our founding fathers knew how fortunate they were to have traveled the rough seas and persevered to overcome overwhelming odds so that they may gather around a table and give thanks for all God had done for them. We are so blessed to be able to celebrate this on a national level each year.

I am thankful each day for the blessings God has given me. I have a lovely family, with a beautiful wife and two very special girls. I am grateful for the work I do and am honored to work in a profession that I chose and enjoy. We live in the greatest country in the world and have freedoms that many would be willing to die for. God is so good. He's so good to me. So what do you have to be thankful for? Take a moment to list a few.

~ DR Fraley

DR Fraley is a filmmaker, actor, and coach with a passion for uniting local filmmakers and producing projects in the Greater Chattanooga area. You can find him at www.Facebook.com/DRFraley2.

April 9

Doctor Gives God Credit

April 9 is my husband's birthday. He is fortunate to be alive. Two years ago, his cardiologist referred him to a hematologist/oncologist because his white bood cell count was high. His diagnosis was chronic mylogenic leukemia. He started treating my husband with a pill that was not available 15 years ago. Therefore, he would be dead now had he developed the leukemia earlier in his life. After two years of treatment, his blood count is normal thanks to a knowledgable doctor who refuses to take credit for the healing. When my husband starting thanking his doctor for all he had done to heal him, his doctor said, "Thank God." My heart is full of gratitude for a doctor who gives God the credit for healing, and I am very grateful that my wonderful husband is in remission.

~ Norma Bonner Elmore

Norma Bonner Elmore, EdD, *is a teacher, singer, pianist, and pageant judge. She loves to read, dance, and travel. She has one son, one grandson, and one great-grandson.*

April 10

Gratitude's Surprising Origins

I am surprised to find myself full of gratitude when I take care of the more mundane parts of life, like cleaning the basement, sweeping, cooking, and exercising. Often I would rather be doing joy-filled activities like shopping or eating homemade apple pie. Yet when I have gratitude for the basics (my garden, my house, my family) I remember with fuller clarity what's truly important in life. Ironically, when I spend time tending to simple things, my fidgety mind and restless soul calm. I breathe more deeply, see more clearly, move more freely, and think more boldly. I am centered and feel held by something greater than myself. I initiate professional "next steps" with confidence and make choices fully grounded in my core values. I am disciplined and can focus for longer periods of time. My head, heart, and belly are aligned so I can live into my dreams, both personal and professional. Gratitude is an essential ingredient for sustainable success. In short, when I focus on gratitude I feel more peace, joy, and compassion in my heart.

~ *Madeline McNeely*

Madeline McNeely, *founder of Conditioning Leaders, provides leadership coaching and consulting. Her company conditions leaders and organizations to do meaningful work for decades. Contact her at www. ConditioningLeaders.com or www.In-BalanceCoaching.com.*

April 11

First Rain in April

The month of April usually ushers in the first rain of the year before the global climate change. Usually, it would come furtively, except for a few gathering gloomy clouds, unaccompanied by the usual tropical rumbling thunder or the unnerving lightning flashes. Like a sprinkling, it would come, but a sprinkling so vast the whole town is touched: a quickie rain. Then the sudden lowering of the temperature would calm all nerves and skin. The welcome change, the welcome coolness on the skin, the change from the scorching heat that seemed to turn the whole body into a furnace and make one want to tear off one's clothes, will tip the mind. Grateful that summer is here; let the birthing begin. All that was nursed, incubated, and dreamt about during the scorching heat, would burst forth, racing to be first to welcome the coolness of summer.

~ *Lucy Irene Vajime*

Lucy Irene Vajime, *lecturer and life coach, is ardent about sharing how to reach within to manifest our dreams. She lives in central Nigeria and can be reached on Facebook.*

April 12

Merlin's Magical Teachings

Out of the blue my girlfriend announced that I needed to get a dog because my heart needed to open more. I defensively answered that nothing was wrong with my heart. I started pondering this idea and thought it was impossible with my travel schedule and already having three cats. A few months later, my friend found my puppy, and two days later he arrived at my house. Merlin is joy on steroids, and he is the happiest creature I have encountered. He has taught me about unconditional love through the way he greets and treats each person—exactly the same way, with unconditional love and enthusiasm. He makes each person feel special. Merlin's loving consistency has taught me to let go of the little and big things in life, and to keep my heart softer and more loving with people. I feel happier, calmer, and more joyful and loving because of Merlin. I am so fortunate to have him in my life, and I give thanks to him every day for his gentle teachings.

~ Bridget Engel

Bridget Engel, angel intuitive and personal life coach, teaches people how to utilize their intuition and Divine Guidance to create big results in their lives.

April 13

I've Seen Enough

My daughter is only 12 years old, but through those years I've seen enough to know that she is special and will do great things, no matter how big or small; that she is compassionate and will help others; that she is talented and will follow her passions; that she is incredibly insightful and will nurture her relationships; that she is honest and will be in touch with what is real; that she is creative and will bravely express herself; that she is beautiful, because she is; that she is loved, because I will always love her and that love will stay with her forever; that I couldn't be more proud of her than I am today, because I've seen enough to know her.

~ Lisa Arvanaghi

Lisa Arvanaghi *lives in San Diego, Calif. She may be reached at LisaArvanaghi@san.rr.com.*

April 14

Rise Up!

Have you wondered if your life can make a difference? As I approached my 70th birthday, I experienced a stronger urgency to fulfill a lifetime dream to publish a book as a positive legacy. A sense of uncertainty exists as I face health challenges that seem to threaten my independence and length of life. The date of my 70th birthday was predetermined and specific. What better way to celebrate than to realize my dream? Just in time, God sent Donna Kozik, who coached me to victory. Imagine the thrill of surprising my family and friends at the party with a gift: my book, *Rise Up! 71 Thoughts of Hope & Inspiration for Women of Value.* While we celebrated a lifetime of love, I also experienced the joy of perseverance and achievement. Not over the hill, but one who is thankful to be alive. Proof of fulfillment of a dream, at any age. The purpose of the book is to encourage women, no matter what stage of life they are in, to rise up. To claim and advocate for their God-given label of Woman of Value. I am thankful that God has allowed me to realize my dream to publish a book, living to see its fulfillment and leaving the message that we are valuable in the eyes of God.

~ *Judi G. Reid*

Judi G. Reid advocates for the respect and dignity of all women. Connect with her at www.WomenOfValue.org or www.Facebook.com/ JudiGReid.

April 15

Endless Love

When we decided to get a puppy for my 8-year-old son, I was terribly afraid of animals. In fact, I would not touch an animal, and no one who knew me would have thought I would own a dog (or any pet). I am a great bird watcher. Soon after King, our Brindle Bullmastiff, was delivered to our front door, he quickly learned the house rules and, when he was ready, attended obedience training. For the first 8 to 10 months, things went fine—meaning I would arrive home from work, look through the mail, and head upstairs. One day I was unable to head up the stairs: King had centered himself on the stairs and would not move. He just sat there, looking past me out the window with his tail wagging. Suddenly my son appeared and said, "King!" He immediately jumped off the stairs. At that moment, I got it. King taught me what it felt like to be ignored and treated like an invisible being. I learned that animals have feelings, and for the next 12 years I experienced deep gratitude for his presence in our family, and his endless love and devotion.

~ *Millie Sunday Jett*

Millie Sunday Jett *is a co-author, speaker, registered nurse, lieutenant colonel (retired), and emotional freedom and healing facilitator. Find her at Facebook.com/Millie.Jett or LinkedIn.com/in/ MillieSundayJett2cu.*

April 16

Horses: Friends and Teachers

Since childhood, horses have blessed me with friendship, unconditional love, and more of an education than I received in any classroom. This valuable lesson from my horse, Trigger, is just one of many I am grateful for. It was a beautiful spring day, and I wanted to spend some quality time bonding with Trigger. I gathered my grooming tools and headed for the pasture, purposely leaving halter and lead rope behind. While I brushed Trigger, he grazed quietly. All was well and peaceful. That is, until I reached for a bottle of fly spray. To show his displeasure, Trigger promptly departed. Every time I approached him, he turned and walked away. Finally he stopped in a fence corner, his rear facing me. In horse language, this isn't a nice gesture! Intuitively, I remembered that by shifting focus from thinking to feeling, I could communicate with Trigger heart-to-heart. I was amazed at how quickly he responded to this new approach. Within seconds, he spun around and softened his stance. This time he didn't move while I used the spray on him. In that moment, without words, I sent Trigger genuine love and appreciation, and he responded by trusting me.

~ Leslie Hagerich

Leslie Hagerich, CPC, *empowers individuals and organizations by getting to the "heart" of what motivates people and performance. You can find her at LeadersEdgeCoaching.com.*

April 17

They Got a *Dog!*

I, Mighty Samson the Cat, lived with my human family and was doing just fine until June 21, 1996. That was the day they brought home this four-footed, white-and-red-colored thing. I heard them describe it as a "Brittany Spaniel mix," whatever that was, whose name was Thor. No matter to the ilk, I knew I had to show Thor who was in charge. The humans set up old milk crates by the windows where Thor could sit and see outside without scratching up the sills. I sabotaged that idea by sprawling my long, sleek gray body the entire length of the crate whenever Thor wanted to look out at the world; he would not dare chance the sharp rebuke of my talons. One day Thor came home from a visit to the vet. He was lethargic and very sleepy. Oh no! The humans did to him what they did to me! As much as I wanted them to believe I disliked Thor, I felt for the poor guy. This was the only time I lay down next to him, offering comfort. Drugged-up Thor would never remember I was kind! I was boss in more ways than one.

~ *Peggy Lee Hanson*

Peggy Lee Hanson mentors those who experience life-changing situations and guides them through their journey using proven strategies. You can reach Peggy at MyDreamArchitect.com.

April 18

Daisy's Love

I vividly remember the day I met my Daisy. She was a 4-month-old stray puppy, and from her distinct features it was clear that she was part Pit Bull. I was gathering my things from my Jeep when I looked up to see her charging at me. I was alone, with no other humans anywhere in sight, and there was no time to seek shelter. As she got to my feet, she literally flopped over on her back, paws up in the air, and smiled as if to say, "Just love me, because I already love you." And I have loved her since that moment. Daisy's love has been such a blessing—not only to me, but to every person she meets. She is so full of love. In fact, she has so much love that my husband and I share her with the world! We take her practically everywhere—nursing homes, schools, community events, local businesses, parks, and parades—and everyone greets her with open arms just as she greets them with an open heart. What a wonderful message she has for the world: everyone deserves to be loved. And for that, I am grateful.

~ *Rhonda Chuyka*

Rhonda Chuyka *teaches high school chemistry and Jazzercise in West Virginia, was named "Teacher of the Year" in 2009 and 2011, and lives to inspire others.*

April 19

No Pacemaker Required

Bandit is our mascot. Tennis is our game. We serve up kindness with Kids Play For Good, acing causes on courts in your backyard and mine. No cause is too big to conquer. Our hearts are stoked by kindness, while our shots are filled with sting. Caring is our armor; it's the sweetest coat of all. We raise our racquets high. Chasing tails and poaching dreams, Bandit leads our champions' team. And like Bandit, we play in the moment to stay in the moment.

Joy is our favorite ball, quick-start tennis our winning format. Mushers for causes nationwide, we make our mark. Pulling together we are top dogs. Playing with heart. Kids at the start. Doing great work. No napping, no yapping. Passion flies our net. Made in America. Made with heart. Serving up the stuff of champions. Bandit stole our hearts, and he'll heal your heart. After all, he's the only service dog taking center court! Kids Play For Good: not for the faint of heart, only for the big of heart.

Bandit is our mascot. Service is our creed. Kindness is our rallying cry. Do you want to join our winning team?

~ *Lynn Morrell*

Lynn Morrell *helps tennis kids nationwide champion kindness and hone their philanthropic muscle online and on court. Visit KidsPlayForGood.org.*

April 20

There She Was

I remember the first time I saw her. She was sitting underneath a citrus tree in our backyard. It was a cold, rainy afternoon, and there was sadness in her eyes. We didn't know where she came from, but she had been visiting our backyard on a regular basis. One day, when my mum came home, she discovered that there were three kittens sunbathing on the grass. They had been hiding in our basement for weeks. The cat who came into our backyard had given birth to these three lovely kittens, and she needed our help looking after them. We gave them a home. Gentle, affectionate Mila has been living with us for about seven years now. I'm very thankful for her sweet companionship and joy over the years. She brought comfort to my family when my dad passed away over a year ago. Thanks, Mila, for the cuddles and smooches. Thanks for the gifts ("pizza" and "sausages") that you left at our doorway. We love and adore you!!

~ Cynthia Hsu

Cynthia Hsu is a designer who loves animals. She works at EmbraceLite, helping people and animals heal. You can reach her at EmbraceLite. com.

April 21

The Silver Lining

My dad was a wonderful man. He was kind, generous, loving, and fun. I was "Daddy's Girl." He was my hero as a child, my saviour as a teen, and my dear friend as an adult. Today is the anniversary of his suicide. Post-traumatic stress disorder and depression stole him from me. His death was the greatest trauma I have ever experienced. I suffered the crisis of unbearable sorrow, hurt, and guilt that often plagues families of suicide victims. As a mother, I also worried about how my grief would affect my newborn son. Although I wish my dad were still here, that event was a catalyst for personal growth and for exploring many different healing methods. It led me to become who I am today and it inspired my passion-filled career—empowering individuals to overcome obstacles, achieve their dreams, and live in joy. I am grateful to my dad for all that he has given me throughout my life. I am grateful for his love, which helped me find peace in his final act, and I am grateful for the silver lining in that terrible black cloud: My dad inspires me daily to cultivate joy in others— what a gift!

~ Shannon Staples

Shannon Staples is a certified life coach and energy worker whose mission is to raise the world's vibration by creating a critical mass of joyful individuals. Reach her at HighVitalityLife.com.

April 22

Eat, Play, Love

Our 9-year-old black-and-white cat named Lowee ("Low-we") is a great teacher of life lessons in our home. She came to us by way of our veterinarian in Charleston, who had rescued her as a tiny stray. I wasn't really looking for another kitten, as we already had three at the time, but this little ball of energy caught my eye. When I called my husband regarding this new addition, he said yes. I replied, "Great, honey!" before he had a chance to change his mind, and Lowee was ours! Since that time Lowee has become the cat that cuddles when we need comfort, plays with imaginary objects when we need entertainment, and grabs kibbles from her sisters (Megan, Misha, and Cattie) when we need to be reminded that sharing is something that takes a little practice. She also tends to act like a puppy dog, so we often call her "Lowee Pup." She follows us around the house as if to say, "Hey, what are we going to do next?"—almost wagging her tail! She is always ready to see us when we arrive home and is the first in bed at night, ready for snuggling. We love all of our cats, but "Lowee Pup" is definitely the most interactive. She keeps us energized and reminds us that life is better when you remember to eat, play, and love!

~ Susan Douglas

Susan Douglas, MD, is a psychiatrist, mother, friend, daughter, entre-preneur, and founder of the No Mommy's Perfect website. Learn more at SusanDouglasMD.com and NoMommysPerfect.com.

April 23

What's in a Name?

There are so many things that mothers teach their children. The most precious lesson I remember is that no matter what possessions you accumulate in life, no one can take your name away from you. When I was younger I didn't really like the first name my parents gave me. I asked my mother why she picked Janet as a name for me. She said that it was from her favorite grandmother's middle name, Jannette. I then decided that Janet was a good name; after all, it was part of my great-grandmother. My middle name is Rose, and my legacy to my two girls is that their middle names are Rose. One of my granddaughters has Rose as her middle name, too. I hope there will be more Roses to come. In our case, names make the family bond stronger. Thanks, Mom, for your guidance and support. I'm also truly grateful for my sweet Roses. I would not have missed this journey for anything! I love you all!

~ *Janet Fuller*

Janet Fuller, *nutritional researcher, self-care advocate, and health coach, has been involved in nutrition and holistic health since the mid-1990s. Learn more at JanetFullerWellness.com.*

April 24

Education, Encouragement, Engagement, Empowerment

We often take for granted the very things that most deserve our gratitude.

~ Cynthia Ozick

D o you take things for granted? Maybe when we're young, we don't know all that life has to offer. Take a moment to pause and appreciate what you have in your life. There's education. Granted, it's required that we go to school, but think how lucky we are to have the ability to learn. We have teachers who care about how much we learn. There are lessons in everything we experience. There's encouragement. There are your friends, family, teachers, neighbors, and employers who all encourage us to stretch and reach and grow. There's engagement. You may think of becoming engaged to be married. But there's also being engaged with what you do, what you believe in, engaged in the world around you, and engaged in achieving your goals. Then there's empowerment. We have the capability to take initiative and make decisions to solve our problems and improve ourselves. I'm very grateful for having the ability to educate, encourage, engage, and empower you to improve your health so you live fabulously and free from mindless eating, fatigue, and stress in your life.

~ *Kim Hiatt*

Kim Hiatt, *author, speaker, and educator, overcame her own health challenges and now helps "overheated" pre- and peri-menopausal women feel "cool" and energetic like their youthful and vibrant selves. Get a free report at www.WhyDoIFeelBad.com.*

April 25

My Big Fast Red Ferrari

In the fall of 1993, following unexpected changes, intense decisions, and life challenges, I was inspired to seriously hunt for a horse again. After owning a number of wonderful horses, delivering two foals, breeding a mare from Montana, and riding as a young girl, I longed to return to the world of kissing velvet noses, smelling barn aromas, and gliding bareback in the sand—moving as one on the clouds through the wind. That is when I met Overlook Ferrari, who, over the next 18 years, became my best friend, soul lover, spiritual advisor, exercise trainer, and teacher of life lessons. My "big baby boy" stood 16.2 hands, with his sorrel red chestnut coat shining like a copper penny in the summer sun. He was a clown, a genius, a guardian, a loner, a free spirit, and a feisty friend. With Arabian tail held high, his elegance and regal presence presided as he became known as the older, wiser leader of the herd; thus, the nickname "King Ferrari" was born.

Dearest Overlook Ferrari,

You opened my heart, supported my soul, and filled my world with joy. There is no separation. We will fly again. With loving gratitude forever,

Your mom,

Amy

~ Amy E. Kelsall

Amy E. Kelsall, PhD, *is an executive/leadership/development coach. She also directs communication and HR Master's degree programs for working adults. Reach her at Amy.Kelsall@du.edu.*

April 26

Made a Mark

The fall of 2013 marked the start of my 20th year of teaching. As I contemplated what I wanted to write about, I started down a path of remembering the many back-to-school September days, the exciting a-ha learning moments reflected on a student's face, and the hundreds, if not thousands, of conversations about the future plans of a nervous soon-to-be high school graduate. Below are the names of 100 former and current students who made a mark on me as an educator. They come from Pennsylvania, Texas, Massachusetts, and California. Each has a story but for now stand united and represent a lifetime of gratitude that every educator has for the young people who changed our lives.

Valerie James Argie Josh Bryan Carlos Justin Geoff Jonathan Gustavo Danny Gilberto Joe Monique Sheri Travis Kateline Anthony Geoffrey Veronica Jeremias Kelcy Cassi Andy Jose Brandon Stacey Albert Gabby Tawny Ryan Ana Whitney Chhandara Phevee Michael Chris Karl Juliana Andres Brandi Megan Vicki Jade Gabriel Larry Christian Sadie Linda Chloe Katy Theresa Quinn William Nicole John Bernardo Terry Madison Adriel Isabell Kevin Lorina Angela Luis Cindy Tia Roger Rudolph Janette Jared Trung Trong Austin Deryk Gianne Avery Fletcher Elisha Chaise-Ann Chelsea Dejon Matt Clarissa Ngan Dawn Lauren Craig Forrest Nick Kristina Betsy Monica Kia Shane David Cole Roxie Kyle Adrian

~ Daniel Kriley

Daniel J. Kriley is a high school theatre teacher and arts management instructor living in Southern California. For more about his school's productions visit MiraMesaTheatre.org.

April 27

No Mask for Harley

Harley, a wonderful yellow Labrador Retriever, is an important part of our family. He entertains us every day with his own special habits. Harley never tries to hide his feelings and doesn't get embarrassed; there's no "mask" to hide anything for this dog. Harley finds amusement everywhere—from doorstops to sticks, to any type of dog toy. When he gets really excited, he does a "wild dog" routine where he spins in circles and just acts goofy. Harley doesn't care what anyone thinks; he just has fun. He is also a creature of habit. If you change his routine (or if there's a different person working at the front desk of the veterinarian's office), he lets you know that he's not happy about the disruption. But as long as you have a dog treat in your pocket, Harley is still your friend. We have learned much from Harley and are grateful to have him in our lives.

~ Beth Sponseller

Beth Sponseller *loves animals and helps pet owners provide optimal nutrition for their furry friends. You can reach her at NutritionForCritters.com.*

April 28

Baby's Story

Bab was her name and, from the first time I visited my friend, Bab would come, lie at my feet, and purr. She was 8 months old then. Bab has only three full legs, due to a mishap at birth. She's a beautiful orange with lots of white patches. My friend moved, leaving her behind. Bab was going to be put out on the street. That was the beginning of our life together, when she was a year old, weighed only five pounds, and had a small meow like a baby. Hence her name became Baby. Now she's 3 and a great companion, content to follow me everywhere, including the bathroom. Baby meets me at the door when I arrive home each day and greets me when I wake up. She's adorable. She shows her displeasure by turning her back on me and limping away slowly for sympathy. When she is playing and running about, one would never know that she only has three legs. She runs up and down the stairs just like any other cat. I love her dearly, and our relationship is unique. Baby gives me love bites as if I am her mother. I truly don't know what I would do without her now.

~ Sharon G. Teed

Sharon G. Teed *has been an inspiring writer since she retired. She lives in Toronto, Canada, and can be contacted via e-mail at Sharon.Teed@ sympatico.ca.*

April 29

Our Golden Angel

People often remark to us that they wish they could live a dog's life. A life filled with playing, eating, sleeping, and begging for more loving! Heck, even our daughter Jill has told us that she wants to come back and live the life that our Merlin has! Merlin Ari LoveJoy, our angel in a Golden Retriever's body, has been a wonderful gift in our lives and is a constant and consistent energy to help create more Love and more Joy in every moment of every day. With his tail wagging, head tilting to one side, and that adoring face that only puppies and children seem to have, he creates magic. It is a magical wisdom that our angel dog, Merlin, inspires in everyone he meets. This magical wisdom is a tribute to the bond of dog to man. Did you know that dog spelled backward is God? Yup, that is the best reminder anyone can have to share in more Love and Joy. Merlin is our constant reminder to live in Love and Joy! May you all live with Love and Joy with your pets. They are precious; cherish their time on this earth with you.

~ Richard and Trisha LoveJoy

Richard and Trisha LoveJoy *are Small Business Consultants and Certified Professional Success Coaches who inspire clients to live their dreams. Contact them at ANewLeafCo@gmail.com.*

April 30

The Exuberance of Children

I am grateful for the exuberance of young children. Their laughter. Their excitement. Their energy. Their unabashed curiosity. Their imagination and ability to play without a care in the world. Youngsters have an amazing gift for bringing light and delight to those who take the time to watch or to interact with them. Their hugs and antics can bring a smile, even on the dreariest of days. Walking down the street. Relaxing at the park. Shopping at the local grocery store. The children I see make me smile. They live in the moment. They experience delight without care or worry about what others will think. They have the courage to explore new worlds. They are unafraid to express their opinions. They share their love unconditionally. Children signify hope. Innocence. Optimism. Joy. Dreams. Enthusiasm. Little ones don't spend their time worrying about the events of yesterday. They are not concerned about tomorrow. They live for today. Children are wonderful role models for all of us. I am immensely grateful that our world is full of children. I can't imagine life without them. Can you?

~ *Diane Sue*

Diane Sue, PhD, *author and school psychologist, offers a free newsletter for parents and grandparents. Receive up-to-date information about children, adolescents, and building positive family relationships by subscribing at www.PathwaysToSuccessfulParenting.com*

May

"He is a wise man who does not grieve for the things which he has not, but rejoices for those which he has."

~ Epictetus

May 1

Lessons from Motherhood

A lesson from my mom: Home is where your mom is.

A lesson from my mother-in-law: Meaningful tradition can be as simple as a special cheese spread, the annual mince pie, and manhattans with the family.

A lesson from my maternal grandma: It's never too late to pick up a hobby. (She started quilting at the age of 70 and handsewed around 25 for her family.)

A lesson from my fraternal grandma: An outrageously huge belly laugh can cure almost anything.

A lesson from my oldest daughter: I can spend a whole afternoon just lying on the grass looking up at the trees and the world will not end.

A lesson from my youngest daughter: Five a.m. snuggles are gifts. Even though they are at 5 a.m.

A lesson from my sister, who was my first contemporary to have kids: Relax. It'll all be okay.

Thank you to *all* of you!

~ Meredith Liepelt

Meredith Liepelt mentors business owners to build buzz, create celebrity, and change the world. Find her at RichLifeMarketing.com.

May 2

Grateful for Love and Growth

I am grateful for my son, who opened my heart and gave me the courage to grow in ways I'd been avoiding. I was eager to do for him what I'd been unwilling to do for myself. I love being his mom.

I am grateful for my family, whose love and wounding have helped me grow me so much.

I am grateful for my friends, my chosen family, who love me more than I ever dreamed of loving myself.

I am grateful for my husband, my best friend and soul mate, whose love heals and who made my dreams of empowered partnership come true, better than I could have ever imagined.

I am grateful for all of these cherished ones, and for my willingness to let their love matter so much that I change and grow—the best way I know to honor their love.

I am grateful for my teachers, who taught me how to grow through love instead of pain.

I am grateful for my happiness and my commitment to learning how to create it from the inside out.

To all of those who love me, you inspire me to be a better me. Thank you. I am grateful for you!

~ *Michele Eisenberg*

Michele Eisenberg lives to love and teach people to create love, happiness, and healthy relationships from the inside out. Connect with Michele and claim your free gift at www.HappyFamilyAcademy.com.

May 3

Remembering My Mom

My mom passed away many years ago. She contributed much to our family—as a wife, homemaker, seamstress, gardener, and artist. She was the quintessential homemaker and always kept the house neat and organized.

My fondest memories are of me studying at the kitchen table while she prepared dinner. That was "me and Mom" time. Whether she made lasagna, Armenian dolma, yogurt soup, pilaf, my favorite baklava, or my morning fried egg and toast, my mom was the best cook ever.

As a seamstress, she made many of my clothes, and I loved to lie on the floor and talk to her while she worked. Her tireless efforts in our garden produced all sorts of fruits and vegetables like figs, apricots, cherry tomatoes, and squash. A favorite of mine was her cactus garden, which had at least 20 different types of cacti.

My mom was also a talented artist. She taught me how to read and write years before I could even attend school. I learned a lot from my mom; that has made me the person I am today.

Although she's not around, I know that a part of her will always be with me.

~ Tara Kachaturoff

Tara Kachaturoff, *an online business manager, host of Michigan Entrepreneur TV, and native of Southern California, resides in Birmingham, Mich. Find her at Twitter.com/TaraKachaturoff.*

May 4

Lessons from Grandma's Lap

"You are special. You will see the world. You can be anything you want to be."

These words of my grandmother, repeated lovingly and frequently into my ear, touched my heart and shaped my destiny. Within the circle of her arms, to the rhythm of her rocking chair, she painted a picture that influenced the way I thought about myself. The smell of her perfume hung over me like holy incense, blessing the potential of all I could become.

As years went by, I watched as she sometimes allowed the pain of life to diminish her own dreams. I learned from these things, too. I learned that forgiving another person is actually a gift to oneself. I learned that fear may feel real, but dissipates in the face of action.

I am not a child anymore. As I turn the page on another day and another chapter in my life, I hear my grandmother's words anew: "You can be anything you want to be." I believed it then. I believe it still. She whispered quiet words of hope and confidence into the heart of this child, changing the course of my life forever. For this, I am eternally grateful.

~ Sherry Wright

Sherry Wright, *Your Own Coach, is a professional coach and "artist" working in the medium of life change, guiding her clients into creating their own living masterpiece. Find out more at YourOwnCoach.com.*

The Power of 5

"Successful people keep moving. They make mistakes, but they don't quit."
~ Conrad Hilton

I conducted a "get things done" program called "The Power of 5." Participants did a lot. I learned a lot.

None of it would have been possible, though, without the leadership of the Power of 5 team captains:

A. Michael Bloom "The Bloomers"
You are a treasure to know, and I love to watch you "blossom" forth as a terrific leader!

Don Craig "Successful Visionaries"
My calm, cool, and steady rock of a captain. Thanks for your dedication!

Tassey Russo "The Shifters"
I appreciate you for jumping into this and going with the flow (and the shifts)!

Martin Salama "The Accelerators"
It's always an honor to be in connection with you and your energy!

Connie Keough Whitesell "Westbound 5 Achievers"
My captain with the positive, "can do" attitude delivered with a smile—thank you!

Kathy Wojcik "Triple A Dreamcatchers"
You are a terrific leader and so conscientious. I appreciate you!

~ Donna Kozik

Donna Kozik *shows people how to Write a Book in a Weekend® and Get Ready for the Shelf™. Pick up a free book planner at FreeBookPlanner.com.*

May 6

What Is a Pet?

What is a pet? Some would say it is a tamed or domesticated animal. Others would comment that a pet is an animal that is usually affectionately cared for that often plays the role of a companion.

A child may be referred to as a teacher's pet. Indeed most anyone who is especially cherished or favored is often referred to as a pet. Adults frequently have pet names for their loved ones as a demonstration of fondness and affection.

To me, a pet means all of the above and so much more. When I think about the dogs, cats, hamsters, gerbils, birds, and even fish that have inhabited my home, I feel the love, companionship, and camaraderie that we shared. I have happy memories, funny pictures, and a great reason to get up in the morning. I get to start my day in gratitude for the unconditional love I receive just for showing up, being me, and sharing my time, attention, and some morsels of food. My pets have provided so much for me that mere words pale in their description of how grateful I feel for them. What is a pet? To me, everything!

~ *Monika Huppertz*

Monika Huppertz *asks, "Are you ready to remove obstacles and leave your restrictive life behind? Step towards your success with purpose and passion!" Learn more at LivingYourTruth.me.*

May 7

Sailing 101

It was a beautiful day in Raleigh, North Carolina; my dad took me and my friend Susan sailing on Kerr Lake. We launched the Super Sunfish and set sail. I was not a stranger to sailing at the age of 8, and I wanted to try. I asked Dad, and without hesitation, he gave me control of the rudder, placing it in my right hand. He observed how quickly I felt at home steering the boat. Then he said, "Here, take this" and placed the sheet, a rope attached to the sail, in my left hand. I was sailing the boat! Next, with one quick motion, my dad grabbed the hand of my friend and jumped off the boat! "Daddy, help!" I yelled as he swam away with my friend at his side. The sailboat rocked wildly; after all dad was 6'4 ½" and 220 pounds. He yelled back, "You can do it!! You have watched me long enough. Bring the boat into shore." I did! I always return to this day when I fear I can't do something. I am so grateful for this lesson from my dad, Lynn Alynn Smith.

~ *Kimberly Smith Lukhard*

Kimberly Smith Lukhard *is a mother, dietitian, teacher, and writer. She has an online teaching/counseling practice. Visit www.KimLukhard.com for great nutrition information, complete with quick tips and recipes.*

May 8

Summer Splendor

As spring turns to summer, the heart warms up with delight to eagerly greet the much-awaited, long-missed, sun-embraced days of summer. Our treasured memories of joyful summers past deepen our gratitude for the days that are no more. Days of orange arm floaties—kept the kiddies afloat and brought about squeals of joy as they knew it was pool time! The pool sparkling as a million-carat aquamarine jewel with the sun's radiance. Excited children jumping in and splashing water at each other and having a merry time. Succulent, deep red watermelon slices—juice dripping down their little arms as soon as they took a bite. Lollipop chicken and corn—barbequed drumsticks and butter-drenched mini corn on the cobs held with tiny porcelain corn skewers. Cooling shaved ice—sweet and fragrant red rose syrup poured onto mountains of shaved ice. There was never enough. Oh, how these sweet precious memories illuminate the heart with love, sparkle the eyes with tears of joy, and bring on an occasional chuckle of laughter. Om Shanti

~ *Jyoti Nebhnani*

Jyoti Nebhnani is a certified health coach and laughter yoga leader. She empowers women to achieve balance and joy in their lives. Find out more at www.NourishingSpoon.com.

May 9

Her Name Means Promise

She came into my life in her old age. At first I was her pet sitter. She is a beautiful silver-coated miniature Poodle named Sheba. Her owner, Idris, had a debilitating stroke and asked me if I would take Sheba permanently. Sheba has lived a full life, starting out as a breeding dog in Texas. After Idris bought her, she entered a life of pampering and playing. It is my joy to love her through her senior years. She is blind in one eye, yet she loves to run fast across the backyard! She also is quite content to sit quietly on my lap while I read a book. It's amazing how God works in the details of our lives. My husband and I were separated, and I was feeling lonely. Sheba came to me and provided that special fur-buddy companionship. Her name means "promise," and I believe she is God's promise to me that everything is going to be okay in my life as well as in Sheba's. We are a blessing to each other. Having her happy spirit and loving presence surrounding me gives me encouragement and helps me stay positive through a difficult time.

~ Nadine Joy Lewis

Nadine Joy Lewis *enjoys taking care of pets in the Eagle Point, Ore. area. She can be reached at HappyDayPetSitting.com.*

May 10

A Year of Authors

I've shown several hundred people how to become published authors this year. A few special ones stood out as those I will always remember, including:

A. Michael Bloom: Watching Michael "write what he knew" was both heart-wrenching and inspiring at the same time. I'm grateful for his openness and compassion in sharing his caregiving journey with readers. (Go Red Sox!)

Claire and Dick Knowles: Their area newspaper said it best with "Wedded Wordsmiths Work to Change Their World." As their books pile up, so does my admiration for this dynamic author duo!

Peg Roach Loyd: This singer-songwriter turned author is a "soul leader" in so many ways. Thank you, Peg, for letting me share your path.

Judi Reid: I smile every time I think of this 70-years-young author and her determination to have her very own book by her birthday. She is truly a woman of value!

Martin Salama: A student of writing who peppered me with so many questions and was open to feedback to make his already-good writing even better. What an honor to work with this author! (When are we doing Friday night dinner?)

~ Donna Kozik

Donna Kozik shows people how to Write a Book in a Weekend® and Get Ready for the Shelf™. Pick up a free book planner at FreeBookPlanner.com.

May 11

My Mother's Secret: Exposed!

What brings a warm smile to my lips and my heart happened when I was a teen. I had received my driver's license a few months prior, and once again, my mother had forgotten to pick some up things from the grocery store. Happy to help my mom and drive the car, I quickly left to get what she needed. Soon I was back with the items in tow. As I was unpacking the bag, I mentioned to my mom how great it was that I had my license and could easily get her what she needed, as she was sure forgetting a lot lately. The smile I received was the one that she used when keeping a secret.

Right then and there, I realized that she was giving me opportunities to get some extra driving practice. It also occurred to me just how smart and clever my mother was. (How many times do kids think that their parents are not cool and not too smart, either?) I felt very much loved and supported. I never looked at my mom in quite the same way again.

~ *Monika Huppertz*

Monika Huppertz asks: "Are you ready to remove obstacles and leave your restrictive life behind?" Step toward your success with purpose and passion at LivingYourTruth.me.

May 12

A Special Museum Trip

One summer day, when I was 7 years old, my mom and I spent the day in Washington, DC, visiting some of the amazing museums with visiting out-of-town cousins. We got up early and took a bus to the subway station, and I had my first ever ride on a train. Once downtown, we took a tour of the FBI Museum, the Air and Space Museum, and the National Gallery of Art. What I remember most was when she proudly took us to see the abstract paintings of her cousin, Morris Louis. She beamed with pride at sharing his work and told us all about how he was a wonderful man who sadly never had his art appreciated while he was alive. She told us that he ignored the naysayers who tried to put him down and always followed his passion.

This was one of many great summer adventures that I gratefully experienced with my mom. She taught me to always explore, try new things, and follow my passion. Although my mom sadly passed away a little over a year ago, I can feel her encouragement and pride with every action I take as I pursue my dreams.

~ *A. Michael Bloom*

A. Michael Bloom, *certified professional coach and Energy Leadership™ Master Practitioner, inspires caregivers and the organizations that support them with practical coping strategies that revitalize careers and save lives. Learn more at www.BloomForCoach.com.*

May 13

Lucky!

It takes a courageous man to marry a kind of quirky, long-single woman with a somewhat sullen teenage son. Courageous, yes, but not necessarily poetic, romantic, or prone to expressing feelings. So, as we stood at the altar, my soon-to-be husband, shocked me. With tears in his eyes he whispered, "I'm the luckiest man in the world." In the years since, he hasn't always felt that way. Quirky women aren't always the easiest to live with! We've experienced heart-wrenching loss and bitter disappointment. We've floundered and fallen. We've dragged ourselves back up. I am especially grateful for the bedrock of this lucky marriage: It turns out we're both a little quirky, and we find real joy in saying, "You make me laugh!" Today, all these years later, his eyes twinkle as he whispers, "I'm still the luckiest man in the world." And although I may tease him saying, "You make me laugh!" inside I'm saying, "It works both ways, babe. It works both ways!" Happy Anniversary!

~ Kamala Murphey

Kamala Murphey *helps weary women reconnect with their own sense of joy and peace. Kamala has earned master's degrees in counseling and theology. Access her free meditations at http://KamalaMurphey. com/GetSet-Meditations.*

May 14

Sister and Brother

Being a mother took some time for me, and not in the usual way, like infertility. Mine was another path. It started in the year 2000. I found out I was pregnant, and we decided she needed to be placed for adoption. A few years later we got married, and a couple more after that we brought our son home. Our son was 2 days old, and we were on our way to a Thanksgiving dinner; my husband and son were waiting for me. When I got into the car I saw my son in the backseat, safely buckled in. I sat right in front of him. For some reason it started to feel like we were driving away from the hospital without our child, again. I sobbed uncontrollably. I am now, and have been ever since that day, very grateful for the honor and joy of being a mother to our son. I am also grateful and thankful for our "daughter's" adoptive mother. She always makes us feel welcome, and she allows us the privilege of our son knowing his sister.

~ Melody Heath-Smith

Melody Heath-Smith *is a married mother of one, an aspiring children's book writer, and currently and always writing a "phantasmagoricle" story. Contact her at MelodyTheWriter@hotmail.com.*

May 15

Thanks to My Intuition!

I love my intuition. It has taught me to let go and follow my heart. Had I not done so, my life path would have been completely different. When friends and family in England wanted me to create stability in my life, to carve out a career and buy a home, my heart told me to trust my intuitive feelings. I did, and those feelings led me on a journey that required my utmost faith. I turned my back on a predictable life, left England, and headed for the United States of America. I was inspired every step of the way to listen to that still, small voice, and it guided me to make decisions that changed the direction of my life. Thanks to my intuition, I realized the deeper meaning of my soul purpose. Thanks to my intuition, I wrote a book that paved the way for greater success in my career. Thanks to my intuition, I met and married my soul mate, a former U.S. Marine and my biggest supporter. I have a lot to be thankful for. My life is blessed, my heart is filled with love, and my intuition continues to navigate me on a miraculous path.

~ Elizabeth Harper

Elizabeth Harper *is an acclaimed metaphysical teacher, color seer, and psychic artist. She is a magazine columnist, a radio personality, and the author of* Wishing. *Explore her coloriscious world at SealedWithLove.com.*

May 16

The Mother's Curse

You may not know it, but you might be a victim of "The Mother's Curse." It goes like this:

You're 3 years old, shopping in the grocery store with Mom. She quickly walks by the "good stuff"—the salty and sugary foods—and stops by the fresh broccoli. You think, "Ugh, not that!" Mom reaches for a big, fat bunch and says, "Mmm, we can have this twice this week." You think about that strong, bitter taste in your mouth. Your stomach flops. Before you can stop yourself, you are whining, "No, Mom. That is yucky! I don't like it! Ewww!" Mom says, "Shhh, stop it. It's really good."

After multiple pleas erupt from your mouth, you drop to the floor and begin screaming loudly, "No, no! *No broccoli!*" Mom looks at the other customers in embarrassment. She leans down and hisses something into your ear that your 3-year-old brain doesn't quite comprehend: "One day, when you are grown up, I hope you have a child that acts just like you."

Many years later, when your child is on the floor screaming "No broccoli!" do you say it, or don't you? My mom said it to me. That curse really works.

~ Susan Veach

Susan Veach *is a graphic designer from Southampton, Pa. She is a bibliophile, traveler, art lover, gardener, mother, and wife.*

Reach her at SusanVeach.com.

May 17

Summers at the Beach

Summer is absolutely the most wonderful time of the year, as it holds so many memories from my childhood. I was born and raised in Southern California, not far from the beach. My most enjoyable memories are of packing up the car on the weekends with all of our beach stuff: towels, clothes, books to read, and, of course, sandwiches and lemonade! We would always go to the main beach at Laguna, walk down at least a thousand rickety wooden stairs, and then find ourselves in this beautiful cove, with lovely, fine sand and the beautiful Pacific Ocean before us. Often we would arrive in the foggy early morning, which was soon to be replaced by the hot afternoon sun. I would spend hours running in and out of the water, collecting seashells, building sand castles, reading books, eating a delicious lunch, and enjoying the best time ever with my family. On occasion, on the way home, with sand in our suits and shoes, and possibly a bit of sunburn on our faces, we would stop by the Sawdust Art Festival to see the local artists. There's nothing more heartwarming than memories of my summers at Laguna.

~ Tara Kachaturoff

Tara Kachaturoff *is an online business manager and the creator, producer, and host of Michigan Entrepreneur TV. A native of Southern California, she currently resides in Birmingham, Michigan.*

May 18

Picnics on the Farm

It was the good ol' summertime growing up on a small farm in Pennsylvania. My favorite memory was the large gatherings of family and friends to picnic. Harvesting the mouth-watering organic produce alongside my parents helped me appreciate wholesome nutrition that we felt blessed to share. Mom would rustle up a smorgasbord with five or six amazing entrees, fresh garden vegetable dishes, and a variety of homemade desserts. While she prepared the feast indoors, Dad and I would ready outside, cutting several acres of grass. We'd set the basketball area, badminton court, croquet wickets, horseshoes (the metal kind), archery targets, bases for a ball game, and groom the horses for rides. My sister, cousin, and I wrote scripts for our annual summertime extravaganza to entertain our guests. One uncle would act as host, improvising and announcing us like Johnny Carson. Five uncles were musicians, each one talented on several different musical instruments. They were our back-up, changing instruments at will. The evening events would continue to the wee hours, with singalongs, laughter, and delightful storytelling. Picnic times were character-building experiences, sharing love and values now passed on by a grateful grandparent.

~ *Susanne Morrone*

Susanne Morrone, C.N.C., LMT, *is an author with decades of experience in natural health coaching and speaking. To learn more about her expertise, visit www.NaturalHealthChat.com.*

May 19

Grapes, Sweet and Sour

Say the word "summer" and my tongue remembers grapes. Growing up, my father grew grapevines in our backyard. I would poke around in the leaves until I saw a bunch, then check to see if they were ripe enough to pick. When they were, the juice would be hot and sweet, and would squirt into my mouth as I bit through the skins. Once I found a ripe bunch, next came the search for worms. Squishy worms hid nearby and camouflaged themselves by eating the grape leaves, which then colored their chubby bodies the same bright green. My big thrill was spotting a worm and snatching the grapes just before it got to them. Then I would close my eyes and relish the lovely, warm, dirty grape taste. I still don't like washed grapes from the refrigerator as well. Today, however, unwashed commercial grapes aren't necessarily safe. Dirt is no longer just dirt. The worms are gone, but now there is the poison that killed them. Maybe that's why I love retasting past grapes in my mind. It's the taste of an easier, safer time when one of the biggest dangers I faced was a worm. Sweet indeed.

~ *Patricia Drury Sidman*

Patricia Drury Sidman *is a writer, actor, storyteller, spiritual advisor, and life coach now living in Lafayette, Louisiana, where it is hot enough for grapes. Reach her at www.Facebook.com/Patricia.Drury.Sidman. Personal.*

May 20

The Neighborhood Children

Those were the days when I'd wake up every morning with excitement and anticipation to quickly get my choir done to prevent being called by any family member to do anything because I had my day planned out already. The fun began as the choir was completed. I began to dig in the ground for the special worms we used to fish, called bait, or prepare a little flour to make a small ball of dough, got my fishing hook ready, and was off to meet with my friends, the neighborhood children—we were going fishing. Sometimes we'd catch plenty and other times the catch would be hard, but we will sat on the bridge over the water with patience or we moved from bridge to bridge in the hot sun. When we decided it was enough, it was then time to bush cook using the fish, we then decided where to cook and what everyone would contribute, then run home for the ingredients and meet at the neighbor's house. Most times it was the Headleys. We delegated the work. The food was then cooked and we'd eat and enjoy. The rest of the day was spent picking tamarind or whatever fruits were available, playing, and bathing in company trench before going home and meeting back in the afternoon to play cheer Sal. It was fun, and I'm grateful to everyone who shared their summer with me.

~ *Melanie Eugene*

Melanie Eugene helps successful plus-size women lose weight and get back in shape. Learn more at Tracobesity.com.

May 21

Thoughts of Gratitude

I am so grateful for all my friends, especially my two best friends, my neighbour, Rose, and my son in the past year. *An extremely rocky ride with a soft landing.* I took a big step—the second biggest move in my adult life. Without their assistance I couldn't have made it. I am so grateful to have these people as they made the ride so smooth. There were many others (too many to mention) who gave gifts making the change an easy transition. The change was from a busy "big city" lifestyle to a more relaxing environment in a small town called Perth. This historic town presents to me more tranquil surroundings, to continue my writing. How can I not be grateful? The move also brings me closer (only an hour away) to my beautiful granddaughters. I am thankful I can see them more often. Topping this, I became a grandma again in August 2013. I am so full of gratitude for these riches that have come my way. I'm bursting at the seams. Life is good, and I am thankful and full of gratitude to everyone who was involved.

~ Sharon G. Teed

Sharon G. Teed *now lives in Perth, Ontario. She is settling in slowly and more inspired than ever to write. She can be reached at Sharon.Teed@sympatico.ca.*

May 22

There's No Roof!

It was May 22, 2011 in Joplin, Missouri and the tornado sirens were blaring. I ran to the only room without windows and hunkered down. The wind ripped through my home of 14 years and I remember looking up and thinking "Hmmm. There's no roof!" My house wasn't the only one, of course. The tornado's path destroyed thousands of homes and businesses and took 161 lives.

Within 24 hours I was grateful to have salvaged my billfold with all contents intact and my car keys. I was thrilled to be able to prove who I said I was and to get where I needed to go when everything else of mine was gone.

I learned that our stuff is just "stuff" and it's our connection to others that matter most. I started the annual Letting Go day as a way for us all to join in spirit and give thanks for our lives. I urge you to release and donate an item that no longer serves you today and give thanks for your own life. As you do, please send a good thought to other communities who have been affected by a natural disaster this year. Thank you!

~ Ann Leach

Ann Leach *is a grief coach and founder of Letting Go Day, an international event happening every May 22. To learn more, visit www.lettinggoday.com.*

May 23

Granny

L ucky me. My mother did not want me home during summer vacations. Each July she put me on a train to the mountains. Granny would meet me at the station with hugs. We'd ride to her three-story home where I had freedom to explore life in her world. Spoiled. Loved. Well-fed.

Every morning we ate homemade biscuits, blackberry jam, and bacon. Oh my goodness. I can almost taste them now.

Granny was an accomplished pianist. After breakfast she tiptoed into her music room and closed the French doors to prevent annoying her husband while she practiced. I sat still on the sofa nearby to observe the grace and ease of her long fingers moving across black and white keys. Listening to her play Chopin and Beethoven created heavenly joy. Oh how I wanted to learn to do the same. My mother refused to provide piano lessons because she "couldn't stand to hear [me] practice." That stance may have made me appreciate Granny's talent more. I learned the impact of using a God-given gift, mastered by self-discipline, practice, and perseverance.

I treasure Granny and the lifetime values she modeled. Through years of summertime visits my life was forever enriched.

~ Judi G. Reid

Judi G. Reid is author of Rise Up! 71 Thoughts of Hope & Inspiration for Women of Value. She advocates for respect and dignity of all women. Learn more at www.WomenOfValue.org.

May 24

Everything Is Love

Although it is hard to put into words what happened during the summer of 1987, it is the one experience that stands out as the most transforming event of my life. I was reading a book by Joel S. Goldsmith called *Practicing the Presence* and started to meditate according to his instructions. I sat down, closed my eyes, and opened up my consciousness with the Bible quote "I and my Father are One." Then I would wait and just stay open. It was only a few days into this practice that something happened: As I had uttered the words "I am my Father are One," I suddenly got flooded with the biggest, deepest, most profound love I had ever experienced. All I could do was fall on my knees and, overwhelmed with gratitude, say: "Thank you! Thank you! Please don't ever let me stray away from You again." The intensity of this experience lasted two to three months, where I saw and realized everything as love, including myself. It changed my life forever and put me on the path of self-realization. It taught me how self-love bridges the gap between who we truly are and who we imagine ourselves to be.

~ *Pernilla Lillarose*

Pernilla Lillarose *is a kindness and consciousness coach, author, meditation teacher, founder of Women Standing For Love, and radio show host. For more information, please go to www.Lillarose.com and www.WomenStandingForLove.com.*

May 25

That Kind of Mother

I always thought I'd be that kind of mother—you know, the kind who always looked sharp and whose children were always well-behaved and well-kept. The kind who knew what her children were thinking just by looking at them, and who would always have the perfect advice for them and other mothers. The kind who could work an eight-hour day, cook a delicious meal, check homework, read bedtime stories, and still have time and energy for hubby. The kind who could spoil her children and still raise compassionate, selfless, and kind adults. Who knew I'd be the kind of mother who'd raise her voice and lose her patience? The kind whose best is sometimes hot dogs and applesauce, and clean but somewhat-wrinkled clothing. The kind who often has no advice to offer, only an understanding heart and a prayer. The kind who knows the value of "no" in growing gracious, compassionate, and generous children. The kind who loves, sacrifices, disciplines, plays, dreams, laughs, cries, believes, prays, does what she can, and learns to do the things that she can't—all for the success and well-being of her children. Yeah, who knew I'd be that kind of mother?

~ *Cherita G. Weatherspoon*

Dr. Cherita Weatherspoon, *mother of four, is an educator, success coach, and author of an upcoming book on parenting. She and her husband host TheChristianMarriageBookClub.com.*

May 26

One Square Mile of Hope

In the summer of 2012 I had taken a trip to the Adirondack Mountains for a woman's conference. A rainy weekend, but nothing could dampen my spirits in this idyllic setting on Fifth Lake. You could look out on the serenity of the day and listen to the loons announcing their presence. On day one of the conference, a woman announced that she taught people how to kayak and had brought many kayaks with her. She offered to teach anyone who wanted to learn. on day three of the conference, although it was still drizzling, I was invited to go kayaking. The teacher was amazing! Moments later, I was snuggled in a kayak, happily paddling across the lake. That began my new obsession. I bought two kayaks, life vests, paddles, and a trailer. I spent many days kayaking. At the end of summer, I returned to the Adirondaks to take part in an event called One Square Mile of Hope. We broke the Guinness World Record, having 1902 kayaks on one square mile of water. We also raised $80,000 for breast cancer research. What am I grateful for? Friends who play big and bring hope to the world.

~ Angela I. Schutz

Angela I. Schutz, *founder of Driven to Succeed Consulting LLC, is a published author, professional speaker, and career coach who is dedicated to helping others empower their lives. Reach her at www.DrivenToSucceed.net.*

May 27

Love Others, Love Yourself

"...A dame so precious, one cannot resist the urge to lean over and place a kiss on the cheek of the one so full of life, the offspring of me and my darling wife..."

~ Daddy

Finding these poetic words, 45 years after my late father wrote them, warmed my heart. I'm grateful for these words of love and the event that launched them: his marriage to my mom on May 27, 1966. My parents, Kathleen and Robert, came from troubled households, but each had a vision of a happier home and quickly began to create it. I was born just 15 months after their marriage and was such a joy that they wanted another child, and my brother was born two years later. They created a loving home, but life wasn't perfect. It never is. They didn't put themselves first enough, but they always loved. They loved everyone: friends, family, and community. My mom continues to be an example of love for all, and I'm thankful that I learned to love others without judgment. Now, I'm grateful and happy to say I have also learned to love myself as they taught me to love others.

~ *Tina Nies*

Tina Nies *is grateful for a simple daily practice that led her to the magic of loving and accepting herself in ways she never thought possible. Learn more at www.40DayLoveFest.com.*

May 28

Our Unique Strengths

I am grateful for the amazing diversity of strengths in this world. It never ceases to amaze me just how different and how essential each of our talents and contributions is. I was reminded again this morning in a conversation with a colleague, who is great at details, structure, and asking the question "why." I, on the other hand, am good at ideas, the big picture, and thinking "why not." This, as it turns out, is an excellent combination.

We all have something very special that is unique to us, be it a skill, our values, or our view of the world. It is often the case that one person's limitations can be perfectly balanced by another person's strengths. Looking around workplaces and families, you see people coming together, each with their unique approach and skills, and their collaboration is truly more than the sum of its parts.

Today, I would like to invite you to pay attention to your own strengths and reflect on how you could use your unique strengths in new ways throughout the day.

If you look out for the talents of those around you, you may find opportunities to acknowledge and appreciate their strengths.

~ Eszter Molnar Mills

Eszter Molnar Mills *is the founder of Formium Development, a strengths-based organizational and leadership development consultancy based in London. You can reach her at www.Formium.co.uk.*

May 29

Summer Rain

I'm grateful for my summertime memory of Garnet, my dearest canine companion, a Westie with extraordinary character, and a summer rain shower. One warm, sunny day, with darkening clouds on the horizon behind us, we ventured out for a stroll down our tree-lined street. We turned around once the sun ducked behind the black clouds. Alas, the wind kicked up and sheets of rain pelted down before we made it home. Garnet was so unimpressed with the rain that he dashed off the sidewalk, straining to the end of his leash, and walked beneath the low-hanging branches, keeping dry as I walked along the sidewalk. The moment he spotted a gap in the trees, he sprinted for the next one. I was laughing so hard! The sight of my fluffy, white dog, running for all he was worth to stay out of the rain, was too precious. Let me tell you: He was so happy to arrive home, somewhat damp and have me wrap him up in a nice thick towel. And I am happy to have this memory to help me smile now that he has passed on.

~ *Susane D. Schuler*

Susane D. Schuler *is a six-sensory artist and author. Uncover your answers to "Who am I?", "Why am I here?", and "Where am I going?" by visiting her website: www.TheTruthTheWayandTheLove.com.*

May 30

Bodysurfing the Pacific

During the 1950s, my struggling actor father loved to take his three little girls on "cheap dates" near our home in Los Angeles, California. After all, it cost next to nothing to load us up in his cherry red Ford convertible, roll the top down, and breeze down Sunset Boulevard to the Pacific Ocean. In fact, the Pacific was like a familiar, doting aunt to us. She welcomed our little bodies, and we learned to catch and ride her waves without the help of surfboards or rafts. My father had been a champion youth swimmer and sailor in Orlando, Florida, and he passed along to us both his passion for the ocean and his knowledge of its treachery. We learned to dive through crunching waves and swim with the stronger currents—"rip tides"—until we could safely traverse them. Mostly, however, I remember the warming comfort of the beach sand after coming out of the chilly ocean, the delicious smell of hot dogs and French fries wafting from the oceanfront venders, the scent of Coppertone on my skin, and the easy camaraderie of a day spent outdoors with my siblings and our beloved dad.

~ *Bonnie Ebsen Jackson*

Bonnie Ebsen Jackson *is an equine writer, teacher, and clinician living in northern Arizona, where she helps new horse owners form better bonds with their animals. Her website is www.NewHorseCoach.com.*

May 31

A Beacon of Beauty

Rockport, Massachusetts, was always a magical place to visit in the summertime. Our family would gather together and host a clambake in my grandmother's backyard. Lobster dripping in butter, steamers, corn on the cob, salad, and linguica sausages were all a part of the mouthwatering menu. We could walk from my grandmother's house to the heart of town, past the fishing boats that bobbed in the harbor and close to the docks near the red fisherman's shack, known as Motif #1. We wandered through the streets and drank in the quaint, weathered fishermen's cottages that had been converted into small, but unique retails shops, selling leather goods, funky jewelry, homemade candy, or artwork that showcased the beauty of the area. We always passed by artists wearing large sun hats and adjusting their easels in the shifting afternoon light as they attempted to capture the landscape in watercolor or oil paints. I loved to sit on the beach and inhale the fresh, salty scent of the Atlantic Ocean mixed with the aroma of fried seafood. My summer days in this little New England fishing village unfolded with a sense of family, beauty, history, and endless possibility.

~ Kerri McManus

Kerri McManus *shows people how to recognize and cultivate their own unique talents. Get in touch at www.Facebook.com/ KerriMcManusWriter.*

June

"There is not a more pleasing exercise of the mind than gratitude. It is accompanied with such an inward satisfaction that the duty is sufficiently rewarded by the performance."

~ Joseph Addison

June 1

Why Birthdays Matter!

June 1 has never been an ordinary day. I've turned that calendar over 66 times, so this June 1 is more than just a circled day on the page-a-day calendar. I'm alive, having survived heart concerns! I'm 66, which means I'm considered "eligible" for Social Security. In all, this day provides a personal reflection that my life has stood for something—something good. And for that, I am most grateful to my creator, to my family, for having substantive work along the way that bolsters my energy, lifts up heartfelt projects, and for continually emerging activities with which to be engaged. Life really is good! My learning is this: I am very grateful for life's gifts. They are too numerous to count. And it is in searching out something beyond myself wherein the real, grateful meaning for my life lies. It is in my giving, not my getting. Viktor Frankl, in Man's Search for Meaning, wrote, "Happiness cannot be pursued; it must ensue." May each of my remaining days ensue another grateful day! Happy Birthday!

~ *Claire Knowles*

Claire Knowles *is an executive business consultant and an Amazon best-selling author of* Lights On! A Reflective Journey. *She writes from a lifetime of developing a keen intuitive sensitivity about people. Learn more at www.LightsOnBook.com.*

June 2

Blessed by My Mentors

I've been so blessed by the women who have served as my mentors throughout the years, teaching me, opening my eyes to the myriad possibilities before me, encouraging me to experiment and experience, supporting my unsure steps as I started my own business, always there for me whenever my steps faltered and I started doubting myself. A huge amount of gratitude goes to Rev. Deborah Bourbon and Linda P. Jones. Thank you for being who you are and for so generously sharing your knowledge. I wouldn't be who I am today or where I am today if it hadn't been for you.

~ Janet Thomasson

Janet Thomasson *helps people discover their purpose, find their path, and step into their power. She can be found at www.JanetThomasson. com.*

June 3

Summer Nights

Summer's sun; fun's just begun; but oh, those summer nights, to loosely quote that "Tell Me More" song from *Grease*. For teens, summer is a fantastic time of year. No school; no homework; fewer duties and commitments. In a word—freedom!

It was the time of year for teenagers to spread their wings and fly. Whether it was getting a taste of the work world earning personal spending money, getting in some extra Harlequin Romance reading, or spending time at the mall with friends, summer was an awesome time of year. And summer nights were always magical. Watching the Canada Day fireworks from a friend's high-rise balcony; the bright colors meeting our gaze against the dark night sky was mesmerizing. Getting to stay up past a usual bed time was simply wonderful. But the paramount thing ever about summer nights was going to the drive-in with your best buds. This epitomized the very essence of freedom. We had wheels; there were food, friends, fun, and frivolity; there were movies o'plenty to watch. What more could teens in the '70s ask for? Tell me more, tell me more. Summer's sun; fun's just begun; but oh, those summer nights!

~ *Monika Dena Huppertz*

Monika Huppertz, life coach, asks, "Are you ready to live your life with purpose and passion? Start a CHANGE reaction in your life and step towards your success!" Get in touch at LivingYourTruth.me or Monika.Huppertz@gmail.com.

June 4

On Our Southern Land

On our southern land a tiny creature called a cicada begins a joyful journey from below the tree line. Their singing voice is a sound for us to rejoice as our summertime arrives. This endless memory of a summertime here in Australia is hearing them play as we walked for miles through a city of business to arrive at a summertime jetty, a place that was close to our hearts, for my brother and me. We would watch the tug boats mighty and small lead in the master ships of coal and maybe a glimpse of Dad. Now I'm a mother, sister, and wife; a friend to many; and a counsellor to those whose minds are in strife. A summertime memory: My mother would say, "Kimmy, you fill your home with much love your house is a lighthouse allowing people to feel safe." Remember a memory of place where the sun shines so bright; feel it fill your soul with warmth, happiness, and light. A balm to the mind rebuilding your sight. Life is like an endless dove carrying a seed of warmth and forgiveness, returning a message of love. The answer is purely all about summertime fun.

~ Kim Lorraine Russell

Kim Lorraine Russell *is an Australian holistic counsellor soul therapist, author, broadcaster, and proud mother of seven children. She offers private consultations, public speaking, educational teachings, and meditations. Visit www.AustraliaSoulTherapy.com or thelighthouse (Facebook), e-mail Therapy@live.com.au, or Skype skimlorraine.*

June 5

Carwashes

What comes to mind when thinking of summer are water and sunshine. There is something magical and healing about both, which I am grateful for. One of my fondest memories was when my girls were young how they loved helping to wash the cars. They had their own little sponges and would work really hard on the tires or as far as they could reach on a door until that was too much work, and then they'd grab the hose and start squirting everything but the car. What starts out as slight irritation on my side turns into wonderful high-pitched squeaks and squeals of laughter that you cannot help but join in. Pretty soon, the soap has dried on the cars, we are all soaked, and our bellies and faces hurt from laughing so hard. Sharing these memories with my girls today makes us all smile and laugh, remembering how good it felt and feels even today. The beautiful gift is that I get to witness them making these same types of memories with their children.

~ Brenda Strong

Brenda Strong *lives in the state of Washington and enjoys spending time with her daughters and grandchildren, and helping people reach a higher state of being through forgiveness, joy, and love.*

June 6

To My Lovely Wife

I was studying in Argentina and took a break to visit my parents in Cochabamba, Bolivia. As many people used to do that time, I went to take a walk at El Prado, a beautiful compound of parks in the middle of the city. Suddenly I saw her and was so impressed by her beauty. I found courage to approach her and started a small conversation. Fortunately she seemed to enjoy my company, so I invited her to go out. We were dating for one week and then I had to return. Life brought surprises to my family, and I ended up living in Costa Rica. Those were pre-Internet days, so communication was extremely difficult. We had not seen each other for nine years, and suddenly she called me. She had become a flight attendant, so she could fly easily. I invited her to Costa Rica and she came. Three days later I proposed her and she said "yes." Thirty-some years later, we are happily married and have an extraordinary family. I am grateful to have gone that Sunday to take a walk in El Prado. This walk changed my life. Thank you, Rosemary.

~ Johnny Tarcica

Johnny Tarcica is the founder and CEO of www.Empleos.net, a leading job portal in Latin America.

June 7

Prepare and Sow

A friend of mine is living in the house I built when I was 20 years old. I called it my Shanti. It was two stories high, with beautiful views of the Oregon forest. From building a house, to gardening, canning, raising animals, midwifing, living without electricity, and relationships, I learned more living on that commune than I ever did in college. My two favorite parts were the afternoon swim in the creek, just hanging out with no worries or hurry, and the nightly campfires of sharing music, stories, and creative thinking. Life was so simple—easy. I drew my house plans on a sheet of paper from a lined notebook.I hunted in secondhand stores for doors and windows; I hand-treated my poles and dug the holes to set my foundation. Then I told everyone around the campfire that I was building my house that weekend. I am not sure anyone thought I could really do it, but on Saturday morning people from town who had watched me gather materials and answered all my questions showed up to help me raise the walls and set the roof. From that day on I have always known I can do it, whatever my dream maybe.

~ Louise Rouse

Louise Rouse *is the founder of Planetary Coaching Academy, offering Holistic Coaching Certification for helping humanity and planetary change. Visit www.PlanetaryCoach.com. Ready to become a coach? Visit www.PlanetaryCoach.com/Calling-To-Serve/.*

June 8

Our Annual Crummy Reunions

For the past 14 summers my husband and I have held a 10-day reunion for his crummy relatives. You may think that's rather tacky of me to call them crummy relatives, and you may be thinking the same about some of your relatives; however, my husband's relatives really are crummy. You see, I married a "Crum," so there are quite a few crummy relatives out there who enjoy coming to the Carlsbad Beach each summer. What started on a whim 14 years ago has continued each year, with the Crummys traveling from New York, Boston, Arizona, Colorado, New Mexico, and Texas. A new generation of Crummys has been born over the years, and now there are eight additional members to this crummy clan. I'm so grateful for the time and effort that all the crummy relatives make to come to our beach town for the sand, the sun, the sea breeze, and the sunsets. With the exception of our daughter, my relatives are deceased, and so I relish in hearing the stories of my husband's childhood with his brother and sister, the updates of all of their children, and a chance to make memories for the future.

~ *Sue Sweeney Crum*

Dr. Sue Sweeney Crum *is a speaker, author, clutter clearing coach, and accredited staging professional. When she's not boogie boarding with her crummy relatives, Sue can be reached at www.SueCrum.com.*

June 9

Summer on the Farm

Summertime brings a lot of work to a farm; it certainly did when I was growing up on my family's Wisconsin dairy farm. I spent my summers doing chores while my city friends spent them swimming at the beach, hanging out with friends, and living the carefree life. How I envied them! Still, there were advantages to living on the farm. My city friends couldn't build a bonfire in the backyard and roast hot dogs and marshmallows on a starry summer night. They didn't get to see the glowing fireflies that glided through the tall grass growing by the creek. Their houses didn't have porches large enough to hold three generations of family members who talked and laughed into the night. Today I realize that growing up on the farm was a blessing. I learned the value of work and family, gratitude for gifts from animals and the earth, and the joy of just being alive. Sometimes I long for those days and the people who shaped me. I am grateful for their sacrifice, for their love, and for those summers on the farm. I wouldn't trade any of them for the world.

~ Laura Weber-Meyers

Laura Weber-Meyers is a life coach who believes that we are each Born to Live it All! You can reach her at LauraWeberMeyers@comcast.net.

June 10

What I Am Grateful For?

While writing this entry, reflections of the past year makes my heart overflow with gratitude for my family, friends, and my healing journey. Last year was one of my most difficult years, full of trials, tribulations, and severe illness, but my growth was exponential. My family and friends nurtured me and supplied me with the love and support that I truly needed. While they held me up, I was able to focus solely on healing. Illness has been my most profound teacher. It accelerated my life lessons. It strengthened me and cultivated parts of my being that needed refinement. It humbled me to appreciate the simple things that are often overlooked and taken for granted. Through physical illness every part of my being has been healed (mind, body, and soul) and I truly feel whole. Illness allowed me to be still long enough to hear the divine voice inside me and heed it. Being still integrates my mind, body, and soul and now they work together as one, dancing to the same tune. Illness has strengthened my inner healer and I have emerged like the Phoenix, living every day aligned in my purpose. The healed is now a healer.

~ *Lisa Lewis*

Dr. Lisa Lewis *is a leading naturopathic physician, acupuncturist, and healthy living expert. She's the author of* Stop Stressing Me Out: 7 Strategies to Overcome Overwhelm and Conquer Disease Naturally.

June 11

Day Trippin'

One of my favorite summertime activities is the day trip. I love spending a day discovering the wonders in my own backyard, so to speak. I think I have seen nearly every attraction in my state, from state parks to amusement parks. If it is within a days drive, I will go. This was particularly fun when my children were teens. They would complain that they had to go—who wants to spend the day with your parent?—but they always seem to have fun once we hit the road. We would sing and laugh as we drove to the day's destination. Part of the fun of the trip is stopping at the little markers or scenic overviews along the way. It is great to sit around now that they are older and reminisce about our trips and the fun things that happened along the way. I encourage you to order your own state's tourist information and plan a day trip or two. It is amazing the fun you can have, but even better is the time that you bond with family or friends and the incredible memories that you make.

~ Shellie A. Couch

Shellie Couch *is a certified Infinite Possibilities Trainer, work-shop creator and facilitator, life coach, and co-author of* Beautiful Seeds of Change *and* Step Into Your Best Life. *Contact her at Shellie.Couch@PracticeLivingJoy.com or www.PracticeLivingJoy.com.*

June 12

The River

At the old hunting cabin perched on the rocks above the Housatonic River belonging to my grandparents, I was an invincible, adventurous queen. It was a mystical, magical world of woods, trails, rocks, river, boat, fishing, animal tracking, card games, books, and freedom. I learned to swim on that river and to row a boat along its edges with my younger siblings as fellow adventurers or, perhaps, reluctant captives. There was an unseen dam around the bend. When the water gates were opened we had to get out of the water quickly or tie ourselves to a rope anchored in a rock. We'd go up river as far as we could, jump in, let the force of the river carry us, or test ourselves as we swam against the current to claim who was mightier than the river. I intensely remember that triumphant moment when I swam across the river unaided. I had to muster great depths of courage to cross the deep, dark river, and this was my moment. Countless precious memories were created at the river, but mostly I remember the joy of summer and the freedom to simply be. I enjoy passing this essence on to our grandchildren.

~ *Megan Paglia-Scheff*

Megan Paglia-Scheff *is a social entrepreneur, artist/dance, author, coach. For more information e-mail MakingMagicEveryDay@gmail.com or visit www.RawYouniverse.com and www.NakedSophia.com.*

June 13

Waking to Dreams

"Your job is now redundant." Who can imagine being grateful to hear those five life-changing words? I certainly didn't. Instead, it was like a blaring alarm clock jolted me from a deep sleep. After tending to my shock and wounded ego, and the rush of all the other unexpected emotions, the dreary fog lifted to reveal my long buried and forgotten dreams. Had it not been for that brief, life-jarring moment, I would never have stepped forward into the life I am living now. When I face an unexpected turn in my life I now smile in eager anticipation, knowing greater things are being asked of me, to stretch and play big. For that, I am grateful. Today, think about those challenges or obstacles that seem to be tugging at your dream life. In what ways do they present the opportunity for you to stretch and grow? What alarm clock is blaring in your life that you can be grateful for?

~ Susan Boras

Susan Boras *enables business leaders to remove their blind spots so they can shine, love what they do, and still have a life! You can reach Susan at Susan@SquareHoleCoaching.com.*

June 14

A Big Nature Hug

I feel so more at peace in my life compared to the past. If I get emotional, the best thing for me to do is go outside in nature. I let my emotions come up and then just be with nature. This makes me more present as I am surrounded by all this beauty. Then gratitude increases, and I become more still and then see more what I am grateful for. A smile appears on my face and in that moment I just am. All the love and peace I feel now are sometimes overwhelming. Tears of joy run down my face, just because I am so grateful for what is already in my life. I wish for others to find this space within them, too. There are so many different ways to get there, and gratitude was definitely one of mine. So just start writing each day about what makes you happy and what you are grateful for, and see what changes in your life. Dad, you passed away three years ago. You have been one of my best mirrors in life; you helped me shape who I am today. Thank you. Love a gratitude, Chantale

~ *Chantale Horst*

Chantale Horst *is a loving mum to Jade and the creator of Gratitude Notes. You can reach her at gratitudenotes.com.au.*

June 15

Magical Journey

"To travel is to live."

~ H.C. Andersen

When I packed my backpack for my solo trip to Bali for one month, this was meant to be my personal journey into power and independence—the ultimate adventure: weeks filled with long walks on the beach, running, exploring my favorite island with all my senses. After having enjoyed the breathtaking views over luscious rice paddies and spectacular sunsets on the beach for two days, all my plans were thwarted due to one careless step on uneven pavement. My left ligament was ruptured, and I had to walk on crutches from that moment on. I was devastated. Everything I had been looking for seemed impossible—until I met the most amazing people who lovingly supported me in all my endeavors, even carried me around when needed, and made sure that I could inhale the magic of Bali in the most empowering and inspiring way. After three weeks, a Balinese healer fixed my foot, and I got to enjoy the remainder of my stay with a renewed sense of gratitude, humility, and friendship. The new friends who helped me out are still an important and enriching part of my life to date.

~ *Elisabeth Balcarczyk*

Elisabeth Balcarczyk, MA, CPCC, *is an Authentic Life & Leadership Coach working with individuals and organizations internationally in form of coaching programs, workshops, and retreats. You can find her at BodyMindSoulCoaching.weebly.com.*

June 16

I'm Grateful for Cancer

Yes, I am grateful for having had cancer. Cancer has taught me many important aspects about myself and about life. First, I've learned to let go, for I am not in total control. There is another force at work. Sure, I can make my own decisions about treatment and therapy, when I'm going to rest, and when I'm going to act. But I am not the only one in control of what happens in my life. I've learned to trust by handing the reins to God. I've also learned:

- I'm not a victim; I have free will choice to act; I am responsible for my decisions and actions.
- To receive by letting others help me.
- To admit past mistakes and ask for forgiveness; and how to forgive and love myself.
- Courage and forward action conquer fear.
- When life's challenges seem daunting and overwhelming, I can dig deeper.
- To honor myself and my life's purpose by acting on what is in my heart, mind, and soul to do in this world with the time I have.

And I've learned that all the time I ever really have is now. I'm not just a survivor, or even three-time survivor. I'm a life-thriver!

~ *Peg Roach Loyd*

Peg Roach Loyd *is an author, blogger, musician, singer/songwriter, and storyteller. Visit her website at www.CellaDawnMusic.com, follow her on Twitter @IrishPegOfAR, or read her blog at www.PegRoachLoyd. Wordpress.com.*

June 17

Summertime

Summer is my second favorite season. To choose a memorable one is hard to do. Going back in time serves me best. I received a puppy for my fourth birthday. Daddy came home with a paper shopping bag with a little white ball of fur in it. She was tidy and I decided to call her Snowball. She grew into her name quite quickly. Then my mother went into the hospital for an operation. The doctor said she needed some "recoup" time away from home chores. Daddy shipped us both off on a train to stay with my grandparents in Toronto. Daddy asked a neighbor to look after Snowball. Summer passed quickly. It was fun to be with my cousins and grandparents. Mom got better fast, and finally it was time to go home. We hadn't seen Daddy or Snowball for six weeks. Imagine my disappointment when Daddy and I went to pick up Snowball and the lady wouldn't return her to me. I cried and cried. She was so cruel. After two weeks of much arguing, Daddy threatened to go to the police. She gave back Snowball. That summer that stands out in my mind as a favorite.

~ *Sharon G. Teed*

Sharon G. Teed *now lives in Perth, Ontario, where she hopes the peace and quiet will inspire her creativity to finish her own book. Contact her at Sharon.Teed@sympatico.ca.*

June 18

Through Windows of Remembrance

The front porch is enclosed now, a result of one of my father's retirement projects. It has large picture windows, though, and I am still able to sit on it and look out at my parents' front yard and beyond, into the fields. I easily can transport myself back to my childhood years; as a teen, this porch became my haven to journey to faraway places, people, and events that just were not part of my everyday world. Summertime was usually filled with work around the house to help the family, from mowing the expansive lawn to picking the homegrown vegetables in our large garden. Not exactly easy summertime living or fun. But my work schedule was mine to set, so I could easily take breaks and relax. That's how I ended up spending so many summer hours on the porch. Quiet, with great vistas and easy breezes, it was the ideal place to pick up a book, relax, and discover what I couldn't get right there at home. One week I would be marching through Civil War battlefields and the next basking in the magnificence of mansions and beachside life in East Hampton. Wait—that was easy living and fun!

~ *Tassey Russo*

Tassey Russo *is a business development strategist and implementation consultant who helps entrepreneurs transform their dreams and ideas into purpose-driven, influential, and highly profitable businesses. She lives in Darnestown, Maryland. Connect with Tassey at www.LevelUpSolutions.com.*

June 19

The Summer of '67

The summer of 1967 brought big changes to my life. I culminated from elementary school, celebrated my 12th birthday, and moved from Los Angeles, California, to Miami, Florida, for the next phase of my life experience. This phase included what my mother referred to as "becoming a woman," having my first best friend, and becoming an entrepreneur. It was just my mother and me, and we were very poor at that time. We did not have a car, a telephone, a television set, or many of the material items that others around us did. I believe this brought us closer, and we enjoyed doing things together like spending Saturdays at the public library and going for walks in nature. That summer I made friends with Tory, the boy next door, and that relationship would end up lasting for almost 40 years, until his accidental death in 2005. Tory introduced me to the world of entrepreneurship, and we made money in a variety of ways, including mowing lawns and raising gerbils to sell to the pet store. Tory taught me some basic business skills that I still use, and for that I will always be grateful to him.

~ Connie Ragen Green

Connie Ragen Green *is a bestselling author and international speaker living in Southern California. She teaches new online entrepreneurs how to build profitable businesses. Find out more at ConnieRagenGreen.com.*

June 20

The Woods

I am fortunate to live in the house I grew up in. Where I live is surrounded by woods—very private—and my home takes on a different personality with each season. Summertime is my favorite season by far. I have a walking path that leads through the woods to a small swimming hole. It is the swimming hole I swam in when I was a kid, took my kids to, and hope to take my grandchildren to. Every morning my three dogs accompany me for a walk on this path, not matter the weather. The path holds a small burial ground for all my dogs and other animals that have passed away. Since this area is an extension of my home, I have begun fixing up the path by planting shrubs, lighting, and a post that includes directional arrow signs with funny names (The Falls, Hogwarts Place, Magical Garden, etc.). I am grateful to walk on this path daily that holds wonderful memories for me and my family.

~ *Doreen R. Dilger*

Doreen R. Dilger *is a business coach, time management and organizing expert, and author who coaches women who work from home who want to get more done and make more money! Learn more at www. DoreenDilger.com.*

June 21

Reflecting Light

As the season turns, I am reminded to be grateful for all that has been, and for all that will be. This is a day of thoughtful reflection. The word reflection has many meanings: a mirror's reflection of a face, the moon's reflection of sunlight, or time pondering the moments of our lives. Sometimes reflection means seeing someone's most beautiful qualities and taking a moment to admire them. They stand out because, in that moment, we get to see our very own qualities, and our hearts are open to enjoy them. Take note of the people and the qualities that you admire. Maybe they are being courageous, adventurous or patient. Possibly you are seeing them as loving, warm, and generous. Take your time and enjoy this. The list you create becomes your own list of core qualities. Try them on, test them out, and find ways to show them off. Importantly, be grateful for the people who reflect them for you to see. People notice how we show up in life. They can see our challenging traits just as easily as our finest and most enduring qualities. What do you want to see when people reflect back to you?

~ Lori L. Gorrell

Lori Gorrell *is a certified professional coach and consultant supporting women in leadership roles to gain clarity and focus on what is most important. Lori can be reached at www.LoriGorrell.com.*

June 22

Summers and Sardines Sandwiches

I am grateful for my summertime memories of going to summer camp for many, many years. My mom was a swim instructor at Camp Redwing in Syracuse, New York. This was a summer camp for inner-city girls at the Girls Club. My sister and I got to go to this camp every summer with her and we loved it. I remember it also making us really appreciate what we had and how much easier our lives were than some of these girls' lives. We were blessed.

I also learned that not everybody was a fan of my lunch choices sometimes. My favorite lunch to pack was a sardine sandwich. We would all go down to the stream to eat every day. When I brought my sardine sandwich, no one would sit next to me! I think they didn't like the smell, and I just didn't understand it. I'd sit by myself by the stream. So, if you are ever eating lunch with a group of people and you want to be by yourself, bring your sardine sandwich!

~ *Kim Kirmmse Toth LCSW, PCC*

Kim Kirmmse Toth's second career is as a business coach working with women "after 50" to build online coaching businesses. Always wanted to be an entrepreneur? Kim can help!

June 23

"I Love You" Spoken from the Heart

My favorite summertime memory was when my two granddaughters came to stay with me for two weeks over the Christmas holidays (summer in Australia). When the youngest granddaughter had her first real conversation with me on the telephone, she finished off with "Love you." I asked my daughter not to tell her to say that to me, as I wanted her to mean it when she said it. Not really understanding why, my daughter agreed. Because of circumstances and distance, the girls were 7 and 10 years old when they first stayed with me on their own. I took them to Wet & Wild, Sea World, ice skating, and swimming, to name a few activities and, being a very fit grandmother, I was able to enjoy all the activities to full measure with them. The first night I kissed them goodnight, they both put their arms around me and said, "I love you, Nanna." I knew they weren't being parrots; they meant it! Driving the girls to the airport for their flight home, I asked what was the highlight of their holiday. "Being with you, Nanna" was the quick reply. My summer was complete. Love cannot be measured!

~ *Elizabeth Collett*

Elizabeth Collett *is a self-employed dance instructor. She has taught in China and the United States, in addition to classes and workshops in Australia. Her instructional DVDs sell worldwide. Learn more at www.LineDance.com.au.*

June 24

Summers in Gearhart with Gram

I'll always remember the wonderful, "beachy" smell greeting us at the entry of our grandparents' house on the Oregon coast. Spending summers at Gearhart were some of my fondest childhood memories. We could really let loose and just be kids when we were there, and Gram would always advocate in our favor: "Oh, let them stay up later," "Come on—the go-karts are waiting," "Let's head to Seaside and have ice cream." Gram was just like one of the kids herself, and after an early morning of clam digging, she'd race us through the spikey beach grass all the way home—with clams flying out of the bucket behind her. At night, we'd head to the "boardwalk" and Gram was the first to hit the trampolines. She raced like a wild woman around the go-kart tracks, delighting in beating the pants off us kids, and she became "Menacing Mary" behind the wheel of the bumper cars. At night, the cards would come out and we would play for hours, and Gram and Mom would sing their silly songs about "carrying moonbeams home in a jar." How I wish I could give my kids those wonderful beach time memories I had as a child!

~ Kim Chaney-Condrin

Kim Chaney-Condrin *is a certified professional organizer and owner of Organize To Order in Sammamish, Wash. She loves dogs, writing, researching, and spending time with family. Connect at www.OrganizeToOrder.com/ Kim@OrganizeToOrder.com.*

June 25

Childhood Summer Memories

As a 7-year-old, the oldest of three siblings, I remember our favorite things to do. We played cowboys and Indians with our stick ponies and bows and arrows. We made eatable mud pies and had tea parties on the lawn. We fished with a long pole for toys in a bag. We cut out paper dolls and played "house" under a sheet tent. Played kick ball, basketball, and tether ball. We hiked in the canyon behind our home, climbed trees, and explored caves. We fed chickens and rabbits only to kill and eat them for dinner. We read funny books to each other. We played hopscotch, jacks, ring around the roses, and jumped rope. At night we lay out on the lawn and counted stars. We knew nothing of videos, texting, electronic games, or social media. We used our unlimited imaginations, enjoyed the warm summers of California, and lived and played outside until the darkness of night forced us to come inside. Those were the days!

~ Linda Strom Medvitz

Linda Strom Medvitz *is currently volunteering at PB Holistic Center as coordinator, doing past life regressions and energy healing sessions. She provides monthly gatherings at Cloudwalk Retreat. sharing Mayan cosmology and ceremonies.*

June 26

Freedom Floating

I swim like a fish. Whenever I tell the story of how I learned to swim, fond memories replay in my mind from a long time ago. At age 7 I experienced post–World War II Germany, which lay in ruins and had no place for children to play. But, we did have our local river with a roped-off section for swimming. One hot summer afternoon my mother, aunt, cousin, and I trekked to the swimming hole. After being equipped with a small circular tube, my cousin and I headed into the river, splashing with joy. As the water got deeper and deeper, I was tippy-toeing, pushed myself up, experiencing my body floating to the surface. Immediately, I had a feeling of freedom and of being held in caring arms. Breathing easily and rhythmically, I floated on my back for as long as I wanted, all the while feeling wonder of a dreamlike state. I relive that moment of joy every time I swim, especially in the Grand Cayman Islands. My work as a flight attendant took me there on long layovers. In the beautiful, calm, warm turquoise waters I snorkeled and floated in heavenly peace.

~ Bettina Sparkles Obernefemann

Bettina Sparkles Obernuefemann *is a retired flight attendant, author, and childhood PTSD survivor with a mission is to inspire trauma victims to cope and hope. Visit BettinaSparkles.com.*

June 27

Summer Visits in Rhode Island

Fond summer memories are of trips taken back east to visit my friends and sister, Lisa, after relocating to Los Angeles. Whether it be a trip around the 4th of July or closer to Labor Day, my trips were filled with nostalgia and good times. Lisa lived in an old summer cottage in Bay Springs, Rhode Island. A quaint home, it was Lisa's pride and joy. The drive was lined with crushed sea shells, and it had a cozy front porch, and a backyard full of Cosmos, sunflowers, and vegetables.

I've always loved summer in Rhode Island, as did my sister. Our visit was casual, our bond strong. A typical day was a trip to the town beach and settling into "her spot." Our days were filled with reading, gabbing, pizza from Vienna bakery, Del's lemonade, and swimming. Evenings were for hanging out with the neighbors for drinks, conversation, laughs, and BBQs. On occasion we'd be side-lined by a storm and hang out watching a movie and eating pop-corn.

I can't think of a better place to grow up than Rhode Island. With all of its gorgeous coastline, I miss it, and I miss my sister. I'm grateful for fond memories of both.

~ Paula D'Andrea

Paula D'Andrea *resides in Los Angeles and still makes an occasional summer trip to Rhode Island. She is a writer, speaker, and coach. Learn more at PaulaDAndrea.com and RockYourLife.tv.*

June 28

Sea, Snacks, and Sunshine

School was out and for nine blissful weeks I was free to relax, and do mostly whatever I wanted with my sister and best friend in St. Maarten. I fondly think back on those days when I was a teenager and feel very grateful for such pleasant memories. These were summers of sand, sea, sweet and salty snacks, and gentle breezes. Some days we would walk along the edge of the lagoon, looking for shells of unusual shapes and colours. We sometimes held contests to see who could collect the most unusual shells. At other times, when it was uncomfortably hot outside, we stayed indoors and ate ice cream. On cool afternoons, we walked to the top of the hill, behind the house, and observed the airplanes as they landed at the nearby airport. Some rainy days, we stayed indoors, reading or telling each other jokes and stories. I remember picnics on the beach when my father and his best friend would roast and serve up the fresh catch of day. The salty and fresh sea air seemed to increase our appetites as we eagerly devoured whatever was cooked. Ah, summertime!

~ Avenelle Warde

Avenelle Warde, founder of ClubE3, where members are enthused by our entertaining and evolutionary approach to education, has a passion for helping children succeed academically. She lives in St. Kitts, West Indies, and has worked in the telecom industry for over 20 years. Tweet her at Twitter.com/aveywar_skn.

June 29

Some Memories Never Lose Their Value

Summers—no school, just parks, tadpoles, dusty feet, fizzy drinks, and the zoo, where one of our kind neighbors worked the gate. (Always sunny—how did that happen?) A city being rebuilt, roads being re-laid, and lots of tar bubbles to pop with fingers and bare toes—and the cranky adults who had to deal with the sticky leftovers.

There's this one summer I remember (with grateful pleasure) for a book. My late mother's best friend always gave us books. This was *Lamb's Tales* from Shakespeare. There have been other editions, the main variation being style of illustration. (I have seen one with flat colors and cartoonesque figures displaying large bodies with tiny heads.) But the one I remember was a delight with beautiful watercolors. Peaseblossom and friends were perfect little girls with wings and pretty dresses flying around an ass's head so real you could count every hair and every petal in his crown of flowers. Dear old Shakespeare. I went to senior high school studies with real enthusiasm for him, a love of words, and a grateful memory of a summer years before.

~ *Barbara Malpass*

Barbara Malpass *is closing on completion of her PhD, then it's on to future projects: parables in haiku for an ebook and Shakespeare for senior primaries with modern graphic illustrations. (Sh-h-h—fingers crossed.)*

June 30

Fireworks on the Fourth

After spending my childhood in Northern Virginia, for a number of years as an adult, I lived too far away to attend the Fourth of July celebration at the Washington Monument. When I moved to Richmond, Virginia, 90 minutes from Washington, DC, I returned to attending the Fourth of July celebration of my fond childhood memories.

I met my husband-to-be in 1994, and it didn't take long to realize he was "the one," and the feeling was mutual. The subject of marriage had come up, but nothing was formalized when, in the summer of 1995, we made plans to visit friends in Northern Virginia, and to attend the fireworks at the Washington Monument on the Fourth as part of our trip. My youngest child, then a teen, was traveling with us. We said goodbye to our friends on the morning of the Fourth and caught the Metro into Washington, DC. We spent a pleasant but uneventful day, and as evening came, we settled into a place on the National Mall with a view of the Monument. We were watching the fireworks when Jon turned to me, out of the blue, and said, "Will you marry me?" Not many people can say there were literally fireworks when the love of their life proposed!

~ *Helen "Sue" Walker*

Helen "Sue" Walker is president of the Richmond Fibromyalgia and Chronic Pain Association and a member of the Leaders Against Pain Coalition of the NFMCPA. Sue lives in Richmond, Virginia, with her husband, Jon, and three beautiful rescued dogs.

July

"*Gratitude makes sense of our past,*
brings peace for today,
and creates a vision for tomorrow."

~ Anonymous

July 1

Grateful for America

What I am grateful for... I am grateful for this beautiful country that allows us to be who and what we want to be freely. I was born into a family of heartlessness, grew up to learn forgiveness and value my life, and cultured an expression of gratitude and love through my craft. I could have grown to hate because that is all I knew for the first 17 years of my life. Although, it took some more years of self-inflicted pain, I eventually saw that others valued me. I could not have learned this nugget if I was born to another country that does not have born-free citizens, since their version of government is heartless and un-nurturing at best. I spent my adult life working (pleasing others) without a creative outlet. The collapsing economy allowed me to culture my love of metal jewelry design. Selling my jewelry on the open market allows for instant feedback. The method of using metal clay is like my life: rudimentary powder that mixes with water to make clay, the flow of design, and the sintering/firing to the end result of pure metal. This free-market government allows me to create my art as an extension of my life.

~ *Jennifer L. Hendricks*

Jennifer L. Hendricks's *jewelry art is formed, sculpted, and refined out of metal clay that, once fired, is solid and 99% pure. Bezel-set gemstones and metalsmithing are incorporated. Get in touch at www.Lavender-Designs.com.*

July 2

God Bless America

When I see an American flag flying, the bigger the better. When I hear "The Star-Spangled Banner" being sung at a baseball game, I shiver with pride and gratitude for this country of my birth. Perhaps it is because I was born to Irish immigrant parents, into a military-serving family; I grew up knowing the sacrifices made and paid to preserve the freedoms we enjoy as one nation under God, indivisible, with liberty and justice for all.

Sure, we may not have it all perfect yet, but our principles are noble and honorable, and nothing to take for granted. I have traveled to other countries and carry many friends and family in my heart from those places, but honestly, we do have it made in the USA!

I hope that all of us have the vision, the gratitude, and the guts to do whatever it takes to preserve and prosper this great nation of ours.

God bless America!

~ *Theresa McMorrow Jordan*

Theresa McMorrow Jordan *is the mother of Jeff and Seth, and has a lifetime vision and mission to see the Earth become more like Heaven. She is a published songwriter and author of the soon-to-be-published* Get Crowned.

July 3

Honoring Our Wedding Vow

Today my husband and I have been married 31 years. This was our vow: I honor the place in you where the entire universe resides, that place of love, light, truth, and peace. When you are in that place in you, and I am in that place in me, there is only one of us. Well, after 16 years, three children, a business failure, and a cancer diagnosis, our marriage appeared to be finished. It simply didn't work out. Divorce was the obvious next step, and we took that step to dissolve our marriage. So we thought. It was an official divorce but we could not figure out how to let go of each other. Needless to say, our divorce didn't work out, either. Another dilemma. After time apart, soul searching, and counseling, we realized we were still in love. We realized we just had a blip on the marriage radar. So we returned our focus to our wedding vow and on the place where we were one rather than separate. We then remarried. The rest is history as we create our future together in this present moment. Today I am grateful for my wedding vow. I have never been happier.

~ *Martha Pasternack*

Martha Pasternack, IAC-MCC *is a fearless living coach. Her passion for witnessing the beauty of love, the mystery of life, healthy healing, peace, and kindness on Earth are integral to her life. For more information, visit CircleOfLifeCoach.com.*

July 4

Happy Birthday, America!

When I hear our national anthem and other renditions thereof tears come to my eyes. This is my favorite holiday. Today is every American's birthday. We really should exchange birthday gifts, don't you think? I want to thank John, George, Thomas, Ben, and their "crew," who had the wherewithal and foresight to be revolutionary in their thinking. Their willingness to move forward in the face of adversity—nay, certain death—to bring forth a more perfect union with liberty and justice for all is astounding. And the women of the revolution, I bow to your dedication. When I watch *John Adams* (2008) and even the musical *1776* (1972), I am awestruck by the astonishing convergence of intelligence and courage each person's declaration of independence produced at a time when it really shouldn't have been possible. Were these revolutionary ideas executed with perfection? Certainly not, but close enough for us to still be a country today. Whichever nation you come from, there are pride and affection. After all, it is your home. As we embrace our individual corners of the world, let's celebrate and honor our similarities as well as our differences with gratitude. May the 4th be with you!

~ Carol Lynn Fletcher

Carol Lynn Fletcher *is an intuitive and author. She helps her clients strengthen their intuitive abilities so they can provide transformative levels of service. Get in touch at Support@EnergeticBiz.com.*

July 5

My Gratitude for Freedom

My gratitude this day goes to the most overlooked members of our society: our veterans. To these men and women I can only say with humility that I am unworthy. Unworthy of the blood shed and lives lost. Unworthy of the sacrifices that you, our country's defenders and protectors, made to allow people like me to live free. I am indebted to you. This indebtedness was the driving force behind my efforts to build a website and write a book to help veterans through the transition back into society. My intent was not only to help military veterans succeed in finding employment, but also to spread awareness to the tremendous struggles military veterans face upon returning to the private sector. For so many of you, your lives will never be the same. America's heroes have demonstrated in the face of incredible odds that we can count on them. Employers, may I suggest interviewing a veteran for your next opening? I'm sure you will find that our veterans have so much to offer. Veterans, my work can never come close to paying my debt to you, but I hope that you will view my efforts as a partial thank you. My gratitude!

~ Russ Hovendick

Russ Hovendick *is the author of three books under the Directional Motivation series and founder of the Directional Motivation organization, which provides free career resources for veterans and others. Learn more at www.DirectionalMotivation.com.*

July 6

Independence Day

I awoke to the warmth of the rays flowing in on the tail of the sun. The atmosphere is pregnant with excitement and anticipation of the imminent event about to unfold. It's intoxicating. These were my last moments of "freedom"—or so I'm told! I think it all depends on how you define "freedom" within the context of marriage. I was ready. I was really present and in awe of the moments to come. My spirit was alive and vibrant. I was experiencing a profound inner peace. I was radiating love and wrapped in a cloak of unwavering faith in life and trusting in the rich, fulfilling process of marriage on the 4th of July. To most, a wedding on Independence Day is ironic. To me, it was the beginning of a special, sacred lifelong union that would be filled with enchanted adventure, deep discovery, and unfettered growth in relatedness. Marriage is the magic of just being, feeling, loving, and sharing. The freedom of being who you are, with who you are with. I'm grateful for the magical summertime memory of my 4th of July wedding—independence of two hearts uniting to be one.

~ Diana Onuma

Diana Onuma, *a coach and writer, lives in London. She runs the Bodacious Butterfly Program, a heart-based healing practice for spiritually conscious women. Contact her at CircleOfGrowth.co.uk or DianaOnuma.com.*

July 7

Summertime Means Mango Time

"Mummy, we don't want to come in!" My five young children are for once in total agreement. Forget lunchtime. It's August, and they live in the pool. "Please, please, Mummy! Throw fruits!" They laugh and laugh and laugh, and gurgle on their dive for them. I throw plums and apples since they stay firm. But their favorite fruit were mangoes, right from our tree. There was one rule to the enjoyment of mangos: They had to leave the pool—well, sort of, because I see five children sitting side by side on the rim, their feet shuffling the blue water. They laugh and laugh and laugh, only like children can while they rip and peel the mango skin and sink their teeth into the warm, soft, yellow mango flesh. Sweet juice runs from their mouths in small streams, drips onto their bellies, and runs across brown thighs, which glisten in the sun. They smile with glee, exposing their white teeth, which are now packed with strings of yellow fiber. "Mummy! We want to come in!" Their hands are stretched out, covered with remnants of sticky mango juice. I laugh out loud and want to embrace my adorable children—but the garden hose was a better idea.

~ Angelika Christie, ND

Angelika Christie, ND, *is known as a trendsetter in personal development. Her insights are highly innovative and goal oriented toward her clients' greatest success. Angelika is a dynamic speaker, multiple bestselling author, and certified life-transformation coach. Learn more at www.FreedomWhisperer.com or www.Facebook.com/FreedomWhisperer.*

July 8

"You Made My Day!"

It was summertime. I was going to the beach, together with a friend of mine. But even though it was summertime, it happened to be a cold, windy, cloudy day. All people were dressed up warmly, covered in layers of warm clothes. They were taking a walk, or having a drink somewhere inside. But I wanted to take a swim in the sea! So I took the courage to get in my bathing suit. I took a run and dived in the waves of the sea! Woohoo, it was so exciting—the cold water touching my skin, the waves running over me. It felt so alive! When I got out of the water, a man behind a fish stall called me. He said, "You are so brave, taking a swim in the sea under these weather conditions. You just made my day! I used to give away a free portion of fried fish to someone every day. Today I would like to give this fish to you. You really deserve it." Now this man really made my day! It was the best fried fish I ever ate in my life. And I still remember that special moment today.

~ *Saskia Fokkink*

Saskia Fokkink *is an international life coach, inspiring and guiding others to live the life of their dreams. Visit her website at www.SaskiaLifeCoaching.com or contact her directly at Saskia@SaskiaLifeCoaching.com.*

July 9

My Magical Summer

In June 2000, Hollyhurst Cottage Inn officially was born. Owning/running a B&B at one of the prettiest beaches on the Cape had never been something I'd expected or planned to do. But, here I was. Creating her out of a neglected Victorian had been a marvel. Once I made the decision to go for it, people and opportunities came out of the woodwork! I had help bookkeeping, website making—anything that didn't come naturally for me! The result was the prettiest, happiest, place I could imagine. Guests came to spend their vacation here, a special event (birthday, anniversary) here, to have a spur-of-the-moment weekend getaway here. They arrived, I checked them in, and then I left them alone. I set up coffee and muffins on the buffet in the mornings, and didn't see much of them until the morning of their departure. There was always a smile on their faces. They would sit, over coffee, and tell me what a great time they had, how relaxed they felt, how comfortable they had been. It always made me feel good to have made someone else feel good. I miss that. Should never have closed. It's time for a little more magic!

~ Alice Rosalie Touchette

Alice Rosalie Touchette *lives in Onset, Mass., with her family of toy poodles in a magical Victorian by the beach. Learn more about Alice's YUEN and Reiki Masteryat www.HollyhurstCottageInn.com or her Facebook (Alice Touchette/Reiki Ragz).*

July 10

The Family Trivia Game

"Are there any questions for the sisters?" my brother, the entertainer of the family, asked at the Great Graetz Gathering in July 2012. My mother has three younger sisters, one of them living in Florida, the others nearby in western Wisconsin. The year Mom turned 70, in 1995, we celebrated with an all-inclusive summertime family picnic. Relatives came from all corners of the U.S. At that time, only two of my cousins could not attend. We had so much fun being together and getting to know the spouses and kids we decided to do it again 17 years later. Our family has doubled since that first great get-together; however, not everyone could attend, our genes even more so spread throughout the country. But all four sisters made it! We had fun and games to pass the time. There was the photo contest where names, places, and the year were to be guessed. And then there was the trivia game. When my brother asked if anyone had a question they wanted answered, the second-oldest sister said, "Well, I want to know who tipped over the chamber pot!" We all laughed hysterically! However, not one sister confessed to the dirty deed.

~ *Peggy Lee Hanson*

Peggy Lee Hanson, *Personal Transition Guidance, LLC, mentors those who experience life-changing situations, and guides them through their journey using self-empowerment tools, compassion, and support. Visit Peggy at www.MyDreamArchitect.com.*

July 11

That Magical Summer

At the age of 15, I made my first transatlantic flight, to visit my father's birthplace in England. How can I describe my emotions upon seeing my first castle? I stood at the foot of the pathway across the moat and tried to imagine what life had been like 600 years before. What were people wearing? What were the smells in the morning air? What would I have been doing, if I had lived there so many centuries before? It was the gateway to so many wonderful memories: seeing the Crown Jewels in the Tower of London, breathtaking and dazzling under the lights, and then looking down on the Traitor's Gate, where prisoners were chained to the wall and left to be drowned by the incoming tide; stopping at a country pub for lunch and having the horse corralled behind the pub try to eat the buttons off my jacket; seeing King Arthur's Round Table and castle ruins; hearing a poltergeist's ghostly footsteps at the top of the stairs of the place where my father was born. PPure magic! I am eternally grateful for the opportunity to step into history, that magical summer of 1970.

~ *Patti Smith*

Patti Smith *lives in Barrie, Ontario, Canada with her beloved husband, Paul, and Jack Russell Terrier, Sheba. She is a speaker, author, and coach. Reach Patti at www.AwesomeWealthyWoman.com.*

July 12

Summer Breeze and Sunshine Memories

Bonfires on the beach, clam digs, swimming, and cooking marshmallows over a campfire are a few of my sweetest and precious memories of summer vacations on Prince Edward Island, Canada. My family roots are on the island and I never stop loving it. Prince Edward Island is widely known as the "Garden of the Gulf." The island is tranquil and draped in velvety green rolling hills, board walks, ocean coves, and the sounds of gentle surf. With childhood excitement and energy I remember the days playing on the beach. The water is a spiritual connection for me. It grounds me. One of my favorite summertime hobbies is beachcombing. With vivid clarity I can recall when the tide is out, collecting shells and feeling the cool red sand in my toes with the warm summer gulf breeze on my face. Life is grand. It is here on this small Canadian island that I feel so at home. I am blessed and so fortunate to have this treasured island to visit. What I believe for sure is that my dream of a summer home on this island will soon come to pass. For now, my memories stay alive in pictures and vacations.

~ *Debra Moser*

Debra Moser *is a certified life coach, writer, and veteran. Living in Ottawa, Canada, Debra is committed to empower her clients to live their best life with kindness and gratitude.*

July 13

The Friendly Skies?

My preteen summers were spent flying, by myself, to visit both sets of grandparents halfway across the country. On one trip, I fell asleep, awakening just as the final passengers were leaving the airplane, which I found confusing. I was accustomed to being the first off the plane, being delivered to my relatives before the mass exit of passengers. Evidently, my assigned stewardess had forgotten all about me. My anxious grandparents stormed their way against the exiting passengers to find me sitting all alone, quietly reading my book. Having flown by myself for so many years, I decided to just wait for my stewardess. I was fairly content, but my grandparents obviously were not happy! I'll never forget the look on the stewardess's face when she realized she "lost" a passenger! And then to be confronted by my 10-gallon-hat-bearing Southern grand-paw who just wanted to "line 'em up and shoot 'em down"! I would venture the airlines never left another child unattended again, especially after my exceptionally expressive grand-paw shared his feelings with everyone in the terminal. I was just glad to see my relatives. I finally finished reading that book, by flashlight under the covers, that night.

~ Shanana "Rain" Golden-Bear

Shanana "Rain" Golden-Bear is the editor/publisher of Desert Messenger, Quartzsite's FREE Community Paper, a Planetary Coach™, joy facilitator, and author. Learn more at www.ChangeWithoutFear.com and www.Twitter.com/QuartzsiteRain.

July 14

Life's Blinks

What Am I grateful for? I am grateful for the times my life has taken an unexpected left turn. Life can change in a blink. It is in those blinks you have a choice to focus on the negative or re-treasure the things in life you've taken for granted. It's in coping with those blinks that you grow and change the things in your life that do not support your health and happiness. There is something good to be found in each of life's blinks. Look for the positive. It's there. Always.

~ Pam Murphy

Pam Murphy, MS, RRT is a holistic nutritionist. Her mission and passion are to inspire and empower people to make healthy choices, which choose life. Learn more at http://EmpowerWellness.blogspot.com.

July 15

A Taste for Life

I don't remember having a happy childhood. Nor was it particularly unhappy. It just was, a series of unfolding experiences, the most memorable, it seems, relating to food! I keenly remember the blissful smell of baking bread imprinted on the salty smell of the sea, a regular feature of our summer holidays when each seaside town had its own local bakery. I miss that smell. Another holiday memory is of my mother producing a small barbeque that we took to the beach and—on one occasion only—had what would now be called a sausage sizzle. How I wanted to repeat the experience but alas, for reasons that were never clear, it was a one-off. Another memory relating to food (maybe that's why I count the enjoyment of good food a major blessing in my life) was the surreptitious eating of the inside of a loaf of bread on the way home from buying it at the local shop. The taste was divine and worth braving my mother's extreme displeasure in finding that only the outside crust remained and her journey to the shop had been in vain. I seem to remember my brother also being involved in this.

~ Justus H. Lewis

Justus H. Lewis, PhD, *life coach, has a lifetime of experience teaching amazing people how to develop strategies and tactics to achieve worthwhile personal goals. Find her at www.JustusLewis.com.au or www.emfmelb.com.*

July 16

Sweet Summer Memories

As a teen during early 1970s, we lived in a small village called Rock City Falls, New York. Summers meant freedom, and days were filled with nature, light, and fun. There was a small dam about a mile away, which was our daily destination! We would pack a lunch, gather our friends, swim, walk through the falls, and do daring stunts. Many weekends, we would all pack into my father's junkie car, which we called the "Captain America" car, due to its red roof, and white and blue on different side panels! We would have at least six neighborhood kids crammed and sitting on each other, acting silly and yelling out the windows. Dad, wearing his Pirates cap, tee shirt, and swim trucks, was leading the singing most of the time! Rock City Falls had multiple areas with decent streams, perfect for family outings! We spent the hottest days there. I can easily recall the delicious smell of hot dogs, burgers, and corn on the cob on the grill! There was tuna macaroni salad, potato salad with egg, and sweet watermelon. Watermelon was fun for several reasons: It tasted sweet, there was always a lot of it, and we would have a contest to see how far we could spit the seeds! We were so tired at the end of the day, we fell into our beds and started early again the next day! Summer days dissolved too quickly, but the sweet memories linger on!

~ Dodi Smith

Dodi Smith spends time between Albany, NY, and Columbia, MD, loving her seven grandchildren, three adult children, and spouse of 39 years. She is enjoying her early retirement and actively pursuing her dream online businesses, involving empowering women and building self-esteem and confidence in women and children. Contact her at DodiSmithEnterprises@gmail.com.

July 17

Down the Shore

Is there a more peaceful place than the beach? Even with all the noises—children giggling, waves crashing, lifeguards' whistles blowing, seagulls cawing—the beach is my happy place, where I feel calm and relaxed no matter the time of day. Early morning, with just me and my coffee? Perfection. Afternoon, with a good book (and extra sunblock!)? Works for me. Evening, taking a walk as the sun goes down and the tide rolls in? What a way to end the day.

I feel like my entire childhood was spent "down the shore," as we say in New Jersey: building sand castles with my brother and cousins, complaining about putting sunblock on (thanks, Mom!), chasing waves, and avoiding jelly fish—all leading up to a night on the boardwalk after the sun set. There is nothing better.

~ Jodi L. Brandon

Jodi L. Brandon is a writer/editor living in suburban Philadelphia. She goes down the shore as often as she can.

July 18

Gus's Lot

My family lived next door to a couple who had no children of their own but were uncle and aunt to many. They owned the land behind our house, their house, and two other homes, creating a private park for the neighbor children to enjoy. We called it "Gus's Lot." It hosted games of softball, tag football, badminton, croquet, and "capture the flag." It had large sassafras trees I'd climb up and perch on for hours, gently moving with the breeze and taking in the sights and sounds of my neighborhood. Gus's Lot was also home to a series of parties he and his wife, Helen, hosted each summer on Memorial Day, July 4th, and Labor Day. The neighborhood kids set up umbrella tables and chairs, and hung rows of lighted Japanese lanterns, providing a festive atmosphere. Our labor was rewarded with as much Coca-Cola as we wanted to enjoy, plus a feast of BBQ ribs, burgers, hot dogs, baked beans, and Loretta's special cheese cake. My favorite memory came at the end of those long summer evenings when those who remained would gather around a table telling jokes and stories, and laughing well into the night.

~ *Peg Roach Loyd*

Peg Roach Loyd *is an author, blogger, musician, singer/songwriter, and storyteller. Visit her website at www.CellaDawnMusic.com, follow her on Twitter @IrishPegOfAR, or read her blog at www. PegRoachLoyd.wordpress.com.*

July 19

The Weeping Willow Tree

I loved summer. It offered more hours to read. At least once a week I rode to the library and came home with a bike basket full of books. The library summer reading program offered prizes for reading a designated number of books, and I always won something. What a joy to be rewarded for my favorite pastime.

My reading spot during those lazy days was under the large weeping willow tree, the focal point in our backyard. I'd lay in my chaise lounge and be transported to some far-off place. During my journey, I'd inhale the fragrance of Mom's rose garden a few feet away. I'd read for hours, occasionally taking a sip of lemonade from the frosty glass that sat on the table next to me. When my eyes needed a rest, I'd watch the goldfish swimming in the fish pond for a few minutes. My own little bit of heaven…

The days marched by too fast, and soon the first day of school arrived. I said goodbye to my weeping willow, knowing it would be waiting to welcome me again the next summer.

~ Joyce Heiser

Joyce Heiser *is living her retirement dream as a published author. She lives in South Dakota with her husband and two rescue tabby cats. Connect with her at LivingMyRetirementDream.com.*

July 20

The Brain Freeze Test

We crowded close to Grandma, watching her fill metal canisters with rich, fresh cream from an uncle's cows, until she shooed us away. Catering to the adults, she threw in sliced strawberries or peaches from her garden. Best of all, in our opinions, were the batches she flavored with cocoa or peanut butter. Granddad lowered the containers into wooden buckets, as cousins demanded "firsties" to turn the crank, while sneaking chips of ice before he had a chance to add the rock salt. Taking turns with the churning, we shared the excitement and wonder of feeling the heavy cream grow thicker as it froze. Around and around we pulled the cranks, until we kids couldn't budge them. Then the men folk sat in the shade, muscling the dashers through the cold treat until they agreed it was frozen solid. We kids rushed the adults through Sunday supper, eyeing the towel-draped churns, anxious for that first blissful taste of frozen sweetness. Finally, Granddad uncovered a churn, slowly pulling the treat-laden dasher free and passing it to Grandma. That was our signal to line up, armed with bowls and spoons. And the first kid shrieking "brain freeze!" proved summer had arrived.

~ *Suzanne Gochenouer*

Suzanne Gochenouer *is grateful for books, peace, and the healing energy of love. She coaches writers, as well anyone seeking a joy-filled life, and blogs at TransformationalEditor.com and PeacemakersPath.com.*

July 21

Connecting to My Essence

I love the feel of the sand between my fingers as I lay on the beach, listening to the sound of the waves pounding up onto the shore. Though the sun is warm, the water has a coolness that makes it difficult to become submerged in it. But I know it is worth the effort so I jump up and down in the ocean until my stomach acclimatises to the temperature. I then take a big breath and dunk my head until I am fully submerged. The water is just beautiful. It is cleansing and refreshing, and invites me to swim and play. I easily tap into the joys of the inner child, leaving any stress and adult worries behind. I could do this every summer and, when winter comes, find somewhere where it is still summer and do it all again. Lying back on the sand, the warmth of the sun is all embracing as it penetrates my skin. It reminds me I am alive, and life is worth living and enjoying. It helps me connect to the awe-inspiring present and connect to the essences of my being. The power of the ocean and the sun is formidable.

~ *Fiona Om Shanti*

Fiona Om Shanti *is a transformational coach, sound healer, and author. Her goal is to inspire people to live their true potential. She can be contacted at www.OnTheWingsofLove.com.au.*

July 22

A Cosmic Seaside Satsang

Warm winds of summer blew in by the Bay of Bengal. A royal procession of bejeweled brahmins strode the shoreline, pausing under a cloud-painted portal, then rose up into the sky, two by two. I stood on the ashram porch overlooking the sea, a young, dreaming yogi standing beside Gracious Guruji. She spoke these words to me: "Cosmic seasons of our lives are like the tides. They wash in, they wash out, they shake you all about—but inevitably, you are washed clean, becoming One with the Ocean of Bliss that is Pure Consciousness itself."

I breathed in deeply, delighting in the breeze. I felt a chakra-tingling Gratitude for all my loved ones, beloveds, friends and familiarities, and my beautiful daughter away at summer camp, exploring and unfolding her self and soul—glowing Gratitude for Life itself, with every precious glimpse of the Divine.

Gracious Guruji sensed it all. Peering pristinely into my heart, she said, "How about some fresh-squeezed mango juice?" "Yes," I cried. "Yes to it all."

Hari Om Shanti, Peace to One in All of You!

~ *Keni Fine*

KENI FINE *aka Swami Pajamananda is a spiritual, creative presence: producer, librettist, lyricist, performer, writer, photographer, creativity coach, eco-evolutionary, and creator of The Light-Hearted Path of Yoga. Visit Facebook.com/kenifine or Facebook/swamipajamananda or connect via Twitter @swamipj.*

July 23

Life's Greatest Lesson

"Give thanks in all circumstances." I could not understand why I have to give thanks in the midst of unfavorable circumstances. On the day of my wedding, my in-laws chose to plant a garden and asked my husband to accompany them, which he refused. Two months after the wedding around midnight we heard footsteps, which sounded like someone wearing big boots trampling on the roof of the house. When we ran outside, to our surprise, we saw and heard nothing. This continued nightly. We prayed but were afraid. We packed our bags and moved one morning. We arrived at the home of a family member who did not accept us; we traveled to another relative who welcomed us and I was grateful. Later she was asked to throw us out. As time passed my husband was unfaithful. It was hard but I forgave him. I was given Isaiah 54:4–17 to read. I remember the tears that flowed at that moment; it poured when I heard the words fear not. I began to fight back on my knees; I cultivated my faith and asked for strength. God answered my prayers. I thank God for blessing my marriage; I am celebrating my 20th wedding anniversary and my 40th birthday.

~ *Melanie Eugene*

Melanie Eugene *helps successful plus-size women lose weight, get back in shape, and look and feel great. Learn more at www.TracObesity.com.*

July 24

Honored and Treasured Cousins

"Cousins are those rare people who ask how we are and then wait to hear the answer."

~ Ed Cunningham

I am grateful for all of my wonderful cousins. As an only child, I longed for family playmates during my childhood. I was raised in the Washington, DC area, hundreds of miles away from my aunts, uncles, and cousins. Holiday trips to stay with out-of-town relatives always brought me great joy—especially for the fun times spent with my cousins. After graduating from college, I relocated to the Boston area, mainly to live closer to these treasured extended family members. I am celebrating the 20th anniversary of my move to this place I call home, which is one of the best life choices I ever made. Over the past few years, several key people in my life, including both parents and a dear cousin, have passed away. I had the privilege of providing caregiving support to all of them. With my loving cousins close by to lend shoulders to cry on, yummy meals to feast on, and encouraging words to cheer me forward, I am filled with determination, gratitude, and strength to experience all that life has to offer.

~ *A. Michael Bloom*

Certified professional coach and Energy Leadership™ master practitioner A. Michael Bloom inspires caregivers and the organizations that support them with practical coping strategies that revitalize careers and save lives. Learn more at www.BloomForCoach.com.

July 25

Coney Island Fries

Eight years old and off to Coney Island on the subway with my friend Dorothy and her father, hauling a huge striped canvas beach umbrella, a jug of grape Kool-Aid, and the best tuna fish sandwiches I ever had. The train smells of hot metal, grime, and Juicy Fruit gum as we screech into station after station. Hot, woven wicker seats that prick our legs and anticipation running high, at last we arrive. The temptation to run in the sand offset by the broken shells that say, "Don't take your shoes off," down to the beach we go. Far enough away to stake the umbrella but close enough to smell the seaweed and salt air, we make a run for the water as fast as we can. But the best is yet to come. Soon we'll be up on the boardwalk, lining up at the hot dog stand for a paper cone of Coney Island crinkle-cut fries. Coins at the ready, we'll reach up to the counter to slide them across in exchange for a piled-high helping of big, fat, salt-and-vinegar-drenched potatoes. Ah, summer!

~ *Mariette D. Edwards*

Mariette D. Edwards *is founder and president of Do Your Great Work, Inc., an executive coaching and creative consulting firm providing career choreography for high achievers. Find her at www.DoYourGreatWork.com.*

July 26

Back Porch Mysteries

I dreaded the end of the school year when I was young. The rest of my classmates were gleefully counting down the days until summer vacation. Not this kid! School represented a haven to me—a fertile breeding ground for luscious learning and a comfort zone of sorts. Why would any kid on earth not look forward to summertime? Try being fair-haired and fair-skinned, for starters. Outdoor activities in the summer meant sunburns and peeling and loads of new freckles. Swell. Oh, and the insanely high levels of humidity invited masses of mosquitoes into my neighborhood. Mosquitoes happen to love me. Enough said. But the summer of 1963 was the greatest! For my 10th birthday in June, I was gifted the entire set of *Nancy Drew Mysteries*. Ahh, the perfect resolve to summertime doldrums. Every morning, I sat on the milk box (we had dairy deliveries in those days) on my parents' back porch—my favorite reading spot. I'm tickled to say I read the entire *Nancy Drew* collection that summer. To this day, nothing beats a good mystery for summertime reading!

~ *Melanie Kissell*

Melanie Kissell *blogs at MelanieKissell.com/blog and shares intimate tidbits about herself at About.me/MelanieKissell.*

July 27

Flying High

I close my eyes and am swept up, up, up on a magic carpet, flying high over a city of mosques. The holy buildings magically appeared below my flying carpet—just like Aladdin!—and I see the bright green of gardens and grassy mounds underneath me. Even the brown and magenta of the tree trunks and roads are beautiful. The gold spires and cream-colored temple towers fit beautifully into the scene as well.   My imagination has developed from the simplicity of just being. Being still. Being quiet. Being grateful. Being love. Being compassionate. Being who I am in that particular moment. The gratitude I feel in my heart, mind, body, and soul cannot be fully explained with mere words. I am blessed in sharing the written and spoken word with those who have perhaps lost their way or are seeking more from life; those who know to their deepest core they have their own special message to share. Yea, though I walk through my own valley of life, with the birds singing high in the cypress trees, with the sun shining brightly lighting the path I am on, I am filled with a grace known to the enlightened and grateful.

~ *Peggy Lee Hanson*

Peggy Lee Hanson, *Personal Transition Guidance, LLC, mentors those who experience life-changing situations and guides them through their journey using self-empowerment tools, compassion, and support. Visit Peggy at www.MyDreamArchitect.com.*

July 28

My Own Personal Fairy Tale

I am grateful for the 28th of July! Not only do my husband and I share the exact same date of birth, this is the day we were married. On our one-year anniversary, I received my master's degree. This is the date I found out I was having my first son through an ultrasound. Whenever we go to renew our licenses, verify medical information, or pass through airport security, I have to clarify there is no mistake; my husband and I have the same birth date. We tried to time the arrival of our last child so he could be born on our birth date. I realized God had a sense of humor, when our son was born on June 28, exactly one month earlier. The joke among our friends and family is what reason would we have to forget each others' birthday or anniversary, unless we both came down with amnesia. Each year is more exciting and amazing. I always anticipate what new things are to come for us!

~ Anitra S. White

Anitra S. White *is a wife, mother, certified family and business coach, founder of Anew Life Coaching, Anitra White Unlimited, and published author with a BA in humanities and an MBA in human resources management. Please contact her at AnitraWhiteWrites@gmail.com.*

July 29

In the Air

Some 40 years have passed, and yet I can step outside and suddenly be back. In the cool of the breeze, I'm 7 again. Breathing in the night air, I'm pleasantly captured by memories of my summer at the beach. Salty air and mist on my face; it's San Diego and it's my summer vacation. Every year my parents, Pierre, our poodle, I, and an occasional friend would house ourselves in a bottom-floor room facing the pool at Surfer Beach.

In the vast starry sky, I'm swept back to the corner Jack-in-the-Box, visions of the hotel's Coke dispenser, and the bucket to fill up at the ice machine. Sunny days collecting sea shells, watching for sand crabs in the bubbly wet sand, and eyeing for sand dollars were some of my treasured activities. The Creator can stop me in my tracks, in the simplest of blessings, whisking my senses back to warm sandy toes and salty wet skin. It's in the air that my memories linger on. It's these moments I hold dear. I thank you Lord Jesus.

~ Patricia Hayes

Patricia Hayes *serves and inspires in the name of Jesus Christ. She is a wife and mother of two. Find her at www.ConnectYourEverything.com.*

July 30

My African Holiday Diary

Summertime is a wonderful time of the year especially when you anticipate flying to South Africa. There I felt the warmth of family and friends, when I went with my husband and three children, in 2008 after an absence of many years. Then as the hot African sun shone down on my face I visited the Elephant Sanctuary and tasted African cuisine, saw some cheeky meerkats, and interacted with elephants by touching them and walking hand-to-trunk with them. At the Lion Park I saw magnificantly powerful lions and went to Cub World, where you can touch lion cubs and jackals in an enclosed area. There are also other animals, one of which is a tame giraffe called Gambit who likes a snack! Later I went to the Johannesburg Zoo, which has over three hundred species of animal. Then I went on one of the largest hot air balloons on the continent and saw panaramic views over Johannesburg. During my time there I went to Durban and swam in the Atlantic Ocean, met with family, and went to uShaka Marine World, which has sharks, dolphines, seals, penguins and other marine life. This truly was a cherished memory of my holiday in Africa.

~ *Melanie G. Robinson*

Melanie G. Robinson *is married and has three children. She loves her family and friends, and enjoys holidays, good food, reading, music, and movies. Follow her on Facebook at www.Facebook.com/MelanieGRobinson , on Twitter at www.Twitter.com/MelGRobinson, and at MelanieGRobinson.DTRVacations.com.*

July 31

Thankful to Just Be

Gratitude—so simple and important but sometimes forgotten. I don't mean for it to happen and it kind of insidiously sneaks up on me, then I realize I need to slow down and be grateful. Life seems so fast-paced at times (of my own doing), but I frequently thank God for my blessings, which come in different forms. Blessings like unexpected delightful laughter from my children, an unsolicited thank-you from a client, or the chance to "just be." I'm grateful for the opportunity to provide excellent customer care and also to teach my clients to put the right procedures in place to do the same for their own clients and customers. I'm grateful to be a co-author of this gratitude book—what an honor to help so many people! I recall part of my excerpt from last year: "I feel happier when I help people"—and it really is true. It brings joy on many levels, to me and to those I help. Gratefulness lends itself to helping more people, and so today and every day, I'd like to take a moment to "just be" and envelop myself in gratitude.

~ *Michaelle Dvornik*

Michaelle Dvornik *and her team at Speedscription provide the "prescription for customer care" to ensure repeat business and long term client retention for companies, small business owners, and personal clients.*

August

"Gratitude is the sign of noble souls."

~ Aesop

August 1

Shuffleboard at the Beach

E very summer our family would head down from Toronto, Canada, to Wildwood Beach in New Jersey. This was a great annual vacation with three generations (four adults and two children) packed into one small Hillman car. The drive took two long days with an exciting overnight stay at a roadside motel. I was one of the children.

I loved our two weeks at the seashore, as I got to do special things with my grandparents. I learned to play shuffleboard with them. I was good at it. This sport was not available in Toronto, so I only got a chance to play during our two-week vacation. I so looked forward to refreshing my skills and being tutored by Grandpa. He was a master at the game. I was not involved with many sports because of some health limitations, but I could play shuffleboard. I felt happy being good at this sport. Grandpa knew this, so he and Grandma selflessly spent many hours helping me get good at the game. My self-esteem and confidence got a boost every summer vacation. My grandparents were proud of me and my shuffleboard skills. I loved them for helping me feel valued and special.

~ *Carol Davies*

Carol Davies, *the Passion Motivator, knows happiness is a choice. She joyfully helps stressed entrepreneurs find their passion in life and design their best life plan at ThePassionMotivator.com.*

August 2

A Reason and Season

"People come into your life for a reason, a season or a lifetime…."

~ Unknown Author

Arriving at my family's beachfront cottage, an unexpected greeter welcomed us: Missy. She entered my summer as if she'd always been there—like best buds, long before "BFF" meant anything. Despite being a few years older, Missy instantly accepted me with an awe-filled infectious confidence. She stretched me, showing me to the edge of my comfort zone and gently guiding me past boundaries I'd never dared dream before. I paddled further out into the open ocean, I water-skied with the big kids, and I explored the beach miles beyond my parents' instructions. I embraced my independence on my terms, finding my footing at an young age when I could have easily faltered. Weeks of freedom passed too quickly. Riding back on the ferry, we said our good-byes: sharing hugs, trading phone numbers, and promising with the best of intentions to stay in touch. Then, just as suddenly as she appeared, Missy strided off with the sassy swagger I now possessed, too. My friendship with Missy lasted only one precious season, but with an honored reason. Thank you, my long lost friend.

~ *Whitney McMillan*

Whitney McMillan, *best-selling author of* Rock Your Overwhelm: Live in Clarity, Balance and Freedom, *life and business coach, workshop facilitator, and motivational speaker, supports busy gals to live Overwhelm Freedom! Visit www.WhitneyMcMillan.com.*

August 3

My First Summer Sail

Most of my childhood summers were spent with my dad, and one of my fondest memories was taking a cruise with him to the Bahamas. It would be our last father/daughter vacation before he remarried. I remember how exciting it was to go on a boat for the first time, as I explored endless amenities to choose from. Stumbling upon the game room kept me busy for hours playing Ms. Pac-Man, determined to beat the high score, of course. It was there I met a new girlfriend, and we were inseparable for the remainder of the trip! Swimming, movies, beach time, fancy dinners, playing hide and seek (yes, on the ship), deck activities—you name it, we did it! I think I even won $50 at a game of bingo one night! Staying up late and waking up on the ocean was heavenly. I had never seen such breathtaking, crystal-blue water, while evenings brought radiant sunsets and more stars than I could count in the sky. Now all grown up, I cherish my one-on-one, quality time with my dad! He pulled out all the stops, making this tropical adventure fun, relaxing, and very dear to my heart!

~ *Michelle Dawnn*

Michelle Dawnn *is a visionary life coach specializing in self-image development. Her vision mapping techniques transform lives, giving clients a positive view of their future. Find more info at www.MichelleDawnn.com.*

August 4

Childhood Neighborhood in Summer

When I was a child, my family used to live in a small subdivision that was about two kilometers away from the centre of the city and had only one street that ended in the rice fields. During summertime, I used to play with boys— my brother, my cousins, and our neighbours—who were all about my age. We would fly our own kites and play "tip" on the narrow footpaths of the rice fields. Then we would climb some fruit trees, ride a bike, or play in the middle of the lone road. Sometimes, we would play rubber bands and marbles on the soil, but I never played "spider fights" on sticks, which the boys seemed to enjoy! On the weekends, my family would go with our cousins to the beach for a picnic and some games. Most of us kids would jump on the waves with floating tyre interiors and later play volleyball. When we were teenagers, we would sit on benches under the mango tree in our backyard learning how to play the guitar with the help of chord books and an old guitar. Summer time was always fun and memorable when I was growing up.

~ Roslyn Rajasingam

Roslyn Rajasingam*, a published article writer, has managed training, employment, and seniors programs while being involved in church-based ministries. She lives in Sydney, Australia, and can be contacted via www.RoslynRajasingam.com/Contact-Us.*

August 5

Through Grief to Gratitude

This day is precious to me. It was the birthday for both my mother and her father, my grandfather. My grandfather died at an all-day singing when he was leading a song titled "I'll Live On." I was playing the piano and saw him fall backward onto the dusty wood floor. The dust swirled around him and turned green as it mingled with his spirit/aura leaving his body; I felt amazing peace in my heart and was filled with gratitude. My mother inspired me to live life with no regrets. She would wash dishes when it was my turn so I could practice piano or sing. She was my role model. I was grief stricken at their deaths, but I am filled with gratitude that these two people were in my life.

~ Norma Bonner Elmore

Norma Bonner Elmore, EdD, *is a teacher, singer, pianist, and pageant judge. She loves to read, dance, and travel. She lives in Alabama with her husband, Joe.*

August 6

My First Long Trip

I was 9 when I first met my grandmother in the summer of 1969. She lived in a remote village in South India, while we grew up in city in North India. Travelling a long distance of 1650 miles for 36 hours by train with my older sister was not only enjoyable, but I think that was the only time I received the most attention. I feel so special even now! Even though I am over 50 years now, the thought of my first long summer vacation is bringing out the description from a 9-year-old child. I loved gazing at vendors in the train station, bathing in clean river water, and eating fresh food prepared and fed by my grandmother.

To sum up my experience in short, here it is:

S—I was impressed with the simplicity of villager's lifestyle.

U—I found villagers more understanding and compassionate.

M—Watching the travellers, vendors, and beautiful scenery seemed magical to me.

M—The memory of my first long summer trip is vivid and makes me feel centered and calm.

E—I experienced the real world during my first long-distance travel in my life.

R—It was a true rest and recuperation.

~ *Lalitha Brahma*

Lalitha Brahma's *passion is to help individuals realize, utilize, and strengthen their entrepreneurial selves. For her articles and free e-zine, please visit www.ElbeeServicesLLC.com.*

August 7

Crab Fishing

Have you ever been stirred by the magic of a balmy summer night to spontaneously step outside your comfort zone—and into the sublime? I don't recall the drive up to Gunnamatta surf beach or back. I just remember the exhilaration as my partner and I trekked along unbeaten miles of massive sand dunes toward towering cliffs, surrounded by hauntingly shaped rocks and invigorating pools of water as the tide receded to expose a bounty of crabs, all in the light of a majestic full moon and sparkling stars above. Antonio and I felt dwarfed by, yet deeply connected to, this mystical tapestry of the Universe, as we immersed ourselves in our comical quest for crabs—cut short by a fierce wind mysteriously rising from the open sea. It ricocheted off the steep cliffs with such momentum that we scurried like crabs ourselves back to the car, laughing so hard that the sand flew into our mouths as it lashed against our bodies. We returned home exhausted with exactly a dozen crabs. But what a magical memory of spontaneously stepping outside our comfort zone into the sublime that balmy summer night!

~ Marina Makushev

Marina Makushev *lives in Australia and established ReVIBE-olution to empower people into more uplifting ways of being through clinical hypnotherapy, resilience training, meditation, tai chi/qigong, art therapy, Zumba, and drum circles.*

August 8

We Had a Convoy!

When you grow up in a large, close-knit family complete with aunts, uncles, cousins, parents, three brothers, and a sister thrown in for good measure, vacations can turn into productions. That was certainly the case the year we decided to go on a grand camping adventure and traveled from our small hometown in northern Ohio to Claytor Lake State Park in Virginia. While that distance may seem negligible today, to a young girl back then it felt like an adventure. Five families set out in cars with campers and boats in tow. Using CB radios (ancient Twitter-like audio communication devices) to "chat" throughout the trip, we heard truckers announce that we had a convoy! We were a mini-parade of family life traveling down the highway. Each morning we awoke to a local boy's invitation to "Get your Roanoke Times." And each night we fell asleep to the crackle of a campfire and the music of nature. Before the trip was over, we would experience a real beach (complete with beach music!), horseback riding, camp-site friendships, a country church, and all things summer. Almost 50 years later, wood smoke and beach smells still bring back memories of that time and place.

~ *Kathi C. Laughman*

Kathi C. Laughman *is an author, inspirational speaker, and certified life coach. Her mission is to inspire, facilitate, and invest in the success of others. Learn more at www.MackenzieCircle.com.*

August 9

The Mount Apo Adventure

"Yee-haw! I finally made it!" Standing on top of a huge boulder, I took in the panoramic view around me. From this unobstructed vantage point, I could see most of Mindanao, its verdant rainforests, its rugged mountain ranges, and its pastel blue skies. As I stood at the summit, I was certain I could do almost anything I set my mind to! This exhilarating feeling wiped out my exhaustion of the past two days when our team started our arduous ascent to majestic Mount Apo, the Philippines' highest mountain. From this dizzying height, it didn't matter now that on day one, I lost my foothold on a fallen coconut log and slid into the freezing Marbel River. And the "killer 90° trail" didn't seem that daunting anymore from up there. Gazing over this breathtaking scenery, I know I will always remember:

- The powerful flight of the critically endangered Pithecophaga jefferyi (the Philippine eagle,)

- The crystal-clear waters of Lake Venado reflecting the peak of Mount Apo,

- The lichen-covered giant trees reaching up to the sky,

- The plethora of distinctive sounds from forest animals, and

- The spectacular nighttime show of shooting stars.

What an unforgettable adventure!

~ Leah Arriola

Leah Arriola lives in Ontario, Canada.

August 10

Childhood Summers

Some of my most cherished memories living in Washington, DC, have to be those long humid summers in the mid-6os. Back in those days we had three whole months of summer vacation and plenty of time to be with family and friends, from sun up to sun down. On those scorching hot days the city would open up the fire hydrants in the neighborhood so that we could cool off. For most of us, our houses were hotter than being outside. After the sun dried us off, we could always depend on the familiar sound of the ice cream truck to bring us cold popsicles and frozen custard. On some weekends when it was too hot to stay in the house, we would pile in our four-door Chevrolet and drive to Haines Point, where we would watch boats sail up and down the Potomac River. We stayed out there for hours, and no one ever bothered us, nor were we told to go home when it started getting late. On most nights the park would be crowded, and families and couples would often dauntlessly fall asleep on blankets enjoying the cool breezes coming off the river.

~ *Audrienne Roberts Womack*

Audrienne Roberts Womack *has written short stories for several anthologies, published three books, and leads empowerment seminars for women. She lives in Washington, DC, with her husband, seven children, and two grandchildren. Learn more at www.ARWomack.com.*

August 11

Hiking

Hiking brings me into the moment and in touch with my soul. The sun sparkles on a meandering creek and the unexpected twists and turns of a rocky, tree-limbed-based trail. The unexpected swooping by of a bright red cardinal and the leaves crunching nearby under the hooves of a startled deer. A killer incline that never seems to summit, then an unexpected dropoff to miles of rolling hills below. The fresh air, natural beauty, and a physical challenge. All bring with them a fresh sense of perspective, appreciation, and peace.

~ *Connie Whitesell*

Connie Whitesell lives in St. Louis, Missouri.

August 12

A Monopoly Tradition

As a single, working, older grandmother, I had little time to spend with my wonderful grandsons. So when they were 5 and 9 and I had some summer days, we needed something fun to do. Dredging up memories of my childhood and hot summer days playing Monopoly with friends, I relived the excitement. Vivid scenes of how we laughed, argued, spent hours trying to win and outsmart the other ran through my mind. My boys and I needed to start a Monopoly tradition. Now, my grandsons were not into video games. They rode bikes, shot their airsoft guns, climbed trees, and raised pigs for 4H. Indoor board games were not on their horizon. With trepidation we went shopping and purchased Monopoly. We spent time figuring out the rules. Then we tweaked the rules to fit our style. Some long games had to be cut short sometimes, and there were tears when someone could not make a deal or lost money. But, when one or the other won there was jubilation. Now, years later, we have happy memories of summertime Monopoly games. Whenever I visit with them there is one question that inevitably gets asked: "Do you want to play, Grandma?"

~ *Patricia Medeiros*

Patricia Medeiros, MFT, *encourages personal growth in children, adults, couples, and families. As a marriage and family therapist, speaker, educator, spiritual advisor, and author, psychology and spirituality are integrated. E-mail PM@WordFromTheHeart.com.*

August 13

Down the Shore

My favorite memories of summer are our family vacations down the shore. We'd all pile into our station wagon and off we would go to Manasquan, for two weeks every year. Visions of penny arcades, kiddie rides, Asbury Park, and Point Pleasant danced in our heads. As a family, we would sit together on our blanket, under the umbrella, on the beach, building sand castles, running to and from the ocean waves. Dad and I would fish from the jetty almost daily. Every evening my sisters and I would each be handed a roll of pennies to spend on the sundry games along the boardwalk (pinball, skeeball, penny-games). Mom and Dad strolled hand-in-hand as we walked to the inlet and watched the boats returning from a day at sea. We were often treated to ice cream cones or a slice of pizza on the return trip past the arcade. Writing this, I vividly remember those times. Over time, my sisters and I had families of our own and moved to distant states, and our parents have passed away. When summer approaches, I revel in these memories—a smile on my face. We were blessed with these times together!

~ *Warren L. Henderson, Jr.*

Warren L. Henderson, Jr., *is the owner of Bridges 2 Empowerment, life coaching and author of 3dB Of Life: Transformational Lessons in Cycles of Success. E-mail Warren at WarrenHCL@gmail.com.*

August 14

Tsquared: Conversations of Commitment

We met in high school. He was an athlete and Student Congress president; I was on the yearbook and newspaper staffs. Honestly, we were not people others would think to see as a couple. But that summer of 1975, he and I both happened to be at the county fair with friends. We stopped to talk and, without realizing it, our friends had slipped away; we only saw and heard each other. Now, 38 years later, we're still together, still in love. We've been married 31 years and have three remarkable children. Through these years, we've grown together, from teenagers and college students to young professionals, parents, and, now, leaders and entrepreneurs. The vows "in sickness and in health, in good times and in bad" have certainly been realized through the years. We don't have a lot of common interests and, especially because of work, likely spend too much time apart, but we have held firm to our vows and our commitment to each other. Together we are solid as a rock, totally supportive of the other. This is our strength, our way forward. I am forever grateful for this man, Tom Mariani, and our love and life together.

~ *Tassey A. Russo*

Tassey Russo *is a business development strategist and implementation consultant who helps entrepreneurs transform their dreams and ideas into purpose-driven, influential, and highly profitable businesses. Learn more at www.LevelUpSolutions.com.*

August 15

Ten Alegria

On December 30, 1993, a beautiful baby girl was born with very little blonde hair and bright blue eyes. No pomp. No circumstance. Just us.

A nurse was there, trying to convince me you shouldn't be mine. I am grateful for that one night in the hospital when you slept on my chest without a care in the world. It was in those hours that I realized the moxie I was made of.

I had kept this pregnancy a secret for six months and appreciated those few months of having my daughter all to myself. I appreciated the learning that came with becoming a mother, though I had hardly ever held a child before.

Th ough it hurt being a single mother, I have come to appreciate that circumstance as a blessing in disguise. And, later, a man willing to step up to the plate and become the dad she deserved came into our lives. It has been 18 years of ups and downs, good times and bad. But one thing I know with all of my being: I wouldn't have traded my sweet pea for the world.

To my daughter Allie: ten alegria. I wish you an elated, eternal joy.

~ Lauren L. Darr

Lauren L. Darr *is mother to Allie and Zachary and wife to Brad. In her spare time, she runs a company as a marketing consultant. Find her at www.LaurenOriginals.com.*

August 16

A Village

"It takes a village to raise a child" is an old African proverb. In addition to my therapy practice, giving retreats and talks, and preparing couples for marriage, I am part of a village that raises children. This village is called "school." Working in a parochial school with children in grades K–8 is a great blessing. What I teach is not a graded subject. The children are told that what we talk about will be graded by the lives they live. Any assigned homework is not done in an evening, a semester, or a year. The homework that I give is for a lifetime. I teach character development. The results of the lessons are long in coming, but the value is life lasting. Currently, lessons are based on six core values: respect, love, hospitality, justice, compassion, and patience. Within my lessons are other virtues like responsibility, gratitude, self-discipline, and courage. Included are ways to handle common issues like bullying, anger, decision-making, and self-esteem. Being another voice in a village to share my gifts with youngsters who need so much guidance to grow up to be all that God has created them to be is beyond blessing. I am very grateful.

~ *Patricia Medeiros, MFT*

Patricia Medeiros *encourages personal growth in children, adults, couples, and families. As a marriage and family therapist, speaker, educator, spiritual advisor, and author, psychology and spirituality are integrated. Contact her at PM@WordFromTheHeart.com.*

August 17

Vested in Gratitude

It was a special birthday. My daughter, Robyn, flew home. She's in New York. We rarely get to be one-on-one, so I was relishing the time. We laughed our heads off and ran around the entire time. We did some of our favorite activities, which are shopping and dining. We took a day trip to a quaint town, Yellow Springs, Ohio. We strolled in and out of the art shops. Simple pleasures. I saw a tie-dyed vest—a 60s throwback—and tried it on. I liked it but, being practical, I deliberated over the purchase, asking the clerk to hold it. When I went back, the store was closed. "Oh well," I thought, "maybe it was not meant to be." Today I went to the mailbox and saw a bulky package. Since I noticed it was from Yellow Springs, I tore it open. There was my colorful vest! To my surprise, Robyn had sneaked back and found the store's name. She collaborated with the clerk by e-mailing and sending pictures back and forth. She asked the clerk to include a handwritten message for the card, then had it mailed. For what this vest means, I am grateful.

~ Barb Girson

Barb Girson, *direct-selling expert, sales coach, and speaker/trainer, helps companies, teams, and entrepreneurs gain confidence, get into action, and grow sales. For sales tips and articles, reach Barb at www.MySalesTactics.com.*

August 18

A New Kind of Fulfillment

L ife is temporary and we are mere mortals. Despite know-ing that, no wife expects to be a widow. Death has a way of sneaking in on you and robbing you of your loved ones. As I found out from personal experience, it is the first time you really face the truth that whether you live or die is not in our hands but in He who created us. After 23 years of walking with God through the grief and loss of my late husband, George, I am able to say that God does heal. He does take away the sting of death, and in Him you can find your way back to building a fulfilling life. I discovered my path to a new kind of fulfillment by being busy helping other and giving them hope for the future. One aspect of this taking the bold step of sharing my life experience by writing a book. I thank God for giving me good health and a blessed family life, and for being able to use my experiences of marriage and widowhood to touch other people's lives.

~ *Isabella G. Matheka*

Isabella G. Matheka *is an entrepreneur and author of Reflections of a Widow. She lives in Nairobi, Kenya. E-mail her at bellageor@gmail.com.*

August 19

Sisters: Pure Niceness

I am grateful for family and friends, and the opportunity to spend the summer of 2012 with my sister. It was one of the most invigorating, spell bounding, emotionally empowering events of our lives. There is an incredible beauty of the space overlooking the Caribbean, with a great family atmosphere, music, and an international mix of poets and storytellers. The audiences are large and welcoming. It is also the most significant festival of artists of African Diaspora, going forth in the spirit of joy and generosity. We especially enjoyed the sun, sea, music, and food combined with good humor and merriment of the people that went all the way into the night until the sun came up. Calabash is a literary writers festival of some of the world's best authors reading their most important works a yearly get-together that is held in Treasure Beach, a small, rural, un-touristy community of down-to-earth, rural Jamaicans who have opened their lives to welcome visitors wanting a simple, vacation experience. People from all walks of life come to the festival to a beautiful setting with the sea crashing behind you as you enjoy the view of the sea while enjoying fresh, juicy fruits.

~ *Melissa Rowe*

Melissa Rowe *supports women in supporting themselves. She provides opportunities to reclaim their greatness and personal power, and take action. She enables women in recognizing their power from within. E-mail her at mrowe45@hotmail.com.*

August 20

Memories of Summers Past

How many of use still carry out the same summertime routines of our childhood, whether we live them out ourselves or through the experiences of our children? Summertime is a season looked forward to by all. I can never get enough of the aroma of food cooking on a grill, laughter, and getting together with friends and families telling stories of summers past. Time on the beach and a great fireworks display is my favorite summertime combination. An activity involving the joys of water in the full mid-day sun or even an occasional summer rainstorm followed by a rainbow sounds nice. Who doesn't love a summer fair, a trip to the farmer's market, or laying out in an open field enjoying the living canvas that God and Mother Nature have created for us? Best of all are the tropical location getaways designed to help get us through the autumns and long winters. The other three seasons are far from my mind. I am trying to savor summer one day at a time!

~ Anitra S. White

Anitra S. White *is a wife, mother, certified family and business coach, founder of Anew Life Coaching, Anitra White Unlimited, and published author with a BA in humanities and an MBA in human resources management. Please contact her at AnitraWhiteWrites@gmail.com.*

August 21

Summer Highlights

The summer sun makes it a beautiful day; it brings warmth and joy to the heart. When the sun is out we can choose to do anything we like. Childhood memories include my dad grilling his famous legendary double hamburgers, stuffed with cheese and onions, baked potatoes, my mom's sliced tomatoes, zucchini with melted cheese, and fresh fruit salad. It's always been a special time, and so good that I've kept the tradition going and I've passed it on to my children. Another memory was when my grandfather made homemade ice cream. It doesn't compare to anything out there. I dream about having it again someday. More summer highlights include riding in friends of our family's boat, hitting the waves with a lot of laughter; it was so refreshing and freeing to the soul to be outside on the big wide open lake. When I was at horseback riding camp, we had evening campfires and sang songs; "Kumbaya My Lord" was a favorite. There were other day camps that were filled with making crafts and swimming. I'm grateful for my summertime memories and love summer because it's great to be outdoors.

~ Linda A. Zimmerman

Linda A. Zimmerman *is a life/spiritual coach/author/speaker at Live Heart Inspired. Her story teeming with adversity, Linda has learned to live her life commanded by her heart. Contact her at LiveHeartInspired@gmail.com or visit www.LiveHeartInspired.com.*

August 22

"Simply Elegant" Moments

"Simply elegant" moments occur unexpectedly through the course of the day or night. In a split second they rush in with simplicity and awareness. They are warm. They are silent. They center my day with gratitude. Here are some of my favorites. I hope you discover yours.

1.) Watching bunny whiskers twitching.

2.) Smiling briefly after pulling a cotton blanket over myself, on a summer night that turned cold.

3.) Realizing a five-minute chance to roll in the grass with my dog.

4.) Whispering gently, while kissing the nose of my horse.

5.) Playing early-evening golf amid bird chatter and deer sightings.

6.) Hearing the camera shutter when I have captured a perfect composition.

7.) Feeling a finely woven tapestry over and over again.

8.) Sipping a new wine and "knowing" it is destined to become a favorite.

9.) Savoring reactions of others, upon the presentation of a small unexpected gift.

10.) Creating my own new recipes and discovering they are delicious.

11.) Remembering—everything in a flood of smells and a touch of classic car leather.

12.) Realizing only silence in a crowded, noisy restaurant.

13.) Listening to what the raindrops are saying.

~ *Amy E. Kelsall, Ph.D.*

Amy Kelsall *is an academic director at the University of Denver. She is a coach, photographer, animal lover, golfer, and traveler. Reach her at Amy.Kelsall@du.edu.*

August 23

Four Seasons of Summer

Sun mixed with songs, sand, and Surf is what makes summertime memories so special, or so I thought. In Australia summer isn't just sunshine and lazy, crazy holiday season; it's also that very merry festive season. And while bombarded with Christmas scenes involving snow, in the land down under we can be fairly sure sunshine will be the order of the day.

One summer I decided to try something different and took my daughter to visit her favourite Aunty, who had moved to our southernmost state, Tasmania. An early-morning wake-up call and despite pouring rain and zero visibility, our host's planned boat trip was still on. Puzzlement at why we would venture out in such miserable weather turned to confusion when reminded to take hat, sunglasses, and sunscreen. "You're joking," I said, but soon discovered otherwise as we experienced an incredible "four seasons in one day." The miraculous weather continued to deliver the unexpected, making that amazing summertime experience my favourite, as it was filled with not just songs, sun, sand, and surf, but also snow! Yes, surprising as it sounds, that summer we got to experience a white Christmas, something I'd never thought possible in an Australian summer.

~ *Faye Grant-Williams*

Faye Grant-Williams *is an accredited film and TV scriptwriter who lives in the world's most isolated city of Perth, Western Australia. You can reach her on www.LinkedIn.com, www.Twitter.com/FayesFAQs, or www.Facebook.com/FayesFAQs.*

August 24

Embracing Gratitude

I feel so grateful for each and every moment of life! I appreciate my health, my family, and friends! I'm grateful for the warmth of the sun on my face and the purifying rain. I'm full of gratitude whenever I can serve others. Everything happens for a reason! There are no coincidences. There's a purpose for everyone I've connected with. I'm grateful for all of the smiles, encouragement, and kind gestures I've received. There are many learning experiences that I may not have understood at the time, that I am so grateful for today. I benefit from meditating on meaningful things with clear intentions, in a calm setting. I am grateful for the ability to empower others to go after their dreams. I am grateful for the miracles that occur all over the world. And finally, I am grateful for the opportunities that come with the new beginning of each new day, and the chance to make smarter decisions in my life! I embrace the now, and delight in the expectations of each and every beautiful day God has granted me. Each day is another opportunity to pay kindness forward with a heart full of Gratitude.

~ *Tracey Doctor*

Tracey Doctor's journey from hair health specialist and holistic health consultant expanded into the unique work she is now doing as a life wellness coach and radio talk show host.

Learn more at www.AmazingWoman-TalkRadio.com.

August 25

Summer Rebirth

I love summertime. Thoughts of the summer season get us through the cold whiteness of winter. It is nature's yearly rebirth. Baby ducks on the lake, birds singing, baby rabbits and squirrels hopping and playing in the yard. Gardens growing. Flowers blooming. Nature's kaleidoscope of beauty. I call summer nature's gratitude attitude: a thank-you for life. Life is good. Summertime is full of life!

~ *Pam Murphy*

Pam Murphy, MS, RRT, *is a holistic nutritionist. Her mission and passion are to inspire and empower people to make healthy choices which choose life. Learn more at EmpowerWellness.blogspot.com.*

August 26

Huckleberry's Lessons

I watch him in his twilight years, a gentle creature who stays close to me now. His eyesight waning, his hearing fading, he stays close to me. He doesn't always greet me when I get home, but he stays close to me when I am home. So different from when he moved in: his shadow frightened him; he lashed out frequently. We worked hard together meeting every challenge, overcoming the fear of unknownobjects or people or dogs. Slowly he learned to let go.

He has a built-in pack of followers: people who visit him, people who want him near—their own version of therapy. As they scratch him, he gently rests a paw on an arm…or a shoulder…and he gently nudges for more. He tests more simply now: *How long can I sleep on the sofa before I'm caught? If I slowly stretch my way off the sofa, will she laugh enough to forget to reprimand me?* It's said I saved him, yet he saved me more. He taught me the power of calm and peacefulness in transforming both his life and mine. Together we greet every day—me, so grateful for his presence in my life, and Huckleberry, so close to me now.

~ Lee Ann Seaman

Lee Ann Seaman *lives in Minneapolis, Minn., and has operated Twin Cities Concierge, a personal concierge service, for over 14 years. Her e-mail address is LAS@TCConcierge.com.*

August 27

Memories of Camp Trailfinder

My favorite summertime memories were at Camp Trail-finder located on Kawagama Lake near Dorset, Ontario, Canada. My sister and I went there for a few summers. The camp staff was awesome, and I enjoyed meeting new friends each summer and greeting returning ones. The camp was co-ed and had many activities. My favorites were water skiing, kayaking, canoeing, swimming, and English-style horseback riding. We used to have games and talent night where campers would sing or dress up and do skits. My favorite evening activities were sitting around a huge campfire singing songs and eating smores. The fellowship, view of the stars and mesmerizing fire in beautiful cottage country were awesome. In 1979 I became a junior camp counselor and really enjoyed it. I was leading young girls in camp activities and actually getting paid to do what I truly enjoyed. It was my dream job and in line with my passion for nature.

I'm thankful my parents sent me to the camp and savour wonderful memories about my experiences at Camp Trailfinder because I saw it as my summer home. I joined the camp Facebook page and enjoy looking at pictures that former campers have posted.

~ Avery Thurman

Avery Thurman *is a nurse, a stock and options student and trader, and budding author who has contributed stories to The Gratitude Book Project series. E-mail her at Avery.T31@gmail.com.*

August 28

Let Love In

I am eternally grateful for my "small in stature but large in heart" feline, Princess Pushkins. She has helped me overcome fear, shown me unconditional love, and healed my relationships beyond my wildest dreams. When I moved into my apartment in Hove East Sussex 11 years ago, I was unhappy in singledom. Pushkins turned up at my windowsill ready to love and to be loved. She playfully nudged and nestled, laid Sphinx-like on my sleeping belly, and became my alarm clock. We became buddies, so when I started dating Symon, she checked his suitability instantly with fierce bats of her claws and wild scratches. Symon, a lifelong animal lover, was undeterred by her kitty tests as our relationship blossomed. Three years later, happily married now, something drastic happened to Pushkins: her heart opened, and she became a soft, purring lap cat. We all felt this love. She began to assist me in my healing and therapy practice, too. Witches are said to have familiars, and there she was! Today Princess Pushkins is a grand old lady. She continues to help me run the Gratitude Group and never fails to bring joy, love, and healing to all those she meets.

~ Ann E. O'keife

Ann O'keife is a healer, therapist, rune expert, artist, and writer. She facilitates a monthly gratitude group in Shoreham West Sussex. Learn more at www.LivingLifeFully.net.

August 29

A Soulful Soothing

I was newly married with a new job and new house. To my delight, I also got an adorable Chihuahua who could sing like an angel and had love in his eyes. One day, my husband worked on the car while I put a cover on the coach. My Chihuahua snuck out of the house. I searched all over for him. To my horror, he made it to the neighbor's yard and was killed by their dog. I cried for three days. My sister insisted that I get another Chihuahua—not to replace him, but to help me heal. She was right. My new puppy had a different personality, but helped heal my aching soul. Ironically, my sister passed away later, which broke my heart. I was left with her two dogs, who could not replace her but again helped to heal my aching soul. I still have her dogs and mine, and they are all truly a soothing blessing.

~ *Terri L. Cunkle*

Terri L. Cunkle is a teacher, creative business owner, and writer. Find her books at Creativity101.com.

August 30

The Race Horse Reunion

My most memorable reunion debuted in the backwoods of Mississippi. At 6 years old, 1964 was indelibly etched in my mind. The anchors of the Clark clan lived a half-mile deep in a secluded area. D.D. (grandfather) and Madear (grandmother) were committed to godly principles and family. Born to this union were three sons and four daughters. Endeavoring to keep traditions alive, some traveled long distances. Anticipation soared at the welcome home sound of cars crossing over the cattle gap. Shortly, my aunts would prepare scrumptious dishes. My cousins and I would play tag and go on explorations. Jubilation! Suspended on tree swings! After dinner, we dashed down the hill out back into a plush field, lined with wild fruit trees: apricot, plum, and apple. Soon we would journey to the pond another half-mile, frolicking and dodging snakes. Upon return, I desired to ride Tony, a red racehorse that Daddy raised from a colt. Obligingly, Daddy lifted me up. However, I slid onto the other side and plummeted to the ground. Immediately, Tony lifted his front left leg and waited for Daddy to remove me from under him. This glorious day did not end in tragedy. I'm so grateful!

~ Patrick Elizabeth Clark Sims

Patrick Elizabeth Clark Sims *is an evangelist, co-founder of Manna Ministries/Kingdom Designs & Services, radio talk show host, and author. Visit www.MannaMinistries.net or e-mail Manna@MannaMinistries.net.*

August 31

YOLI-BU

You were not present when I was born. You did not see me take my first steps and you did not hear me speak my first words. However, the gift of knowing you has proven to be one of the greatest treasures that I have ever encountered. You are my friend. You are my confidant You have been there for me when I have needed you the most. You have celebrated with me when I have felt the ultimate happiness and have wept with me when I have experienced the deepest of sorrows. Like the butterfly, I have gone through the process of metamorphosis before your very eyes. The girl encased within the cocoon broke free, developing into a mature and confident woman. You assisted greatly with this process and have taught me everything that you know. You have continued to guide me and encourage me throughout the years, and I hold you very dear to my heart. Even though we are not related by blood, the bonds of love and respect that have formed between us will never be severed. I am truly thankful for having you in my life.

~ *Barbara B. Romero*

Barbara B. Romero *works in an educational institution as an academic advisor and part-time instructor. She finds inspiration in the simple things and enjoys helping others.*

September

"Gratitude is not only the greatest of virtues, but the parent of all the others."

~ Marcus Tullius Cicero

September 1

I Am Grateful for My Gifts

It is easy to become disheartened when life doesn't fit our agendas. Having to experience a heartbreak, a health issue, a money problem, or a loss of opportunity, can darken our perspective and optimism. There can be a negative "snowball" effect, a downward spiral, as we become focused on what is not going well. What I find preferable is to focus on my service and what I can do for others. You may have heard the saying "I felt sorry for myself because I had no shoes, until I saw a man who had no feet." I am grateful for my intuitive and healing gifts that allow me to help another, to get my mind off my own issues and channel the energy of the Divine for another. My service has saved me countless times, allowing me to detach from the "poor me" consciousness and attune to the wisdom, love, and healing that pour through me instead. There is a saying in the healing world: "Give a healing, get a healing." When I let go of my agenda, my intuitive gifts can be used in service to all, and I benefit as well.

~ Holly Shantara

Holly Shantara *is a transformational "LifeStar" mentor, coach, consultant, and author. She specializes in showing emerging leaders how to master their gifts and follow their life calling in extraordinary ways. Visit www.HollyShantara.com.*

September 2

Gift of Angels

Maggie, a wild Australian magpie, was a bird on a mission. As a chick he made friends with our dogs, Scotty and Benny, along a country lane by letting them tap him on the chest. Their remarkable friendship attracted attention again months later when Maggie sought Benny's help in dealing with adversaries.After the dogs died, Maggie dispelled our sorrow by singing the sweetest songs. His melodious voice had the magical ability to just dissolve the pain in my heart. Together with his sisters, Cindy and Tammie, his beautiful songs filled the air with the most magnificent carols, and one never felt alone. Maggie's rowdy antics, superb negotiating skills, and friends from other bird species around our yard entertained us for hours. Contrary to all popular tales about magpie aggression, Maggie with his mate,Vicky, trusted us with their children, as did his foster parents, Fatty and Molly. I thank Maggie daily for opening our lives to the incredibly rich, loving relationships that exist among wild bird communities in the backyard, and for letting us into their extended family to share that love and awareness. I thank Scotty and Benny for gifting us this incredible legacy.

~ *Gitie House*

Gitie House *is a co-discoverer of the Principle of Goodness, and writes about communicating and building relationships with wild birds in the backyard at WingedHearts.org.*

September 3

Self-Trained Service Dog

My dog and I both feel a deep gratitude for each other—she because I rescued her from a difficult life with an uncertain future as a stray, and I because she has taught me that dogs can have special qualities. I've had dogs before, but I'm a "cat person" and always regarded dogs as mostly eating and barking machines. Babe, despite having lost a leg due to cruelty, has shown through her remarkable intelligence that she could have been a service dog. She takes care of me.After another dog knocked me down (and out) last year, she now waits with me at the top of the stairs until the coast is clear, then descends the steps with me in case I need help balancing. She alerts me to visitors before I hear them, and calls to me when the cats are having a dispute. She shakes her head to jingle her tags when she wants to go out because I might not know one bark from another. She walks with me without a leash, and always waits to be invited back into the house. I didn't have to train her. She's been training me!

~ RJ Peters

Dr. RJ Peters, *a retired physician, established a rescue shelter in 2002. She can be reached at Twitter.com/DrBert, and her dog is at ADogWith-3Legs.blogspot.com.*

September 4

Tribute to Olivia

My Dear Sweet Girl,

Although you only touched my life for a few short years, your contributions were profound. Through your traumatic story as a rescue dog from the mountains of North Georgia, to your life in the Arizona desert, everyone will soon know what the life of a "bait" dog is like. Helpless, homeless, and unloved, you came to me as a beam of light, teacher, healer, and messenger dog. Your love, affection, and relentless connection to me has changed my life forever. My heart now holds a special place for all rescue dogs, and especially all "bait" dogs. Your message will be heard throughout the world so that other dogs will not have to endure the life you led before coming to live with me. My tribute to you is work to rid the world of the blood sport of dog-baiting. Your message will be heard. You trusted me when you trusted no other. Love prevails, Olivia. Thank you for coming into my life. I will always miss you, but I know that you are watching from above.

~ Lynne M. McCarthy

Lynne M. McCarthy, ASID, is an interior designer, author, and intuitive reader. She specializes in designing environments for dogs. Find out more at zDogz.com.

September 5

The Gift of Life

A t 6:24 p.m. on September 5, 1964, my mother performed her labor of love. At that moment, I, baby Jennifer, was born. What a glorious day! Since that time, to that same date in 2014, I have breathed in the beauty of my life for 17, 885 days. The journey I have been traveling is a wonderful adventure story filled with colorful characters, delicious dialogue, and exciting plot twists. Along the way I have celebrated tremendous highs and endured heartbreaking lows. And I wouldn't change a second of it. Each day when I rise, I take a deep breath and speak these words aloud: "Thank you for this new day where anything and everything is possible! Today I will be the best I can be personally, professionally, emotionally, physically, and spiritually. And so it shall be. Thank you!" Then I bound out of bed to continue my journey. I am so grateful for the life I have lived thus far. And, can't wait for what is lying ahead for the next 17,885 days. ~ Peace ~

~ Jennifer Carlevatti Aderhold

Jennifer Carlevatti Aderhold *is the publisher of www.BeABestseller. com, an online community and free, information-packed, weekly inbox magazine dedicated to elevating the voices of entrepreneurial authors around the world.*

September 6

Puppy Teaches Self-Love

I am grateful that in 2002 a tiny, four-legged teacher bounced into my life. Chloe was my new Yellow Labrador puppy, and she showed me what real self-love looked like. The full-length mirror in my bedroom had always been my nemesis. Each trip past it triggered instant self-scrutiny. Like a frog I once saw on Animal Planet who flung out its tongue and snatched a bug so fast I couldn't see it happen until it had been replayed in slow motion, my mind would fling out tiny lashes of judgment so fast I couldn't see how they diminished me: "I look fat." "Bad hair day." "New wrinkles." One day Chloe noticed herself in the mirror for the first time. Her reaction was simple. She paused, gave her little face a quick lick, right on the mirror, and walked on. I was stunned. With one quick lick of her puppy tongue, Chloe had caused the frog tongue in my mind to be replayed in slow motion. For the first time, I saw how to stop rejecting myself. Chloe's puppy mind had no self-rejection; she met herself with the same open-hearted love and acceptance she offered to everyone, unconditionally. Now I could, too.

~ *Martia Nelson*

Martia Nelson, *life coach and author of* Coming Home: The Return to True Self, *guides professionals into richer, more joyful lives. For a free gift, visit MartiaNelson.com.*

September 7

Unconditional Love

I have had the gift of experiencing unconditional love from my mom, Marilyn Evelyn Hayden, since being born on Christmas Day, 40-some years ago.

Through the trials and tribulations of my life, not once have I ever doubted Mom's unconditional love. As a toddler, when Mom napped, I attempted to catch fish from the aquarium, while dragging all of the aquarium pebbles to the shag carpet.

Mom still loved me.

As a first-grade student, I was painfully shy and afraid to go to school. Mom encouraged me, knowing I was ready for school and would succeed.

Mom always assumed I would complete my university education and, thanks to Mom's belief in me, I have achieved a bachelor of science degree and a master of arts degree. Mom shared her unconditional love when she gave up her husband, her home, and her job for several months to help me recover from severe injuries, as a result of a devastating car crash. I have been blessed with Mom's unconditional love, and this has helped me to create a life I love.

Mom loves me unconditionally, as I unconditionally love Mom.

~ Cristy Hayden

Cristy Hayden *is a creative nonfiction writer, certified professional résumé writer, and career coach from Calgary, Alberta. You can reach her at CalgaryCris@gmail.com.*

September 8

My Hairball Professor

Mindfulness is the psychological practice of being completely attentive to the present moment. It involves being consciously aware of one's own thoughts, feelings, sensations, and behaviors, without making judgments. Mindfulness is a useful quality for dealing with many personal psychological issues. My Hairball Professor taught me mindfulness. Watching my cat, it occurred to me that he did not try to be other than "cat." He did what was present at the moment for him to do: sleep, eat, watch, work (prowl), or play. Yesterday was gone; there were no tears. The future held no fear. When he came to an obstacle, he went around, crawled under, jumped over, or turned back. Intuition guided his movements. At an unfamiliar sound, he listened to, investigated, or ignored it. Wanting affection, he rubbed against the object of his attention. His comings and goings were timely. His energy was conserved by satisfying curiosity and watching his surroundings with studied detachment. Observing my Hairball Professor taught me that ruminating over the past or worrying about the future wasted time and energy. It is essential is to be present to each moment and to respond intuitively. He modeled mindfulness effortlessly, without words, by simply being "cat."

~ *Patricia Medeiros*

Patricia Medeiros *encourages personal growth in children, adults, couples, and families. A counselor, speaker, educator, spiritual advisor, and author, she is at Patricia@WordFromTheHeart.com.*

September 9

Country Boy

At nearly a hundred acres, the family farm is far from large, but big enough that it lent itself to a childhood of exploring and fun. Now that I call urban San Diego home, every day I see the contrast of my life then and now.

The farm was never the sole income for our family, but it did provide some extra help when college tuition was due each September. My visits back to the farm are usually limited to one or two times a year at most and always refresh my memory of what it was like living there for the first 20 years of my life.

The farm was a lot of work. Summers were spent clearing brush around the fences, weeding the garden, and moving massive piles of oats from one spot on the barn floor to another spot five feet away. Winters involved hours of feeding and bedding cows and chickens, and carrying wood from stacks in the yard to the wood burning stove that heated the house.

I used to resent my life there. Now I cherish my upbringing. It grounded me. It built a strong work ethic in me and a deep respect for my parents. Thank god I'm a country boy at heart.

~ *Daniel Kriley*

Daniel J. Kriley *is a high school theatre and arts management instructor living in Southern California. Find him at Facebook.com/Daniel.Kriley.*

September 10

My Best Backyard Buddies

I love animals, especially the small and precious red squirrels who inhabit our backyard. I've observed several generations over the years and look forward to their cute little babies every spring. Fiercely independent, quick, funny, and full of their distinctive personalities, they've brought me hours of joy and laughter as I've watched their crazy antics. From pulling insulation out of the attic for their nests to carrying away large apples and corncobs many times their size, they never cease to amaze me with their energy and creativity. In summer, we gather black walnuts, acorns, and chestnuts to feed them through the snowy winter, although they engage in their own rigorous nut gathering. At Christmastime, we set out a small stocking filled with acorns to include them in the holiday cheer. We talk about them as family, and I'm always concerned with their well-being. I truly love my little friends. They've taught me much:

Be determined—no matter what.

Go for the goal (the nut) and be focused.

Every day is a gift, so jump around and be happy.

Take time to relax; you don't always need to search for nuts. Enjoy today—it's all you have!

~ *Tara Kachaturoff*

Tara Kachaturoff is an online business manager and host of Michigan Entrepreneur TV. A Southern California native, she resides in Birmingham, Mich. Find her at Twitter.com/TaraKachaturoff.

September 11

9/11: Subdued or Celebration?

September 11 is my birthday. Like for others born on this day, it can be a day of celebration or it can also be a subdued day. The fact is I could make this a sad tale; I have enough sorrow to go around. I choose rather to appreciate 9/11 as a day of true, unconditional love and celebration because of the events of 9/11/2001. They have taught me to appreciate and celebrate what's important. I actually see my September 11 birthday as more special with every year that passes. I choose to remember those I love and have lost and whose love will always beat in my heart. Unconditional love is the greatest gift to give and receive no matter what day it is. It is the gift I enjoy giving most to others and to myself. From it all things are possible. Lucky for me I've had great teachers, human and furry alike, to teach me what true unconditional love is. I choose September 11 as a day to celebrate because it is the day I was born and I make a difference in the world just by being here. We all do no matter what day it is.

~ Julie A. Hawkins

Julie Hawkins is a trainer, author, life and spiritual coach, akashic reader, and conscious channel. Julie teaches women how to confidently "take charge" of their lives. Find her at www.JulieHawkins.com.

September 12

WOW

Wow, how my life has changed since my first entry in The Gratitude Book Project® back in 2010! I had been recently divorced and was very much unsure of myself. I was grateful to have my life back and had been using the practice of gratitude for a long time; however, my self-esteem had taken a huge hit. After years of being verbally whipped, he finally did it physically, and that wake-up call finally got me out.

I have a completely new life. I help others who suffer from the damages of verbal abuse to heal and live a joyful life by getting rid of fear, anxiety, and shame.

One of my greatest joys is my own radio show, *Joyful Living Radio*. Can I say *extreme gratitude*? Oh, yes, I can! Being able to share joy and bring awareness so there will be less abuse in the world is something that I express gratitude for every day!

My favorite gratitude practice is the Gratitude Walk. I learned this from my amazing friend Alycia Schlesinger. While walking briskly and listening to inspiring music, you say what you're grateful for out loud! Try it. It's fun and empowering, with remarkable results!

~ *Gwen Lepard*

Gwen Lepard *is host of* Joyful Living Radio, *Master Healer, speaker, joy authority, Master NLP Practitioner, hypnotherapist, creator of "Be the Sun…3 Keys to Joy" and the Quantum Joy Experience.*

September 13

Who's the Babysitter?

I will never forget my mother's laughter as our local greengrocer asked, "What's Susan got in that infant seat, a dog?" "No, my granddaughter," Mom replied.

Kayla was the first single-parent adoption in town. The first four months were laced with bouts of incessant crying, day and night. A CAT scan diagnosed Kayla with severe disabilities caused from drug use by her biological mother. My beautiful baby was not going to walk, talk, or play—ever! Through all the sleepless times, my mother was there. We literally took turns sleeping and caring for Kayla. I came home from teaching one afternoon to find my mother asleep in her recliner, holding Kayla, who was wide awake. I quickly snapped a picture of Kayla babysitting Grandma. At 9 months old, Kayla was placed in a top residential facility nearby, due to the need for constant nursing care. She's still there, brightening people's lives with her smile!

My mother passed away when Kayla was 2, so she never got to meet her other two beautiful granddaughters, Kayanna and Kaylene. Without my mother's love and support, and God's helping hand, I would not have made it through those first nine months.

~ Susan Ottaway

Susan Ottaway lives in Union City, Pa. She has two adorable grandchildren, a master's degree in special education, and three dogs, and is on Facebook.

September 14

Trevor, Our Wonder Dog

Trevor came to us as a newborn. He joined a family of 11 kids, tots through teens, plus our parents. Trevor was pretty, noble, part Beagle, part other breeds, and part human. He played football with the kids and meant business. He could catch touchdown passes with the flair of an NFL star, and he did not like to lose. He jumped, blocked, and tackled with enthusiasm. *Lessons learned: Show enthusiasm, learn the skills, get down to business. Show a little flair.*

Trevor played baseball, but could not bat. However, he could scoop up ground balls, run the bases with glee, and cheer on the team. *Lessons learned: Find your place. Do your best. Cheer!*

Trevor followed the family to school. "Trevor is here!" was a frequent shout on the playground. He "guarded" the baby of the family around strangers and relinquished his post when all was well. When someone was ill, Trevor stayed at his or her side. *Lessons learned: Take care of your people and be there for them.*

Trevor made the cover of the local Sunday magazine. A photographer followed him for hours and miles. *Lessons learned: You never know when fame will come. Be ready!*

~ *Trish Ostroski*

Trish Ostroski *is a hypnotherapist ("Sleep with Me and Wake Up Your Life") and a writer, speaker, and memory trainer from Los Angeles. Contact Trish@RainbowHypno.com.*

September 15

The Soundtrack of Life

Today, on my 60th birthday, I am grateful for the love of music that permeates the spirit of our family, that was passed on from our dad and underscores the milestones of our lives. Like colorful threads coursing through a tapestry, the sound of piano keys played in just the right order or a guitar riff played in a souful way takes us back, and in one moment can alter our mood and perspectives. Hearing the words from the Jewel song "When you are standing in deep water and bailing yourself out with a straw," I am transported to a hospital room in Kansas filled with fear and determination that my daughter would win her battle against cancer. Casting Crowns sing "Voice of Truth" and I'm overflowing with pride, reminded of the loving family man my son has become. My brothers play guitar alternating rhythm and lead, and suddenly Dad, who passed in 2001, is present in the room. My adult children, on opposite sides of the political and religious spectrum, play music together harmonizing as only siblings can do—and it gives me goose bumps. So thankful am I for the melodies and lyrics that are the soundtrack of my life.

~ Cindy Barnard

Cindy Barnard, RN, CPCC, is the author of Leader for Life: Lessons Learned as a Fortune 500 Executive, a Nurse, a Waitress, a Taco Bell Manager, and a Mom.

September 16

Life Lessons

I had been without a horse in my life for more then 10 years before Digger, a gorgeous Palomino Quarter Horse gelding with a laundry list of physical ailments and deep-seated trust issues, was offered to me. Digger's luck was almost as impressive as his conformational flaws. He was rescued at least twice, that I know of, from certain death by kindhearted individuals who saw in his imperfect form a bright, inquisitive personality who just wanted a safe place to belong. I believe that Digger came into my life to give me a chance to rediscover who I am and how to be me again. I am convinced that all the animals that have come into my life have brought with them life lessons that I needed to learn. In some cases they carried life lessons that I didn't even know I needed to learn, and sometimes I was absolutely oblivious to the wellspring of knowledge each animal was presenting to me. Then there are those rare occasions when the lightbulb turns on and it all comes together in a grand moment of clarity. This was one of those moments. I rescued him, and he rescued me.

~ Michelle Larsen

Michelle Larsen lives in Santa Rosa, Calif.

September 17

My Furry Love Ball

He just showed up, literally on my doorstep, a voyager I thought, because the word stray didn't seem to fit that tiny gray-and-white fur ball with big ears. I couldn't bear to hear him cry, so in he came, at least for the night. After a can of tuna, he curled up contentedly on my shoulder and purred himself and me to sleep. I awoke to see the charming heart-shaped marking on his head and his beautiful green eyes gazing lovingly into mine. Busy with college and work, I had never realized something was missing from my life, but at that moment I knew it had been Sinbad. Since my landlord did not allow pets, I offered to pay "rent" for him. Our building then became "no pets, except Sinbad." He quickly became a combination son and best friend. When we play fought together, ironically I wore a dog hand puppet. Of course I always let him win. I can still imagine his warm cheek gently nuzzling mine. Sinbad, my beautiful boy, thank you for 11 love-filled years.

~ Helen M. Thamm

Helen M. Thamm, APRN, CPC, *is a career success coach, creator of NurseCareerSuccess.com, and author of* How to Manage With a Magic Wand.

September 18

The Gift of Eyesight

God has blessed us with many beautiful senses: sight, hearing, taste, smell, and touch. I value all of these senses, and the one I'm most grateful for is the gift of sight. I have had incidences with both eyes that could have caused me to lose my eyesight. Being nearsighted, I'm very grateful for corrective lenses so I can see clearly. The gift of sight allows me to live independently and enables me do my job, drive my car, travel alone, read a book, and even take online courses on my computer. Independence is very important, especially if someone lives alone. My vision also enables me to see the beauty of life. I look out my window and enjoy seeing the flowers on my lilac tree, and watching the birds eating from the bird feeder and playing in the bird bath. I love to take walks in nature and see the trees, water, and wildlife. I appreciate the sites I see when traveling. I enjoy viewing the smiles, laughter, and gestures of the people who light up my life. I also love watching my cat's eyes and playfulness. Thank you, God, for the precious gift of eyesight!

~ *Avery Thurman*

Avery Thurman *is a nurse, stock and options student and new trader, and budding author who has contributed stories to The Gratitude Book Project series. E-mail her at Avery.T31@gmail.com.*

September 19

The Impact

After game of Monopoly with my grandsons, I was headed home to recuperate. A large motorhome just ahead of me blocked my view, so I passed him on the outside lane. Now I could see the road clearly. Surprisingly, my mirror indicated the motorhome was moving into my lane. There was no room. His right front bumper collided with my left rear panel. Jackknifed across his front bumper, his grill pressed against the driver's side of my Honda. "Oh, is this how it ends." Uncharacteristically calm, noticing brakes applied. The motorhome began to veer toward the center divider. As we left pavement, rocky soil was beneath. "Please, Lord, let him stop before he hits the divider," was my prayer. Feeling oddly safe and secure, as if the interior of my car was encapsulated in velvet, it was like I was in the Palm of His Hand. There was absolutely no fear. The vehicles stopped 200 feet from initial impact. "Fire" I thought, jumped across the console, and exited on the passenger side. I was intact. This miraculous impact with God and the motorhome has purpose. I am grateful for things that impact my life and my work with Him.

~ *Patricia Medeiros*

Patricia Medeiros *encourages personal growth in children, adults, couples, and families. As a marriage and family therapist, speaker, educator, spiritual advisor, and author, psychology and spirituality are integrated.*

September 20

Fred

Fred was a mutt—a 65-pound sable-and-white Lab mix. Fred took responsibility for keeping everything dangerous away from "his people," such as leaves, snow, and the neighbor's cat. When he heard fireworks or thunder, he hid under the bed, which was no small feat, considering his size. When the doorbell rang, Fred barked ferociously, lunging and baring his teeth to protect us from the unknown. When I answered the door, he hid under the bed. When my sons got rambunctious and ran around, Fred hid under the bed. One time I forgot about a loaf of frozen bread left on the counter. The next day, I went into the laundry room and found the chewed up bread bag on the floor. I held up the bag and asked, "Did you do this?" Fred put his ears down and did a walk of shame. He hid under the bed.

When I went to bed each night, Fred squeezed under the bed directly beneath me. We both felt safe and protected. Fred shared 10 years of my adult life, good and bad. No matter what happened, Fred was always there—usually under the bed. I still miss that soft snore.

~ Susan Veach

Susan Veach *is a graphic designer from Southampton, Pennsylvania. She is a bibliophile, traveler, art lover, gardener, mother, and wife. Reach her at SusanVeach.com.*

September 21

Tears, Cheers, and Lessons

Dear Kids,

With God's help, I gave you life. In love, I cared for you and kissed your "owwies." I took you to the emergency room and made you potato soup so you would feel better. My heart ached for you when the world hurt you. I worried about you when you faced the challenges of growing up, choosing good friends, and making the right choices. I was excited for you when you went off to college and earned your degrees. I was three feet off the ground when you landed your first jobs. With pride, I gave you to the world, so you could give to it. I cried tears of joy when you married your spouses. Words can't express the love I have for you. For most of those things of motherhood, I was fairly prepared. What I was not prepared for was what you did for me. You taught me unconditional love. You taught me about priorities in life and the meaning of sacrifice. You taught me what a gift it is to be a mother. It's a funny thing: I thought I was going to be the teacher. It turns out you were.

Love,

Mom

~ *Susan Brownell*

Susan Brownell *founded and writes for the award-winning website SanctuaryForCancerCaregivers.com. She lives her passion of virtually supporting cancer caregivers when they need help the most.*

September 22

My Autumn Gem!

Today, September 22, is the first full day of Autumn, and my husband Ed's birthday. His beautiful green eyes remind me of everything I loved about him and this time of year. On July 2, 2013, everything changed. He often said, "We have something very special, 38 years together and 36 years of marriage. Who does that anymore? We have two beautiful daughters and four grandchildren. What an absolutely awesome family I have." We were going to get through his Hep-C and liver cancer together. We did get through it; we just didn't get around it. If love, lots of tears, and a great attitude were enough, he would still be here. But, God had other plans. He picks the very best to come join him. So, he chose my Ed. He was the logical one. Always looking to the Lord for answers, and always looking for the common good in any situation. He always said, "Look on the bright side." I am the lucky one to have him watching over me now from "the bright side." I will always have the days, the hours, the years, and the moments of him forever and always stamped in my heart.

~ Barbara Rae Zak

Barbara Rae Zak is owner/author of GoalForTheGreen.com. Barbara has successfully integrated her daily work with developmentally disabled adults into her passion for writing and blogging.

September 23

My Clutch Poodle

Biscuit was just the right size—the perfect companion. Because I always carried him tucked like a clutch purse under my arm and propped on my hip, a friend called him the "Clutch Poodle." Biscuit enjoyed riding shotgun, lazing around, and scavenging sweets, especially chocolate. As a puppy, Biscuit was attacked by the dog next door. This attack resulted in lifelong internal injuries, so his mischievous behavior was often excused. Despite his injuries, he took his job of guarding the house very seriously—from under the bed! I'm grateful for Biscuit's unconditional love. We miss his sashay of a walk, his quiet begging, and his soft brown eyes. He was beloved.

~ *Melisse Campbell*

Melisse Campbell *is an artist and purveyor of antiques who photographs, paints, writes, and designs. Her work has been featured in national publications. Visit MelisseCampbell.com.*

September 24

A True Love Story

She was beautiful—black and brown, with a posture filled with a pride and grace that very few believed a Dachshund could have. Her name was Nickan, and when I made my entrance in the autumn of 1965 she had already been in the family for a few months. My mother quickly learned that if I was crying she just had to put the little dog in my crib; when Nickan licked my feet, I became calm again. We were companions for almost 16 years, and during that time she was the sole being that gave me the neverending consolation of always being there, always understanding. She ran away from home a few times, and on one horrendous occasion she was stolen from outside the supermarket, but she always managed to find her way back home.

The last days of her life were awful. She was unconscious on a thick blanket in my parents' room, and we took turns caring for her. When she finally let go, the grief almost tore my heart into pieces. But today my heart is filled with gratitude. Nickan, thank you for being the first love of my life.

~ *Kicki Pallin Serby*

Kicki Pallin Serby *worked as a radio host for Swedish radio for many years. She now studies sustainability in Uppsala, Sweden. Find her at Twitter.com/KickiPS.*

September 25

A Soul on Fire

A situation marked by near tragedy can sometimes ignite us to express appreciation for the blessings present in our life and for the good things to come. It was Tuesday, September 25, 2012, when I experienced my soul on fire with gratitude.

My cousin called from Cleveland, Ohio, around 3:00 pm. The call itself was not unusual, though the message she delivered initially confounded me. She said her brother's home in Pound, Virginia, burned down; however, he and his family were safe.

Later that week the details were told to me. A neighbor told my cousin's wife that soon after she and the two grand-boys (ages 4 and 3) left for the store she saw smoke, and then fire, followed by an explosion. Their neighbors were generous beyond imagination, bringing money, clothes, and toys, and even offered them a place to stay.

A shift in focus from what you don't have to what you do is often the spark that attracts new sources of abundance into your life. A soul on fire with gratitude ensures you will have the burning passion and strength to overcome whatever obstacles you may face.

~ *Millie Sunday Jett*

Millie Sunday Jett *is an author, speaker, registered nurse, lieutenant colonel (retired), and emotional freedom and healing facilitator based in Detroit, Michigan. Find her at Facebook.com/Millie.Jett or LinkedIn.com/in/MillieSundayJett2cu.*

September 26

Legacy

I feel most grateful and alive when I allow myself to be present to "what is" and truly feel my feelings, coupled with taking intentional action.

When grief from loss pierces me, it brings my lens of awareness into sharp focus. At the recent graveside funeral of a lifelong friend, all my senses were at full volume.

The comforting blanket of my dear brother's arm around my back was cherished, along with the precious sight of my beloved parents, sister, and friends. With yearning, I savored the rare gift of desert rain sprinkling upon my upturned face.

The cloud murals on the blue sky canvas, above the canopy of pine trees laden with cones and needles, added grace. The fresh smell of rain and moist earth pervaded.

Our voices painted vivid, deeply personalized portraits as we mourned the loss, and celebrated the life and legacy of this extraordinary man. This brought hugs, waves of tears, smiles, and bursts of bittersweet laughter.

As soul-searching and communion tenderized my heart, it sparked me to fully commit to a meaningful, collaborative project.

What am I feeling right now? What is one positive action, even baby step, I will take today?

~ *Suzanne Brier*

Suzanne Brier *is an experienced holistic teacher, coach, and speaker who shows clients how to manifest well-being, abundance, joy, and empowerment. Find her at www.OasisStation.com.*

September 27

His Name Was Lucky

Someone had thrown this darling kitten out a car window, clipping off part of his tail, and he hadn't been adopted. He was just waiting for us. Our granddaughter and I decided to give him a new name. I wanted Ziggy, and she wanted Wiggles (he likes to dance), so we named him Ziggle. Ziggle acts like a polished gentleman. He loves to lead the way when walking from room to room. He's so affectionate, and he loves to hold hands! If my hands are anywhere near him, he places his paw on me as though to say, "Aren't we wonderful together?" And, while hard to believe, he caresses my face with his paws and draws me near to lick my nose. I sometimes wonder if we were partners in another life. Ziggle loves to lay on my husband's upper chest, snuggling along his neck. It's heartwarming to hear Ty chuckle in delight. I take cues from Ziggle, too. If someone visits and Ziggle doesn't come around, I know the person isn't likely to be invited back. Ziggle is our guardian and friend, and our lives are more blessed and fulfilled since he came to live with us.

~ Diana Garber

Diana Garber is changing the world one business, one home, one person at a time. This Master Feng Shui Practitioner can be found at IntuitiveConcepts.com.

September 28

A Blessing in Our Life

On Saturday, July 3rd, Stephanie and I were thinking about a "big" way to celebrate Independence Day. We decided that freeing a dog from a cage would fit the bill, so we headed to the animal rescue shelter. As we walked down the rows of cages, several dogs barked loudly, and many charged the front of the cages. We then passed a cage where a 6-year-old Beagle named Toby was quietly sitting in the back corner. He looked frightened, but when I bent down to the cage, Toby cautiously approached. He was gentle and quiet, and we learned that he'd been abandoned twice before. Our hearts melted at the sight of his sweet face, soft floppy ears, and quiet demeanor. Toby seemed perfect, and we took him home. Luckily, it turns out that Toby enjoys sitting on the couch and early bedtimes as much as we do, and he's even learned to love kayaking! Toby is truly a member of our family. We set out on July 3rd to bring happiness and independence to a dog, and in the end it is our hearts that have grown larger and more full of love! Thanks, Toby, for being the perfect dog for these empty-nesters.

~ *Jim Palmer*

Jim Palmer *is known internationally as "The Newsletter Guru" and author of* The Magic of Newsletter Marketing *and* Stick Like Glue! *Learn more at NewsletterGuru.TV.*

September 29

The Entertainer

Entertaining—that's an understatement. Ever since the day Simba, my handsome, loveable red tabby, entered my life it has been anything but boring. Simba routinely jumps on the bed in the middle of the night. One particular night, Simba had been exploring the inner workings of the fireplace. I opened my eyes to discover his white belly and paws covered in soot, and so was my white comforter. As I lay there in disbelief I wondered how in the world he managed to pry open the fireplace glass doors— and whether this going to be a frequent occurrence. Luckily, Simba moved on to the kitchen. He loves exploring the kitchen cabinets, so I decided to designate one kitchen cabinet "all things Simba." Occasionally, I have discovered Simba's Ziploc bag of treats scattered all over the kitchen floor. What amazes me is his ability to open the bag. I just wish he would learn how to clean up after himself. (There's always hope.) Each day Simba continues to amaze me with his talents. I am forever grateful for the joy that he has brought into my life, and I could not have asked for a more amazing companion.

~ Joan S. Epstein

Joan S. Epstein is a green living coach. You can reach her at Inspire-GreenLiving.com.

September 30

With Love from Kannik

Last week we learned that our dog, Kannik, had an inoperable tumor. In a few days, our 12-year-old Alaskan Malamute changed from an energetic dog into a shell of her former self. Although she was running a month ago, by last Thursday she was no longer able to stand. Watching her fail was heartwrenching, and we made the difficult decision to help her. In the moment of her death, I held her and whispered my love into her ear, as I have done so many times over the years. Her long, white fur smelled like a wool sweater. She was comfortable in my arms, and her warm, brown-eyed gaze was calm and content. There wasn't time to think between the moment she was here and the next when she was gone. In the blink of an eye she was no longer with us. As her body relaxed, I was left holding onto a part of her that was no longer whole. Instantly I missed her and felt the tearing pain that comes from having to say goodbye. She is gone now, but my memories remain. I will always cherish the time I had with my beautiful Kannik.

~ *Kelli O'Brien Corasanti*

Kelli O'Brien Corasanti *is an author, personal trainer, life transformation coach, business owner, and mom who lives in upstate New York. Find her at FindingMyWayBackToMe.com.*

October

"*Gratitude is a vaccine, an antitoxin, and an antiseptic.*"

~John Henry Jowett

October 1

What's in a Name?

B ettina, the name I used most of my life, is an Italian derivative of Elizabeth, like Betty or Tina, and means "of the house of Elijah." During my PTSD recovery, which began 28 years ago, my friend Anne Sermons suggested I meditate to find a spiritual name that would define my new purpose in life. My blind buddy, Ron, phoned within a week and greeted me cheerfully, "Hello, sparkle eyes." He hadn't called me that before. "Do you really think I sparkle?" "Of course, you do," he assured me. "I see Light around you right now." Ever since, I've introduced myself as Bettina Sparkles. I kept the old name to honor my little childhood trauma survivor, who saw the world through the eyes of fear and carried a heavy cross of guilt, shame, blame, and self-hatred. Sparkles stands for the new me who once was lost but now has found, forgave the past and loves her Self. Bettina Sparkles is grateful for each day and desires to be God's instrument of peace by joining all other sparkles on Earth to extend His Love.

~ *Bettina Sparkles Obernuefemann*

Bettina Sparkles Obernuefemann *is a retired flight attendant and author, with a mission to inspire trauma survivors to cope and hope. Visit BettinaSparkles.com.*

October 2

Always Turns Out Right

How many times have you spent sleepless nights mulling over a decision you need to make, second-guessing yourself if it's the right one, obsessing over the what-ifs that play out as offshoots of this decision? According to psychologists, you are a "maximizer" if you study all the options available before reaching a decision you consider to be the best one. And you are a "satisficer" if you opt for an acceptable choice rather than an optimal one once the requirements are satisfied. Whether you are one or the other or a mixture of both, you may have noticed something. In some cases, even if you made a "wrong" decision, when you look back at the consequences of that decision, you realize that the course of action you took actually unfolded in a much better, satisfying outcome surpassing the doubts you had at one time. I know because this happened to me! Though I am not quite sure how and why my experience successfully pans out the way it does, I would like to think that there are no mistakes in life, only lessons. I am grateful that whichever way we go, it always turns out right!

~ *Leah Arriola*

Leah Arriola *lives in Ontario, Canada.*

October 3

Harvesting

Gratitude for me is:

- The voice of my grandmother, which I continue to be guided by each day.
- Going to work and feeling fulfilled albeit tired at the end of the day.
- My daughters and our continuing ability to support each other through difficult times.
- My friends who celebrate and support our differences.
- My longevity and good health.
- Eating a meal cooked by my family, nourishing each other through our bellies and hearts with recipes handed down by our grandparents.
- Understanding the importance of worshiping God.
- Knowing I have what I need and accepting that things do eventually work out.
- My love of the arts. I thank my actor ex-husband for that.
- Embracing the many lessons of diversity.
- Appreciating the music I play on my old upright piano. It still has much to give, as do I.
- Having sisters and brothers who still understand and love each other even when we disagree.

~ Bernice N. Gordon

Bernice Gordon, MA, RN, MA *is a registered nurse who goes to work daily at a leading hospital in New York City. She proudly admits to being a senior citizen. She has two wonderful daughters whom she cherishes and four grandchildren whom she adores.*

October 4

Leap of Faith

Two years ago, my husband and I took a big leap of faith when we moved 2,300 miles from Indiana to Beaumont, California, leaving behind my husband's hometown and many friends and family.

It is not an exaggeration to say jaws dropped when we made our announcement. I had worked at the same job for 16 years and realized I needed a change, and my husband supported me. Since arriving in California, I have been more aware of my blessings than ever before.

It is too long a story to write here, but after much stress, we were able to purchase our dream home. When my brother-in-law visited, he commented on how we went from a small, plain home in Indiana to a palace in California. At that point, my "old soul" husband replied that we were content in Indiana, and we do not measure our happiness by the square footage of a house. I'm not doing it justice in this vignette, but at that moment I fell even more in love with Brad.

I am so grateful for our financial success, but I'm incredibly blessed to be married to such a kind, loving, wise teacher and friend.

~ *Teresa A. Castleman*

Teresa A. Castleman *is happily married to Brad C. Castleman. Teresa loves cats, golfing, and reality television. She can be reached at Facebook.com/Teresa.Castleman.*

October 5

Life as a Present

A s I sit comfortably in my car driving around the scenic hills to work, I wonder about the small things in life. The rain drizzles down the windscreen tempting me to turn the wipers on. I notice the colours of the autumn leaves that have floated from the trees. Each leaf seems to float as though gently, gracefully finding its place amongst the rubble on the side of the road. I am reminded that everything is grace. A large semi trailer suddenly swerves, pulling out in front of me and causing me to brake suddenly. His actions may appear an inconvenience, yet I am grateful that in his own way he has slowed me down. I could get caught in emotion about being stuck behind him, crawling around the hills at a snail's pace, concerned whether I will be late for work. But I choose to accept that there is a bigger picture. Perhaps I was driving too fast. Perhaps he has slowed me down and prevented an accident. With grace I am returned to the present. Living in the moment is definitely a present. I thank the truck driver and arrive safely and on time for work.

~ Fiona Om Shanti

Fiona Om Shanti *is a transformational coach, sound healer, and author. Her goal is to inspire others to reach their full potential. She can be contacted at www.OnTheWingsofLove.com.au.*

October 6

I Am...What?

"I am...what?" I asked the doctor, my face pale and eyes crazed. "You mean this is not the flu?" All I could think about at that moment, back in 1982, was my little 5-month-old baby, Christopher, at home, and wondered how in the world I would ever handle two babies just 13 months apart!

Little did I know back then that this jaw-dropping, daunting news would turn out to be the best thing in my life!

My daughter, Lindsey, was born in June 1983, and yes, that first year was an overwhelming blur of diapers, doctors' appointments, and car seats, but these two tiny gifts soon became the greatest joys and lights of my life.

Now, watching them from afar, all grown up and living happy and successful lives, I can only look back with the deepest joy, pride, and gratitude.

I am one of the few lucky women to be blessed with an amazing mother of my own (whom I miss each and every day), as well as children I could not be more proud of. When God looks down and sees true, unconditional love, She smiles—and magic is created.

~ *Mary Armstrong Hines*

Mary Armstrong Hines *is a teacher and social worker in the San Francisco Bay area. She can be reached at MaryH11@att.net.*

October 7

Light

"Love is not consolation. It is light."

~ Nietzsche

I don't like to sleep in complete darkness. I always tell people there is plenty of time for that after I'm dead. I'm not afraid of the dark; I just love light.

From the first time I could climb a ladder, I took over Dad's job of stringing Christmas lights on snow-covered blue spruces in single-digit temperatures. The best part came after finishing the job when my siblings and I all piled into the station wagon with Mom behind the wheel and we drove up and down the road admiring our work. Lights reassure me.

My mom loves light, too—all kinds of lights: Christmas and other holiday lights, garden lights, electric fireplaces, candles, IKEA and Target decorative lights, novelty lights. She even has a solar-powered decorative garden gnome light.

She had an unimaginable dark day in her life when I was not yet two-years-old, and I think light has been a source of comfort for her ever since. Her bravery moving past this and never wavering in her love for her children is why she has always been one of the greatest lights in my life. Now that the miles between us are great, I find I surround myself with lights. They are a shining reminder whenever I look at them that my mom is thinking of me, and I of her.

~ Daniel Kriley

Daniel J. Kriley is a high school theatre and arts management instructor living in Southern California. Find him at Facebook.com/Daniel.Kriley.

October 8

My Forever Love

The rain held off. The early October flowers were a stunning carpet of color bracketing the aisle to our outdoor ceremony. Everyone said, "Wait until you see Paul"—the catering manager, our minister, my father. Then they'd smile mysteriously and leave me to wonder what, exactly, I was going to see out in the courtyard. The moment finally came, and I stepped onto the path leading me to my beloved. I was so happy to have my father escort me on this most special of days, and we set off, arm-in-arm, while the music played and he shared some final words of wisdom. At last! We rounded the bend and I could see, standing straight ahead of me, the man it had taken so many years to find. He was so incredibly handsome and self-possessed, standing tall, in a relaxed yet commanding stance, and the sun shone on him, seeming to create a halo around him. All eyes, including his, were on the bride, but mine were only on him. I wanted to run down the aisle and jump into his arms. We were wed on October 8, 2005. Happy Anniversary, my always and forever love.

~ *Patti Smith*

Patti Smith *lives in Barrie, Ontario, Canada, with her beloved husband, Paul, and Jack Russell Terrier, Sheba. She is a speaker, author, and coach. Reach Patti at AwesomeWealthyWoman.com.*

October 9

The Power of Love

I have a small four-legged friend whom I love very much, but he has quite a tale for the short years he's been on the planet! In 2006 I adopted him as a 7-month old kitten from the ASPCA. After about six months together I went on vacation and left Snuggleafuagus in the care of my neighbors. Since Snuggleafuagus was so shy he didn't interact with them much. When I got home Snuggleafuagus stopped eating, drinking, peeing, and pooping. I took him to a vet who did lab work and gave him a fatal diagnosis. I couldn't believe it so I took him to another vet, who also gave him a death sentence. Finally I had a vet come do a house call. He suggested a supplement that I dilute in Snuggleafuagus's food. When the vet Left, the last thing he said was that he saw cases of cancer and FIP (feline infectious peritonitis) resolve with the supplement. Snuggleafuagus was diagnosed with FIP so I was very motivated to give it to him! Eight years later Snuggleafuagus is still alive today—and he's thriving! He is still a snuggly little one. I am so grateful he is in my life!

~ *Aine M. Sweeney*

Dr. Aine Sweeney, DC, DACAN *is a doctor of chiropractic and diplomate in chiropractic neurology. Learn more about her at www.NonForceChiropratic.com, or contact her at Chiropractic@dr.com.*

October 10

Azza

She came into my life at a time when I must have needed her most. I say "must have needed" because I really didn't believe, at that time, I needed her at all. I was busy with school, work, and my own chaotic life, and I didn't want to take on any more responsibility. But I did, and she is Azza: Azza, my sweet pea! My heart! My sweet-za! She has been there for me since the day I saw her in the kennel at the humane society, and she will be there for me until her body goes. She makes me laugh, smile, and cry. I am grateful to have her in my life. I appreciate the joy she gives me. I appreciate her everything—her stubbornness, craziness, and silliness. She is my peace. Without her, who knows where I might be. She keeps me on track, and I need that. Being responsible for her is helping me stabilize my life. I really needed her, and for her I am grateful!

~ *Bonnie Baker*

Bonnie Baker *is an outdoor enthusiast enjoying the ride of life! She loves the ocean, music, her dog, and spending time with family and friends.*

October 11

Can Parents Be Heroes?

My parents are my heroes. Every day, I thank God for giving them to me. While my parents were not perfect, in my eyes they were! Like every teenager, I didn't like them much. But as I got older, I realized how lucky I was and how grateful I should be to my parents. The most important thing my parents showed me was what marriage should be. They were married for 52 years. My father always came first in my mother's life, and vice-versa. My three siblings and I came second. Some may be appalled at this. I feel it made our family stronger, seeing the absolute love, respect, and devotion they had for each other. They lit up whenever the saw each other. I get so sad when people I know complain about how their parents nag them. What I wouldn't give to have my parents around to nag me. My parents are both gone now. My mom passed away in 2010 and my father passed away in July 2013. Still, I am so grateful because I know they are together, and one day I will be able to be with them again and see their love continue forever.

~ *Julie Anne Clune*

Julie Anne Clune *was born and raised in the Chicagoland area. She graduated from Loras College. She lives in Naperville, Illinois, with her husband and three handsome boys, and works for SpeedScription.*

October 12

My Beloved First Kitten

One day when I was 12, I was sitting on the porch, and a wild cat and her two kittens came up. They were afraid of humans. To avoid scaring them, I put food out and sat very quietly watching them eat, attempting to earn their trust. I tried to pet them periodically, and one day, to my delight, the male kitten jumped on my lap for the first time and let me pet him. I was getting cold, as it was fall, and I wanted to put him down so I could go inside, but I was afraid that would scare him. When I finally picked him up and put him on the stair, he wasn't scared. My parents didn't like cats, but because I spent many hours sitting on the porch taming the male kitten, they let me keep him because I earned it. That was one of the most joyous days of my life; I gained the trust of a wild kitten who became my pet and trusted friend. I'm middle-aged now and love and enjoy my two 10-year-old cats.

~ Avery Thurman

Avery Thurman *is a nurse with entrepreneurial goals. She loves being with her friends, spending time with her pets, and traveling. Find her at Facebook.com/AveryThurman.*

October 13

My Loyal Friend Rusty

Our dog, Rusty, has been our loving companion for 15½ years. He is a sweet, mild-mannered friend who is slowing down physically, but he still does his best to show his affection and loyalty. When I look at him, I see the Cocker Spaniel puppy we found at the animal shelter who paced along the inside of the enclosure looking pleadingly at us for acceptance. I see the young dog who frolicked on walks and loved to chase the tennis balls we threw for him. He would jump up on the bed and snuggle with us, wanting nothing more than to be close, be loved, and share his affection. I see the shameless beggar looking at the treat cabinet and at us alternately until we rewarded him for his endless optimism. Rusty can't jump up anymore, so he finds familiar places to sleep and walk, where his failing eyesight doesn't hold him back. I am so grateful to have enjoyed his company these many years. When it is his time to depart, it will leave a hole in my heart that will be difficult to fill.

~ *Douglas Brennecke*

Douglas Brennecke *is a San Diego, Calif., mortgage originator who listens to his clients, educates them, and tells them the truth. Reach him at DougBrennecke.com.*

October 14

Magical Moments

I am grateful for the magical moments in my life, such as:
- The first rays of the morning sun
- The sound of the birds happily chirping away as I take an early morning walk
- A barefoot walk on the sandy beaches of Mombasa, Kenya
- The sight of the snow peaks of Mount Kilimanjaro, Kenya/Tanzania border
- An unexpected squeeze of my hand from my wife as we take a leisurely walk
- When my daughter Amy says "You're the best daddy in the world!"
- When my daughter Joy lets out a happy shriek, runs to open the door, and gives me a big hug.
- Money flowing in—just in time, exactly when I needed it
- Receiving payment from a perfect and happy client
- My client out from the blue deciding to pay up-front three months in advance for my services
- The perfect idea just popping into mind for an article or how help a client solve a problem
- Finding the perfect parking space in a seemingly full parking lot!
- Finding a long-lost item
- A smile and a cheery wave from a happy stranger

~ James N. Karundu

James N. Karundu *is a motivational speaker, business growth mentor for entrepreneurs, and author of* 7 Keys for Success Beyond Chance, GO FOR IT, *and* Stepping Stones for Top Achievers.

October 15

My Transcending Love Story

Today is my husband's birth date. On our very first date in 1993 we spent all day at a strawberry festival; it felt as if I knew him all my life. At the same time, I was intrigued by this specimen of a man that I did not have a clue could exist outside of a fairy tale. He was a gentleman, soft spoken, gentle, thoughtful, and very willing to share his history with me. There was something very special about him that despite my traditional upbringing, we moved in together that summer, a few months later. Michael has been an unwavering pillar of love and joy in my life. With him I learned to be a loving woman, wife, and mother. He has always kept a safe, gentle, and patient space for me to dive deep within me over and over again; so that I might also be able to communicate with him from the soft, loving space that I cried and prayed for so long to be able to reciprocate to him. I am eternally grateful for October 15, 1971, when the love of my life took his first breath to meet with me again in this lifetime.

~ Raquel Meyer

*Life coach **Raquel Meyer** founded Integrated Authenticity. She coaches how to connect with your authentic essence so that you may see, listen, speak, and feel from your heart, too. Learn more at www.IntegratedAuthenticity.com.*

October 16

Therapy Seizure Cats

Diagnosed with an inoperable brain tumor in 2002, I wanted something to help me feel better. I decided to get a kitten as a companion and brought 6-week-old BooBoo Kitty home. Six months later BooBoo's mother had another litter, and I brought home MewMew Kitty. They are my angels. They talk all the time, and I love it when they line up their toys or place them in a perfect circle on the floor. Most importantly, for the last eight years they have been therapy cats for me. After saving my life several times, they were certified by my neurologist as therapy seizure cats! When I have a seizure they wake me up by biting my nose, licking me, and even putting their paws in my mouth. They are always on the alert for my health. In May 2009 my apartment building burned in a four-alarm fire. I actually suffered a stroke because I believed they perished in the fire. When firefighters went back the next morning to search again, they found BooBoo and MewMew hidden under the bed, alive and well.

~ *Glen Schallman*

Glen Schallman, *born with an inoperable brain tumor, is a 52-year-old survivor, miracle, and hero! Friend him on Facebook to see pictures of his cats.*

October 17

Puppy Love

There is something magical about seeing a Golden or Labrador Retriever puppy that makes your heart melt and your brain useless. You will buy one, so buyer beware! We bought our second Golden puppy for our two young children as a holiday surprise. My husband made an excuse on Christmas morning to run out and get some milk, and he came home with a box with a big red bow on top. I will never forget the wonder of them excitedly opening that box and seeing that adorable ball of fur wiggling out to survey his new surroundings. Thus began our 14-year love affair with MacGyver, who grabbed our heartstrings from day one and never let go. Our current princess is a Yellow Lab named Maggie May, who is 1½ years old. As empty-nesters, we struggled with getting another dog versus enjoying our footloose freedom. We decided that life without a dog was just not quite complete, and we could not be happier with our decision. She brings so much joy, love, and innocence into our lives—and watching her run to catch a ball in the sparkling ocean surf is simply the best.

~ *Mary Armstrong Hines*

Mary Armstrong Hines *is a teacher and social worker in the San Francisco Bay Area and can be reached at MaryH11@att.net.*

October 18

I Enjoy Contemplating This

Rare treasures can occasionally be found in dumping grounds. So it was with Char. Hidden among the typical finds at the animal shelter was a pedigree Basenji. Curious about this breed, we read about it. The Basenji was supposedly employed by Egyptian pharaohs and their households during hunting expeditions. The Basenji's unique characteristic—it doesn't bark—made it the ideal dog for locating animals without revealing the pharaoh and his fellow hunters to the prey. True to form, Char didn't bark. However, unlike her ancestors, she wasn't employed in hunting escapades. Instead, friendly, affectionate Char became a beloved member of an American Jewish household.

Rare treasures can also be found among biblical verses. For example, consider Exodus 11:7: "And against the Children of Israel no dog shall whet its tongue." At the time when the Hebrew slaves were about to leave Egypt, God informed them that no dog would bark, thereby concealing their imminent escape. Could it be that the dogs alluded to in this particular verse were Basenjis? Is it possible that ancestors of Char were present when our family's ancestors were liberated from ancient Egypt? I enjoy contemplating this.

~ *Tziporah Wishky*

Tziporah Wishky, *from New Jersey, lives in Israel. She is a Torah teacher and life coach to women worldwide. Learn more at IStillHaveMyLife. com.*

October 19

Oscar the Teacher Dog!

I am privileged to share Oscar's home. Oscar is a 5½ pound Maltese. He allows five cats, my husband, and me to share his space. He runs the house according to his schedule and routine, but never hesitates to take a break for a chicken treat and is ready to go for a ride whenever we say "bye-bye the car." He is intelligent, loves to play, and has a contagious attitude toward life. Of course, he's beautiful. As my momma always said, "Pretty is as pretty does." And he knows how to do pretty! Oscar is my teacher, my coach, and my mentor all rolled up into one little package. He has taught me that simple things can be just as fantastic or better than expensive things. He doesn't care that I traded down when I bought my last car. He is as happy in a basic hotel room as he is in a luxury suite. Oscar also taught me about love—pure, unconditional, nonjudgmental love. That's a beautiful lesson to learn. He taught me that there's always a reason to wiggle with happiness. Oscar is always there for me on the good days and the great days. With Oscar in my life, there are no bad days!

~ Sylvia Myers

Sylvia Myers is a virtual assistant who loves working with Infusionsoft while in the company of Oscar. You can find her at SylviaMyers.com.

October 20

The Gift of Grace

Grace. Defined as favour, goodwill, or mercy, it is something that has blessed my life abundantly. Deeply moved by it as I am each time, even more deeply am I humbled by it. It is the most precious gift; and awareness of this inspires my deepest awe and gratitude. Grace has manifested itself variously, unpredictably, over the years. From Divine ministering to the innermost achings of soul—such as through the miraculous provision of Chico, my boy cat who soothes me through depression; or the synchronicity in the deaths of my dad and Ponchik, my little girl cat, who mirrored each other's gentleness, purity, and unconditional love for me; to giftings of incredible kindness by people—and repeatedly by those who knew I had nothing to give back: my sister, brother-in-law, Marlyse and Michael, Joe, Steve and Helen, Manuela, Ian especially. I'm grateful also to Antonio, my partner, for his steadfast support, loving patience, and wisdom. My deepest thanks, however, goes to my mother for propelling my search for self—to discover even pain holds grace. Divine Love breathes even there. Grace. For me, the gift of refreshing, acceptance, charity, and encouragement. May I be such a gift to others.

~ *Marina Makushev*

Marina Makushev *lives in Australia and established ReVIBE-olution to empower people into more uplifting ways of being through clinical hypnotherapy, resilience training, meditation, tai chi/qigong, art therapy, zumba, and drum circles.*

October 21

Little Black Kitty

Buka, my cat, is the reason I am writing here today. She helped me through one of the toughest times in my life. We had a crisis pregnancy in 2001; our baby girl was placed in a loving home via open adoption. Then along came Buka, born in May of the same year. She was abandoned, and I remember someone saying that since I already had two cats, I should be strong like I was with our baby girl and give this cat to the shelter. Those words helped me keep this wonderful little black kitty. She was very small and she was very smelly, but she was my muse. After the adoption, she helped my healing process. Buka was always right there, ready to snuggle. She came running anytime she heard me crying, even when I was silent. Sadly, she passed away in October 2008. I miss her every day! I would like to take this opportunity to thank her for being in my life, for helping me heal, for being a big inspiration, and for helping me become the writer I am today!

~ Melody Heath-Smith

Melody Heath-Smith *is a married mother of one. As an aspiring children's book creator, she is writing a "phantasmagorical" story. Contact her at MelodyTheWriter@hotmail.com.*

October 22

Is it Negotiable?

Years ago my daughter and I were looking to rent a second home. We had moved to a new city a year before with only two bags and a teddy bear. During that time we often felt alone—after all, we didn't know many people, and everything was different, even the stars in the sky. One day we spotted some puppies for sale. It was love at first sight with one white puppy making an extra effort to get our attention! Apple became part of our family. She was there to make us laugh every day and help us through the rough times. She followed us and stood by our sides many times, filled a void, and helped us grow. That day when we were looking for a new home, we asked if they allowed pets and were told no. The woman asked, "Is it negotiable? Could you give the dog away?" Negotiable?! Would you trade someone who stays by your side at all times—no questions asked, no judgments made— in exchange for some empty walls? In unison, we gladly said, "No!" That home was not meant to be ours, as giving away Apple was certainly not negotiable.

~ Shahar Boyayan

Shahar Boyayan is an innovative marketing advisor for entrepreneurs, and is crazy for animals and geocaching.

October 23

Baby Grackle Lessons

My young son and his friend found two baby grackles in our yard. I entered the scene too late to prevent contact, so we became responsible for them. We called on the local naturalist, who whipped up baby grackle food for us to feed them. She offered to keep us supplied as long as needed. We fixed up an old aquarium with sticks, leaves, and some soft clothes inside the house for these newcomers to our family. We named them D.J. and Charlie. We used a chopstick tip to feed them mouthfuls of food, and droppers to serve them water. Very soon D.J. and Charlie needed to fly, so we took them outside. Not knowing what would happen, we watched in amazement as they perched on the lilac bush by the porch door, calling insistently to be fed. Eventually the "every two hour" feedings lessened. Hungry from unsuccessful food forays, they would return to us, and we would rejoice that they were still alive.

Sadly, these valiant grackles died too soon. Caring for them increased my respect for wild creatures. I am grateful for the responsibility, our commitment and adaptability, and the connection and trust we shared. They touched our hearts and changed our lives.

~ Carol B. Gailey

Carol B. Gailey, a licensed spiritual healer, facilitates healing and wholeness using tuning forks aligned to the ancient Solfeggio frequencies. You can find her at Facebook.com/Carol.Gailey528.

October 24

Friends in Ironic Places

I find it ironic that some of the people I've been warned to stay away from are the very vessels God has used somehow, usually in a big way. One example is a man I heard about off and on through high school named Scot. My best friend made him out to be a freak and a pervert.

Fast-forward 20 years. Imagine my surprise when I learned that the owner of my son's karate school was that same freak! Well, to this day, Scot has enriched my life in many ways. He has helped restore me spiritually and emotionally. He is also a brilliant attorney, pastor, and life coach.

Ironically, my "best friend" who told me about Scot won't speak to me today, while Scot is helping me with a serious crisis in my life. I'm grateful, not just for Scot's friendship, but for the brain and good discernment God gave me that caused me to give him and others the benefit of the doubt.

~ Nicole Bissett deRochemont

Nicole Bissett deRochemont *resides with her husband, Harry, and her son, Eddie. Her writing has appeared in Behind Our Eyes, an anthology on disabilities and in numerous magazines. You can reach her at NicoleBissett1969@gmail.com.*

October 25

Reality TV

Oh, how I love reality TV!
My sister watches these shows with an eye for the "I'd never" and "Oh, that's a really good idea" moments. Mostly, I am just filled with gratitude that my life is not as out of control as some of these individuals'. But then there are those private moments when I am alone in my car or wandering through a grocery store when crazy reality TV thinking takes over and I begin to wonder.

What if my life was a reality TV show? How many hours would they have to record to find an hour of entertainment? Would I behave differently if I had a camera crew following me all day?

Would my show be a collection of moments when everything is going right, and viewers would be bored to tears? Or would post-production and editing gather the most humiliating and shameful "scenes" from my day, when everything is falling apart, and viewers would be riveted?

I'm so grateful for the multitude of reality shows because, the truth is, I really am starring in my own reality show—minus the cameras.

~ Anonymous

October 26

We Only Live Once

Life can be tough. Sometimes we might feel like giving up or think that nothing is worth living for. We might feel sad, lonely, and hopeless. But the truth is we only live once. We are here to learn as much as we can, meet as many amazing people as we can, and experience many emotions. The choice is ours; we can do good things or bad. Rather than complaining to God about how miserable we are and about how horrible our life is, we should practice being grateful. After all, we are alive, right?

It is difficult to do, but we should also be grateful for our problems and troubles. I think they are what shape us and ultimately make us stronger. That said, I want to let you know that I am grateful for having the dad that I have. He has surely made me suffer a lot because of his unfortunate drug addiction, but I am grateful that he is my dad. I wouldn't want another; I truly love him with all my heart, and I accept his mistakes and his faults.

~ *Myriam A. Felix*

Myriam A. Felix *was born in Whittier, Calif. She is a Mexican-American only child brought up as a Catholic. She likes psychedelic art and old rock 'n' roll music.*

October 27

Easiest Delivery Ever

It was three weeks and two days before my due date. I started feeling unfamiliar pains, but I was sure it was nothing. There was no way I was going into labor early. Surely the baby would wait. How wrong I was.

Labor was not at all what I had prepared myself for. I was calm and relaxed. I did well with the contractions and even better with the epidural. I guess my partner and I expected lots of stress, screaming, and crying.

Three easy pushes later, my daughter, Tristyn, was on my chest. I don't believe there are words to describe what I felt at that moment, but it was the greatest moment in my life.

As the doctor finished checking the baby, he congratulated me and said, "This was my easiest delivery ever. I shouldn't even be paid for this!"

Even as she was being born, Tristyn was so easy. Even one year later I can honestly say I have never felt like parenting Tristyn was hard work. She is so smart and loving, curious and adventurous. She is truly my light, my life, and my love.

~ Deanna McAdams

Deanna McAdams lives in San Diego, CA. She can be reached at DeannaVA.com.

October 28

Eye of the Beholder

I learned about beauty from a plain, cinnamon-colored cat named Zoe. When I agreed to take Zoe as a kitten, I was already quite enamored of my other cat, Emily, an elegant Angora. Short-haired Zoe wasn't my idea of a pretty cat. Emily liked being an only cat and pushed Zoe around whenever she could. Even when Zoe grew larger, Emily still dominated her.

Zoe never gave up. She slept beside me every night, though further from my face than Emily. She purred in my lap while Emily crowded my chin. I knew I was falling for Zoe when I cheered the day she finally smacked Emily back.

Zoe developed diabetes, and I had to give her insulin injections. She never fought me, purred when I petted her after her shots, and kept snuggling in my lap every evening. Zoe lived her 11 years with such dignified trust and unflagging optimism that she took my breath away. On her last day, I finally realized how profoundly beautiful she was.

I continued to appreciate Emily's physical beauty, as I do the beauty of certain people, but now I value more the beauty of spirit I first saw in Zoe.

~ *Patricia Drury Sidman*

Patricia Drury Sidman *believes in love. She is a professional relationship coach who helps people find and keep loving relationships. Reach her at PatriciaDSidman@gmail.com.*

October 29

Mailbox Encouragement

Encouraging words. I'm thankful for them in whatever form they come: in a card, note, or e-mail, face-to-face, over the phone. I think my favorite way is snail mail—a surprise waiting in my mailbox.

Three weeks after my mom's death, the numbness and shock began to wear off. No matter how I tried to block out the pain, I desperately missed her—my best friend. Out of habit, I lifted my heart in prayer, asking for something to help ease my hurting heart.

Later that day, I hurried to the mailbox when I saw the yellow ball up, indicating mail arrival. I glanced through the stack when I spied a red envelope with an out-of-state return address. Curious, I ripped the envelope open.

I began to read. In the first paragraph, the sender identified herself as a hospice volunteer who visited Mom twice a week. As I continued to read, I let the healing tears flow as I drank in the words that described some of their activities and Mom's impact on her life.

Encouraging words penned by a woman days before—arriving just when I needed them.

~ Joyce Heiser

Joyce Heiser *is living her dream of being a published author. She is widely published, mostly in the inspirational area. You can reach her through JoyceHeiser.com or LivingMyRetirementDream.com.*

October 30

A Woman of Value

There I was. Staring in the mirror. Glowing. I finally liked me. For many years I tried to mimic the models of the world. I bought into lies that we are desirable only as physical satisfiers, starting with the eyes.

Destructive tapes played in my head during critical years of development. Comparisons: Why can't I be more like her? Envy: I want to be as beautiful as she is. Dissatisfaction: I can never look like that. Despair: Why bother? I'm worthless.

Then I attended a seminar with speaker Pat Self. Although I wore my mask well, when we talked, Pat intuitively sensed my downcast spirit. She asked, "Do you ever try to pretend to the outside world that your life is perfect, when on the inside it's in shambles?"

Pat taught me how to replace my mentally destructive tapes with new messages. She explained that my worth is based on how Jesus sees me—not the culture, not my past. I will be thankful forever for our paths crossing. Now I can look in the mirror with a glow of hope and excitement. You and I both are valuable to God, our Creator.

~ *Judi G. Reid*

Judi G. Reid *advocates for women to know they are valuable to God. As a writer and teacher, she illuminates truth behind the lies of our sexualized culture. Learn more at www.WomenOfValue.org.*

October 31

God Bless America

My cup runneth over for gratitude for America, a therapy dog who lives with Ann Deakers of San Diego. Ann and America volunteer in the third grade class my daughter teaches. America has been attending third grade all year, and I expect her to start reading any minute. She's had many stories and books read to her. She doesn't fidget, squirm, or get unfocused. She listens! My daughter, Mindy, put out a call for help last August. Ann and America signed up—and help is exactly what they've done. Showing up consistently week after week has given these struggling readers something to look forward to and count on—someone who hasn't given up on them. Everyone wants to read to America, is on their best behavior when she arrives, and is eager to share stories they've written and words they've learned to read. The kids really revere this dog. Since America can't go across America, can a therapy dog in your community find a way into your local classrooms? The children and teachers would be ever so grateful! My daughter and I certainly are. In years to come, the children of Room 32 will recall with affection and gratitude their memories of reading to America. God bless her!

~ Sue Sweeney Crum

Sue Sweeney Crum *is a public speaker, author, and trainer in the organizing and home staging industry. Visit her at theREDteam.com or SueCrum.com.*

November

*"Gratitude bestows reverence, allowing us to
encounter everyday epiphanies,
those transcendent moments of awe
that change forever how we experience
life and the world."*

~ John Milton

November 1

The Little Things Matter

There are always reasons to be grateful, and the focus often falls on those defining moments in life—the big moments that made a big difference. I believe, though, that the little things matter, and when you're grateful for these, you see the magic that occurs in your life every day.

It's the seemingly insignificant things that are remembered wistfully and that ultimately create gratitude for life's richness. Things like the crunch of fall leaves and the hypnotic pull of a crackling fire. The way freshly baked bread smells and how marshmallows float merrily in hot chocolate. Experiencing the laughter and touch of a friend or lover, or being hugged by your pet. How the perfect summer day can make everything feel peaceful and delicious, or how newly fallen snow makes the earth seem pure and good.

In our hurried world, days slip by quickly into tomorrows. Then one day, you realize you've used up an incredible amount of tomorrows and don't have many left.

Be grateful for the insignificant things, for they make up the moments that make up your days. And I would imagine at the end, when you look back, you will wish for more of them.

~ Jane A. Garee

Jane A. Garee *is a sales trainer, speaker, and author passionate about helping entrepreneurs develop effective sales strategies that don't feel sales-y or pushy. Learn more about Jane at www.JaneGaree.com.*

November 2

Courage from Spirit

When Chris, my life and business partner and best friend, died unexpectedly on December 21, 2010, it was impossible to believe there was much left in my life to live for. At a time when my only daughter and I should have been close, we had a huge falling out and became estranged. I had to move our office and residence, and that meant touching everything that was Chris's. I also had to start thinking about how I would support myself now that Chris's portion of the income was gone.

Over the next year the pain was unbearable, and I felt like dying every day. What got me through was feeling Chris's spirit still with me. This gave me the courage to move forward, often only moment-by-moment. I got professional help emotionally and support from my spiritual family during my absence of faith, and allowed my dearest friends to deeply embrace me. I let my cats need me less, and snuggle and love me more, and I joined a mastermind group for professional business support.

I am grateful every day for Chris's spirit, because it protects and guides me and connects me to my courage.

~ Rev. Julie A. Hawkins

Rev. Julie A. Hawkins *is your "take charge" expert. Julie teaches overwhelmed, stressed out, and exhausted women how to reclaim, connect, and take charge of their lives. Reach her at www.SpiritStudies.com.*

November 3

Jessie, My Angel Cat

One part of my life experience, for which I have immense, ongoing gratitude, is my beloved feline friend, Jessie Justin Joy. Evening ends. Fitting like a perfect puzzle piece between my leg and Ray's, our beloved, Jessie the feline, purrs. His essence spreads through our hearts, filling up the bedroom. In our feline's loving warmth, we melt as one song together. We drop into dream-realms, fluffy and warm. I'm snug with thanks as I wake up the next morning. Now Jessie is nuzzled up against Ray's chest, his face right by Ray's. He kisses Ray on the nose and scampers over to me. Always moving in love, thinking first of everyone else's well-being, Jessie starts my day with a singing meow. He brushes against my face. He jumps off of the bed, looking back to make sure I will follow. We go outside to meditate, to appreciate how sweet life is. Nothing is missing. All needed is here inside of me and surrounding. My kitty, Jessie, shows me how to be in love with now by his own way of contentment. He looks into my eyes like a Buddha. He reminds me that all I know is love.

~ *Laurie Alison Moore*

Dr. Laurie Moore *helps people and animals by phone, by Skype, and in person with her animal communication readings. She is the author of* Healing & Awakening the Heart: Animal Wisdom for Humans. *Learn more at www.Animiracles.com.*

November 4

My Dream Cat, Finally

I lost count of the number of cats I'd looked at in response to our missing cat ad, and I hoped that evening's appointment wouldn't end in another heartbreak. The woman said she'd put the stray in a bedroom to keep him away from her two dogs. She opened the door, and the cat started down the hall. I stared, astonished. About 15 years earlier, I'd fallen in love with the picture of an orange and white tabby on the dust cover of a book, instantly deciding that if I would ever have a cat, I wanted one just like that one. Now, there he was, coming toward me. I could hardly believe it. He stopped at my feet, looked up, and then jumped into my lap. He snuggled down, curled into a ball, and purred contentedly as I began to pet his head. In spite of wandering around the trailer park for more than six weeks, he appeared healthy. I asked the woman a few questions and, satisfied with her answers, a few minutes later the newly named Cuddles and I left for his new home—at my house.

~ *Joyce Heiser*

Joyce Heiser *is a freelance author. She is widely published, mostly in the inspirational area. You can reach her at JoyceHeiser.com.*

November 5

Sophie's Miracle Laugh

Sophie refused to attend my laughter therapy sessions. No amount of pleading from the hospital staff could convince Sophie that laughter could help her with her anger issues. Once when I came close to Sophie she spat on me and yelled, "You're crazy!" Six months to the day that I had begun these "laughing classes," I arrived to find Sophie *inside* the activity room, inches from the doorway. Weeks later there was a woman visitor standing next to Sophie's wheelchair. I introduced myself, and the mystery woman introduced herself as Lena, Sophie's sister. I came to find out that they only had each other, having lost all of their family in the concentration camps in Poland. Lena wanted Sophie to participate in the laughter. Patients participated because they understood the value of bringing more oxygen into their lungs while releasing endorphins into their bodies from the laughter! Then a miracle happened. Sophie laughed out loud! Sophie was looking at a stroke patient who had laughed so hard that tears were falling from his eyes. Sophie laughed *and* she cried. We all laughed and cried together that day. Now we come together to share our laughter and are grateful we can!

~ *Teena Miller*

Teena Miller at *www.LaughingHeartConnection.com* is a laughter therapist who considers it an honor and a blessing to bring laughter to those in need of it!

November 6

Dude, I Am Brody*

I am a happy-go-lucky, big lover-bear kinda 'bro.' I love my life and my peeps. I am feelin their love; all my senses are strong like me. Oakland is my home-town, and, accordin to me, the main capital of Pitbulls and bros in the world. I love bros on 'one.' They always compliment me as the best-looking Pit. We are mobbin' hella barred up, smackin' and scrapin'. I am the king of Pit Bulls for sho."

"I am really grateful for my life. I was the runt of a litter of seven. When I finally popped out, my mom was too exhausted to lick me clean. I was not breathing. My human mommy took me into her front paws and gave me mouth-to-mouth. She loves me so much. I can't believe she could then hold me in one paw, and now I weigh 100-plus pounds. My daddy has a tattoo of the Bay Bridge on his chest. I want a tattoo like that on my belly to show my pride for my homies whenever I roll around. Diggitt? Holler at you later!"

~ *Marlies Janzen*

Marlies Janzen lives in Oakland, Calif. She writes about Brody to improve the reputation of pitbulls as loving companions. Befriend her at Facebook/Marlies.Janzen.

*Editor's Note: This piece is written in "rap style," and we curbed the grammatical and punctuation fixes we'd normally apply. You can look up unknown terms in this piece at UrbanDictionary.com. (We did!)

November 7

Stray Angel

It was almost 20 years ago when I first encountered Indian. He was a gorgeous red Chow, but most couldn't see that through his filthy, matted fur. He was left abandoned and made his home in the fast food restaurant parking lot. I never saw him beg—he was afraid of people—but he was smart and hung out where there was plenty to eat. I was not a real "dog person," but something about this animal stole my heart. I would stop by every evening to see him, carrying with me healthy dog food, water, and bones. After a lifetime of abuse, Indian was reluctant to come near. I was consistent and showed up to our nightly visits, patiently allowing him to get to know me on his terms. It was a back-and-forth dance of forward and retreat as a connection was made between our hearts. Some might say he was just a dog—a dirty, unwanted stray. I say he was an angel, sent just for me, to teach me lessons in trust and compassion.

~ *Kathy "HiKath" Preston*

Kathy "HiKath" Preston *lives in Atlanta, Ga. and would like to share her life with an allergy-free Standard Poodle. Her e-mail is HiKath.Preston@gmail.com.*

November 8

Through Thick and Thin

I didn't get Macey's full story when I adopted her from the Berkeley Humane Society, but I suspect she's a dog who's had her heart broken. She wasn't used to kisses or hugs (barely tolerated them) and had trouble learning to trust people. When we had been together about 3 years, Macey had an encounter with a feral cat that left her in a lot of pain even though she'd barely been scratched. After going to multiple vets, we discovered she had a flesh-eating bacterial infection and she ended up losing all the skin underneath her belly. After staying at Advanced Critical Care in Tustin, California for over a month (thanks, Dr. Mineo!), she came home, all bandaged up and exhausted. The two of us made daily 60-mile round trips for months to get her dressings changed. And then the trips happened every other day and then every 3 days until finally, nearly a year later, she had healed. An interesting side effect of all this is that Macey learned to trust people and is a much sweeter dog, coming to me now and then and laying her head in my lap to be kissed and hugged.

~ Kim Bidwell

Kim Bidwell *is an avid runner, voracious reader, foodie, and devoted dog lover living in Southern California. Connect with her at KimOnFacebook.com.*

November 9

Cougar: From Psycho-Kitty to Cuddlebutt

Cougar had been badly abused (skull fracture, broken tail-bone) before I got him. Friends joked that he was my jealous husband in a past life, because he hated every guy I talked to. The first time he saw my boyfriend kiss me, the cat went ballistic, jumped on his back, and slashed all the way down. Rick was a good sport about it, but the poor guy probably still has scars. Since Cougar thought he was protecting me, Rick forgave him. But he never managed to make friends with the cat.

I also had to teach Cougar how to purr—he cuddled with me at night, and I could tell he was happy, but he often looked confused, as if he was trying to remember something. I realized one night I had never heard him purr, so I made purring sounds. It took several nights, but he finally realized what he was missing—and it was louder than any purr I'd ever heard before. For 12 years after that, he curled up on my neck and purred away. In those 12 years, Cougar went from a raving psycho-kitty to the biggest cuddlebutt I've ever seen.

~ *Debi Schepers*

Debi Schepers *is a freelance writer and editor in Chicago with a penchant for finding and loving strange and/or damaged kitties.*

November 10

Dog Wisdom

One of the greatest things we learned from our two German Shepherds happened at their passing after 13 wonderful years. Scotty was the enthusiastic one, Benny the worrier who made sure everything was running by the rules. Suffering from cancer, Benny slowly got sicker, then Scotty suddenly fell ill and passed within a single week. We were devastated, but Scotty, unable to eat and feeling too uncomfortable to lift himself from his bed, found the strength to put on his "happy clown" face and play the joker. "It's fine," he seemed to say. "I'll bound on ahead, as I always have, and explore the mysterious world beyond the veil." And so he passed, his enthusiasm undimmed. Then Benny, grumpy at times in his youth, transformed into a smiling, wise soul, who comforted us in our loss and kept our spirits up until we could look back on Scotty's life with gladness and gratitude for his unending joy at the worst of times. Benny left us comforted, consoled, and with an insight into death that cannot be spoken, but is nonetheless precious for being a secret shared by two humans and two wise and wonderful dogs.

~ *Ron House*

Ron House *is an author in computing, wild bird communication, ethics, and philosophy, and co-discoverer of the Principle of Goodness. Find him at Ron@PeaceLegacy.org.*

November 11

To Veterans: My Gratitude

My gratitude this day goes to the most overlooked members of our society: our veterans. To these men and women I can only say with humility that I am unworthy. Unworthy of the blood shed and lives lost. Unworthy of the sacrifices that you, our country's defenders and protectors, made to allow people like me to live free. I am indebted to you. This indebtedness was the driving force behind my efforts to build a website and write a book to help veterans through the transition back into society. My intent was not only to help military veterans succeed in finding employment, but also to spread awareness to the tremendous struggles military veterans face upon returning to the private sector. For so many of you, your lives will never be the same. America's heroes have demonstrated in the face of incredible odds that we can count on them. Employers, may I suggest interviewing a veteran for your next opening? I'm sure you will find that our veterans have so much to offer. My work can never come close to paying my debt to you, but I hope that you will view my efforts as a partial thank you. My gratitude!

~ Russ Hovendick

Russ Hovendick *is an award-winning executive recruiter. He is the author of three books and the founder of the Directional Motivation organization, which is dedicated to helping people. Learn more at www.DirectionalMotivation.com.*

November 12

Our Freedom

I am grateful for our United States military servicemen and women who have chosen to serve our country to protect our freedom. It takes special people who have answered their calling to join the military and make a huge sacrifice for themselves and their families—all to make a difference in the world. I love our military and support the families with prayer and gratitude for their time in service and deployment. Now, with this freedom, each of us can choose every day how to live life, feeling it. First, do you take the time to honor and love yourself so you are filled up and let it flow to everyone around you? Opportunities are everywhere. You can help an elderly person out at the store or give the clerk a compliment or smile to make his or her day brighter. It's the little acts of kindness that make life bearable for others when they're in need. When you think of the military and all that they do for freedom, what is the one more deed you can do for people to celebrate it?

~ Linda A. Zimmerman

Linda A. Zimmerman *is a life/spiritual coach, author, and speaker at Live Heart Inspired. Learn more at www.LiveHeartInspired.com. Contact her at LiveHeartInspired@gmail.com.*

November 13

What Makes Me Laugh

I truly love my animals—they make me laugh every day. I have two dogs and two cats. My dogs are Jack and Jasper; Jack is a runner and Jasper is a barker. My cats are Lilly and Prix; Lilly hunts mice and Prix is lazy. Lilly and Jack are best friends. Every time Jack wants to go outside or go for a walk, Lilly is right there beside him. It is the funniest thing to see: me walking my dogs down the street and my cat following. Jasper is all of 9 pounds, much smaller than Lilly, yet he waits next to the door as I let the cats in and then pounces on them. Lilly just takes it. She sits there and waits until he's done. When he moves on to Prix, she hisses and strikes back. Prix is my lazy cat who loves to eat. When she is ready to eat she jumps off the table and walks down the stairs. She is so big you would swear that it sounds like a person walking down the stairs. My animals have such distinct personalities, and they are so much fun that they make each and every day a blast.

~ *Doreen Dilger*

Doreen Dilger *is a home-based business coach who empowers women to create systems to get more done daily. She can be reached at DoreenDilger.com.*

November 14

Reflection

Thinking back on the challenging interactions of this day, I pause to see the reflection of me in the mirror of each. I receive the gift of observing these self-imposed challenges wrought with judgment and frustration, the by-products of ego. Deep breath. What firmly entrenched "buttons" have been pushed? From where did they come? What do I fear? What is true? I am grateful. I am grateful for the gift of the mirrors held by others so that, in the reflection, I might see who I have become. Allowing myself to examine, move through, and release this puzzle of emotion, I am joyfully reminded that I am more. The truth of all that I am towers over those moments of dancing with the ego. I am grateful to know that, if I care to take the time, I can continue my journey back to the all of me, my soul self, my essence. I begin to move with the possibilities of choice, and I am grateful.

~ *Judaline D. Nelson*

Judaline D. Nelson *is a transpersonal therapist/coach assisting people in their journeys toward self. For more information, go to www. ALifeWithinReach.com.*

November 15

California Dreaming

We are grateful that California Dreaming is now a reality. You would not believe me if we told you how many days a year the sun shines in Beaumont, California.

We live two miles from the most wonderful fruit stand, Dowling Orchards.

We can get to the ocean in 75 minutes and to Palm Springs in 30 minutes.

We get to see snow on the mountains but no shoveling required.

We get to giggle from our patio as we watch golfers try to hit out of a brutal fairway sand trap.

We have a quiet, beautiful neighborhood for walking.

The moon is such a presence in our lives due to the lack of clouds.

The cats have more sleeping spots then they can count.

We can watch the sunset from our living room.

Vegas is four hours away, not too close and not too far.

You can grow colorful annuals and desert plants year round, including palm trees.

It is fun to wear shorts in January at noon and then use the gas fireplace that same evening.

And the best thing of all: We can visit my amazing sister, Donna Kozik, in San Diego, whenever we want!

~ Teresa and Brad Castleman

Teresa A. Castleman and **Brad C. Castleman** live in Beaumont, California. Besides the Golden State, they love cats, golfing, sports, and reality television.

November 16

To Those Who Awaken to Motherhood

I woke up that night, finding myself alone in the hospital room. I was suffering post-delivery complications, and was ordered by the doctor to remain under medical observation, leaving my new baby with my mother. The events of the previous weeks rushed back. I remembered my quiet anger at my husband for not being at the clinic; I resented the fact that birth complications had weakened me so, preventing me from taking my final exams. I began to cry bitterly.

Suddenly the image of my baby came to the fore. A soft bundle in my arms, she looks at me, squinting her eyes, her little hands jerking out as though wanting to touch my face. I stopped crying as a strange, warm sensation started to fill my heart, slowly spreading through my veins, reaching my ears, then my eyes. A new wave of tears—loving and longing tears this time—rolled down on my dry lips, washing away my anger and resentment. "What was that?" I asked myself, intrigued. "Was that what people call the maternal bond?" I pondered. Whatever that was, I realized that I now had a new life to cherish and care for.

Nothing else mattered!

~ *Lem H. Truong*

Lem Hoang Truong *shows executives in developing countries how to successfully manage and lead donor-assisted development projects. You can reach her at LTAssociates.com or Truong.HL@cox.net.*

November 17

Lifelong Friends

We can tell the character of people by the company they keep, and we can tell what kind of life they have led by the animals they have adopted. My life included: Feeding the deer by hand when I was about 6 years old.

Watching the cat have her first batch of kittens, and my mare have her first foal, knowing that if they could do it, I could too—and I did, one week later with the exact same ease and speed as they did!

Having my horse come back to me and wait for me to get back on after I had fallen off.

Watching my very small "hardly" dog protect my oldest daughter from an intruder.

Winning my first three-day event.

Hearing the frogs croaking each spring in the pond.

Winning the gold medal for endurance riding.

Walking up to alpacas for the first time and being told that I was the first person who ever walked up to them and got them to respond.

"Christmas Eve," who came to me after my children left home.

Gratitude does not begin to express the blessings and joy with which I have been gifted during my life.

~ Anne Ryan

Anne Ryan *is a "country girl." She uses her knowledge of animals in her coaching practice. Find Anne Ryan, coach at Facebook.com.*

November 18

True Friends Are Blessings

I'm grateful for true friends that helped me through sorrow. On February 9, 2012, I had to euthanize my favorite cat, as he was suffering from kidney disease.

My friend Charlie drove me the half hour to the vet because I was emotionally exhausted. The vet sedated Panther first, so that he would be relaxed, and I could say goodbye and express my love for him. The vet then gave the final injection that ended his wonderful life. I talked and cried all the way back, and Charlie just listened.

I was devastated and cried a lot over the following three days. Thanks to my friends, I didn't have to go through the grief on my own. My friend Ramona invited me to supper one evening, which lifted my spirits. The following day my friend Debra and her friend Wilma took me out to lunch, and we talked and laughed for three hours. My friend Leah wrote and sent a beautiful poem. Another friend left a comforting phone message.

I'm truly grateful for all of my loving and supportive friends in times of need, and that God gave me over 10 years with my beloved cat, Panther.

~ Avery Thurman

Avery Thurman *is a nurse, new entrepreneur, and budding author who has contributed stories to "The Gratitude Book Project®" series. E-mail her at Avery.T37@gmail.com.*

November 19

My "Lucky" Gratitude Secret

I have been called lucky, and I agree I live a charmed life. What I discovered is I intuitively follow the law of attraction, so it's not random luck but specific ways of thinking that create good feelings in my body and attracting more of the same. At the same time, I see others struggle—and create more struggle. Now I know anyone can change the way they think about situations in their lives, even trials. It gives me joy to watch my clients' lives change miraculously when they use a gratitude practice. I am so grateful to have transferred this knowledge from my subconscious to my conscious mind, so I can support others in transforming their lives. If we learn to jump with faith into the fear of the unknown, we discover how trials are actually "growing opportunities." I'm still learning this myself, as when my husband lost his job. Initially, I felt vulnerable and scared. But then my fear motivated me to find the Institute of Integrative Nutrition, become a holistic health coach, and launch a rewarding career. I am grateful as I now support women in reclaiming their bright light and finding their own inner wisdom.

~ Lia Venet

Lia Venet *is a holistic health coach in the Bay Area and founder of Wellness Within Guidance. She specializes in relationships, self-care, and living your authentic life. Find more info at www.WellnessWithinGuidance.com.*

November 20

From Russia with Love

Four years ago I was skiing in Norway. A somewhat large Russian snowboarder accidentally smashed into me, knocking me out and sending me tumbling down the mountainside. A couple weeks later I suffered an internal bleed in my brain resulting in a small stroke. I couldn't move my arm; I was severely confused; I couldn't remember things clearly. As I slowly recovered physically, worse was about to come: post-traumatic stress disorder. Incredible anxiety and stress; I really came to an abrupt halt—*completely stuck!* As a personal development coach, I have always been a strong advocate for positive thinking. I have helped people use the necessary tools to move forward in their personal lives and their career. However, this time I had to turn it all around to myself. What a journey! My experience was a nightmare—a horrible time in my life that I wouldn't wish on anybody. However, it led me to a greater understanding of stress, anxiety, and indeed living constantly in a heightened state of FEAR—which most of the time is False Evidence Appearing Real! I am indeed grateful to my Russian snowboarder for what happened that day! What could have resulted in a long-term disaster actually showed me the way forward in my life and has helped me become an understanding, compassionate, and effective coach.

~ *Vivien Black*

Vivien Black *is a personal development coach specializing in managing stress and anxiety and a motivational speaker. You can find out more about her and her work at www.CreateTimeForYourLife. CoachesConsole.com and www.TipsFromALifeCoach.blogspot.com.*

November 21

Pine Needles and Things

I look to the ground and carefully search the ground for each fallen pine needle, picking them up one at a time, as if they are calling out to me. Most people think of them as useless and dirty, and a chore to be gathered up and thrown away. But I gather them, wash them, and coil them into unique, beautiful, and useful creations. Each time I do, I am thankful, because I am reminded of our creator, Father God, whose eyes search throughout the whole earth looking for people who will call out to Him. Some appear to be useless, broken, and dirty, but He gathers them up, washes them, and, with His love, creates something uniquely beautiful in each of us.

~ *Carmen Haynes*

Carmen Haynes *was a full-time caregiver, when she asked the Lord for something to occupy her time. She now has her own business called Pine Needles and Things.*

November 22

Becoming Grateful

Gratitude is a way of thinking. Gratitude is a habit. Unfortunately, our tendency is to go through our days without noticing all that goes right, and all the luxury and things we have. Instead we notice what goes wrong. We need to change our habits. Try focusing on all that is right. And when something does not go the way we think it should, consider the possibility that maybe we are not seeing the complete picture. Just maybe God knows what is best. We also need to look for ways that the challenges can be used to help us grow and mature. But habits are hard to change. How can we change our way of thinking—our attitudes? Here is an idea to try. Start a list of things for which you are thankful. On the first day, write one item. Stop. Do not write any more. On the second day, add one more item. Continue this, each day adding one item. See how long it takes before you run out of anything to add. Chances are you will never run out. But you will begin looking for those things for which you can be grateful! You will be changed!

~ *Patricia A. Klempke*

Born **Patricia Ann Davison** *in Hampton, Kentucky, Patricia Klempke grew up on a farm near Metropolis, Illinois, and resides in Rockford, Minnesota, with her husband, William. She is retired and enjoys reading and writing.*

November 23

Gratitude Is an Attitude

There are so many things in my life for which I am grateful. Every day when I wake up I am grateful to be alive. I thank God for the new day. No grumbling or complaining about having to get up. As I go through the day, I am grateful for the little things: the warm breeze on my face or the cool wind in my hair; the trees turning bright green in the spring or bursting with color in the fall; the smell of homemade soup cooking on the stove as I walk in the door on a cold, winter day. Every day can be a good day or a bad day, all depending on how I look at it and what I focus on. I think I get this attitude from my dad who would always says, "It's a great day today!" When I asked why, he'd reply, "Because the sun is shining. It's a bad day only when the sun doesn't shine." "But Dad," I'd reply, "it's raining out." His reply would be, "Yes, down here it might be raining, but up above the clouds, the sun is shining bright!"

~ Lisa Thorburn

Lisa Thorburn *grew up in Michigan and is the youngest of six kids. She currently lives and works in Northern California with her husband and two very vocal cats.*

November 24

Embracing Adversity

On this Thanksgiving day, I count my blessings even more for the transformation my life has taken, from being a refugee to now being a professional and a productive citizen of this great nation. I can remember the event as if it happened yesterday. I was about 9 years old when my parents made a courageous decision to risk all of our lives (my parents and their 10 children) in the name of freedom.   We were among thousands of the "boat people" who fled Vietnam by sea after the fall of Saigon in the infamous Vietnam War. For three days and three nights, we were afloat and engulfed in the vastness of the ocean. Nothing but darkness surrounded us with our boat tattered. All we could do was pray. Just when our luck seemed to run out, we spotted land! My family and I stayed in a refugee camp for almost nine months before we set foot in America. Although our lives were difficult in the early years, the struggles brought my family even so much closer to this day. I am extremely grateful for this experience in molding my character to grow from any challenges life puts forth.

~ *Le Doan*

Le Doan, PhD *is a psychologist and certified relationship coach for small business owners, providing "mental-wealth" care whenever and wherever that's convenient for her clients. Reach her at OnDemandPsychotherapy.com.*

November 25

In Mom's Kitchen

I learned many of life's critical lessons while helping in Mom's kitchen.

Here are three favorites:

- Clean up as you go. Rather than waiting until the whole meal was prepared, Mom cleaned up the little messes along the way, making for light work later. Most messes, personal and professional, benefit from this approach. I learned to put things right today rather than tackle mountains of debris tomorrow.

- Recipes make good guides. Mom collected recipes for any tasty dishes she encountered. She never hesitated to make improvements, either, often scribbling notes in cookbook margins about ingredients to add or swap. She invented many sweet and savory goodies for us, too. Mom showed me to seek successful models, trust my senses, and create new things.

- Cooking requires your presence. During my teens, I often wandered away while cooking, only to be called back by Mom's loud admonition: "You can't cook if you're not in the kitchen, Julie!" Great meals require attention, planning, and care, just like great educations, careers, and relationships. I learned to be present—emotionally, mentally, and physically—for what matters.

In Mom's kitchen, I learned more than how to prepare a satisfying meal; I learned how to live a satisfying life.

~ Julie Renee Linkins

Julie Renee Linkins, public speaking coach, conflict resolver, and artist, succeeds because she paid attention in her mother's kitchen. Swap stories with her at JRLinkins@ClearLeadershipCommunication.com.

November 26

Be Grateful Always

During life's rough times it is often hard to be grateful. If you've experienced a job loss, a divorce, or a death of a loved one, gratitude tends to take a back seat to anger, bitterness, hurt, pain, and sadness. Although it may seem counter-intuitive, it's during these times that you should strive to be grateful for what you do have.

Ask yourself these questions:

Did I wake up today? Then be grateful you are around to live another day. A patient dying of cancer in the hospital would be.

Did I eat today? Then be grateful you aren't starving. A child in Africa who hasn't eaten in two days would be.

Am I reading this? Then be grateful you have the ability to read. A woman in Afghanistan where the illiteracy rate is over 70 percent for females would be.

Am I living in a comfortable home? Then be grateful you have somewhere to sleep. A homeless man shivering in the cold would be.

Are you feeling more grateful now? If so, remember that feeling and practice gratitude every day. Life can be hard, but it can also be wonderful. Be grateful. I know I will be.

~ *Diane Adkins*

Diane Adkins *is a divorce recovery specialist, a certified life coach, and an NLP practitioner whose effective strategies and solutions help women move beyond their midlife divorce at www.BetterBeyondDivorce.com.*

November 27

Crisis as an Intervention

"The Chinese use two brush strokes to write the word 'crisis.' One brush stroke stands for danger; the other for opportunity. In a crisis, be aware of the danger—but recognize the opportunity."

~ John F. Kennedy

Some of my life's most pivotal points have been during crisis. Radical shifts in relationships when the familiar fell apart. Entrepreneurial experiences of financial "meltdowns." But I realize they are because of how I've been living life. Each occurrence was my golden opportunity to evaluate and choose: to be realistic and safe, or to risk and commit to give my deepest gifts.

I am again at a crux. By playing it small and safe, I have not become successful or fulfilled. The highest path is one of growth: courage, and a willingness to risk, be uncomfortable, and, ultimately, do whatever it takes to achieve my dreams. There is rich satisfaction in committing to go the distance, liberated from the need to see the entirety of the path before you get there.

I have learned much from crisis. I am grateful for these soul-stretching interventions. As I breathe deeply and swing through the crux, I get to experience what I am truly capable of.

~ *April Asher*

April Asher *supports people in acting on their inner guidance, and in experiencing more happiness and fulfillment in all their relationships! Visit www.ALifeUncommon.com*

November 28

Grateful for Groceries

"I've got to go get groceries."

"I've got to bring the groceries in."

"I've got to put the groceries away."

Sigh.

Then I give myself a little shake and a reminder: I'm grateful for groceries!

I'm grateful that I have a place just blocks away filled with nearly any food I desire, from the basics to exotic cheeses and locally grown vegetables. Aisle after aisle after aisle of food, with no cow milking or garden plowing required.

Then, my Bug nearly bursting with bags, I get to bring them in the house and pile them up on the table and put them away—each item snugly fitting in my refrigerator or cupboard.

I remember there are many out there now who would be grateful for the grocery shopping opportunity I have, along with ancestors of mine who never had it so easy.

So today I'm grateful for groceries—thankful for how convenient and abundant they are!

~ *Donna Kozik*

Donna Kozik *gets people between the covers—book covers, that is! Want to write a book and be on Amazon? Get a free book-writing planner at FreeBookPlanner.com.*

November 29

My Grandparents' Table

I am grateful for what my grandparents taught me about sharing meals. One Sunday afternoon, when I was 11 years old, I had an "a-ha moment" about food.

As we had done for years, three generations (11 of us altogether) gathered around the table at my grandparents' house, chattering and jostling for elbow room, to share a Sunday dinner. My Aunt Mary always sat by the door to the kitchen, popping up so frequently for "just one more thing" that my father complained she was like a jack-in-the box.

Noni and Grandpa had both emigrated from Italy, bringing their deep cultural roots to America. Dinner began with soup, then courses of pasta, vegetables, meat, salad, and dessert. Finally the nut bowl came out, and we took turns using our favorite nutcrackers on walnuts, pecans, almonds, and filberts (hence the term, "soup to nuts").

I had a realization the food on the table was wholesome, real food, prepared from the heart to feed us all. From that day, I have embraced the belief that our meals should begin with fresh, real food as close as possible to how it is raised, and shared in a peaceful environment with a spirit of fellowship and gratitude. This belief has served me well, keeping me healthy and nourished in many ways over the years.

~ Tom Castrigno

Tom Castrigno empowers home cooks to overcome obstacles by teaching them new skills so they can eat better and improve their health. Find Tom, Kindle author and blog writer, at www.AMobileChef.com.

November 30

Never Pass Up Opportunities

It was a warm and breezy, a perfect beach-weather day. Toby and I were scampering in and out of the surf, chasing each other around like a couple of kids, when it happened again: "Awwwwwww…" My spunky, 8-pound Morkie stopped short, a small arch of sand spraying out to the left. He frantically snapped his head from side to side, ears held high, as if to say, "Who said that?" He scrutinized everyone within talking distance, trying to figure out which fabulous person released the universal expression for "look at that adorable little dog." He locked eyes with the suspects and, without hesitation, took off full steam ahead in their direction. He knew they wanted to meet him, and I knew there was no stopping him! He was on a mission. He was on his way to meet the wonderful people who thought he was equally wonderful. I admire Toby's self-confidence. I'm thankful for my little bundle of love and energy, who reminds me daily never to pass up an opportunity to meet new people, to have fun in everything I do, and to be confident in who I am and what I have to offer the world.

~ Shelly Lodes

Shelly Lodes *specializes in helping bed & breakfast owners worldwide fill their rooms. Shelly travels extensively with her dog, Toby. Learn more about their travels at TrippinWithToby.com.*

December

"I would maintain that thanks
are the highest form of thought,
and that gratitude is happiness
doubled by wonder."

~ Gilbert K. Chesterson

December 1

Miles of Gratitude

The Holy Bible contains these words: "The steps of a good man are ordered by the Lord."

One morning I prayed, "Lord, today bring me in touch with those You want me to speak to and with those you want to speak to me." Not much is remembered about the daytime. My "steps" at nighttime led to a telephone conversation with a stranger. It was the weekly conference call for our company, but we didn't know the date had been changed. Eagerly, I dialed. Hearing no one after several minutes, two ladies in the "almost" silence realized that they were not alone on the line. "Hello." And "Hello." The silence was broken and a friendship was born.

We exchanged e-mails and had telephone conversations. Once I said, "My dream is to write a book." She remembered. She coauthored a book and sent it to me. Then I received an e-mail from the publisher of the book.

My gratitude overflows to my fellow Christians who followed the footsteps of Jesus, too. Thank you, God. Thank you to Leila Glenn in Detroit, Michigan, from me, Helen Pulliam, in Metter, Georgia. God ordered our steps so beautifully!

~ Helen Pulliam

Helen Pulliam resides in Metter, Ga. with her husband and Paws, the cat who "adopted" her. Although Helen and her husband are retired, they continue to be pastor and wife of two small churches.

December 2

Thank You, Lord

I am grateful for life and the opportunities strewn in my path. The humble, nondescript, non-extraordinary, yet complete, gracious, and almost-gold-studded, mundane life. I am grateful for my mum. She kindled and nurtured my inspiration. I am grateful for my husband. He accepted me, naïve as I was. He guided my fledgling aspirations and concealed my shortcomings.

I am grateful for our children. They give us joy, love, respect, and the fulfillment any parent could desire.

I am grateful for today, for life, and the three score spent. Each year has opened new vistas, horizons that point to the lighthouse. Like a rose bud, each day opens to these mysteries of life. We are here to learn, to enjoy, and to share. I have shared and received my share. May I feel this way every moment, every day, in every way. Lord, I thank you for all you have given me and, more especially, for the many things I forgot to thank you for.

~ Lucy Irene Vajime

Lucy Irene Vajime *is from Ghana, has lived in Nigeria for over 30 years, is a faculty member at Benue State University, and loves reading, traveling, and classical music.*

December 3

A Precious Gift

When my mother was 85, she had to stop driving. She was heartbroken, as she was fiercely independent, doing her own errands and going on shopping sprees. My brother and I decided a Siamese kitten would be the "purrfect" gift to lift her spirits. Mom was thrilled with her new kitten named Precious. He was creamy white with black points and bright blue eyes. Extremely affectionate, Precious followed Mom all over the house. She played with him, she watched TV with him, and he would jump on her shoulder when she did the dishes. Precious's purrs, rubs, and snuggles made Mom happier now that she had her companion. Several months later, Mom was diagnosed with brain cancer. With home hospice and caregivers, Mom was able to spend the last few months of her life at home with Precious. Precious's engaging personality charmed everyone: the hospice nurse, the caregivers, and Mom's many visitors. When Mom passed away, I became the proud "godmother" to Precious. He is a special cat, and I am so grateful for the joy and affection he brought to Mom during her last year on Earth. It is an honor to be the guardian of this precious gift, Precious!

~ *Vitucci Lyons*

Vitucci Lyons *is an animal minister, writer, speaker, and cat artist. She enjoys spending time with her two cats, Precious and Raggedy Andy.*

December 4

My Darling McBarker

After a miscarriage, my heart needed someone special to love. I visited the local shelter, where I fell hard and fast for a gold-and-white Siberian Husky/German Shepherd mix puppy with big brown eyes.

McBarker was the dearest friend in all the world: my pillow, my clown, my confidant, my dance partner, my partner in crime, my sing-along buddy, and my kiss-my-tears-away friend. He was a protector of kitties and a companion to our two wonderful sons.

Mick grew to 65 pounds of unbridled energy. His impulsive nature got him into all kinds of trouble, like the time he lifted his leg on our freshly cut Christmas tree. Once he was so excited to come in that he failed to notice the screen door was closed and bounded right through it.

He would sit, speak, and give his paw, but I never could get him to roll over. He'd bark for his treat when I sang the Meaty Bone song. Otherwise he would obey commands only after filing a verbal complaint in his Husky way: "roo, roo, rooooooo!"

I'm so grateful that McBarker helped me through a heartbreaking time and cheered my heart for many years.

~ Stasia Kuntz

Stasia Kuntz *lives happily in Paxton, Mass. with her husband and an Australian Shepherd. A proud mother and grandmother, Stasia enjoys art, writing, music, and nature.*

December 5

Your Best Life Yet

Life is precious and should not be squandered. If we are to leave this world a better place, then it is not only our responsibility, but our duty, to be and live to our highest potential. Destiny lies in your hands alone. Put fear aside and forge ahead; never settle for less than is possible. For that possibility alone, I am so thankful to be born into a country where women can pursue their dreams and a better life for their families.

I'm grateful for a being born into a country that believes in life, liberty, and the pursuit of happiness. These intangibles are so easily taken for granted. Too many have paid the highest price that enables us to continue living and participating in a free society. Life is far too short. Live. Create. Enjoy.

My business has been a pursuit of creating a life well lived—realizing my dreams of foreign travel, helping other women find work they are passionate about, and being around like-minded inspirational people.

I invite you to join me on the journey for a life well lived.

~ *Sandra Lee Williams*

Sandra Lee Williams *currently resides in the Pacific Northwest. Her passions are traveling, and helping women 50+ start a business they are passionate about and live the lifestyle they've always dreamed about. Learn more at www.SandraLeeWilliams.com.*

December 6

My Canine Is Feline

Kona is clearly a dog. But don't try to convince her of that. She looks like a dog and barks like a dog, but she believes she's a cat. Having a doggie bed for Kona is almost a joke. Her comfy spot to take a snooze is on the back of the couch or under a piece of furniture. Her favorite foods are tuna, salmon, and shrimp. She looks at me rather indignantly when I put dog kibble in her bowl. Kona can curl up in a ball so tight, she shrinks to half her size. And she grooms herself all day long. Good thing, too, because she hates to be near water. Giving her a bath is a formidable challenge. No fortress is a challenge for Kona. Her cat-like agility is unsurpassed. She can take one swift leap, from a complete standstill, and perch herself on top of a fence or wall. Once she's up there, she can maneuver across with the confidence and precision of a tightrope walker. Kona is pretty persnickety, but she's also loyal, protective, and lovable. My little Jack Russell/Whippet mix is the coolest cat on the block!

~ *Melanie Kissell*

Melanie Kissell *shares shoestring marketing strategies with mompreneurs who want to ditch the corporate world and work from home. You can find her at MelanieKissell.com.*

December 7

Unanswered Prayers

Yes, I'm grateful for not always getting the things I wanted and prayed so hard for. I'm a practicing Christian, so what I pray for I should receive, right? Apparently God doesn't always think so. Sometimes what I want and what is best for me are two different things, and sometimes God has a completely different plan from anything I might have in mind for myself and others. I prayed to get into medical school after college and that didn't pan out. After graduate school I prayed for a particular job I really wanted. That didn't happen, either. In hindsight, those paths would not have been the blessings I thought them to be. I've prayed for relationships that didn't work out; I later learned God really did me a favor there! I've also prayed that loved ones with illnesses would be healed. They weren't. But their tired bodies departed this world peacefully and they left legacies of dignity, courage, and strength. So if your prayers aren't always answered in the way you'd like, please remember that sometimes the true blessing is not receiving what we want. More than likely you'll get what you truly need.

~ Leslie Nelson

Leslie Nelson *is a writer, speaker, and mentor. She enjoys making spiritual concepts practical and accessible, and helping others develop personally and professionally. Contact her at CoachLeslie.Nelson@gmail.com.*

December 8

Up from the Ashes

My heart stopped and did a free-fall down to my feet. Things seemed to be happening in slow motion. The Pit Bull came out of nowhere—up from the canyon. He had Phoenix by the neck and was starting to shake him from side to side in his big, powerful jaws. I saw the fear in Phoenix's eyes and felt it spread throughout my entire body, yet I could not move.

I saw my mother out of my peripheral vision. She was moving toward our white, button-nosed Malti-Poo with amazing speed and simultaneously pulling back his leash. She managed to startle the Pit Bull and scooped the whimpering, terrified Phoenix out of what surely would have been the jaws of death. I found my feet and moved toward the Pit Bull with a ferocity I didn't know I had. These actions were enough to get the Pit Bull to open his mouth enough to free our precious boy.

Phoenix is back to his former self—his running, playing, loving, energetic, sweet self. He is again interested in the world. He has confirmed some life lessons I have been working on: Let the past be the past, and let the present be a present.

~ Nikki L. Goodman

Nikki L. Goodman *owns MyVintageDiamondRings.com and is passionate about loving animals.*

December 9

Friendship, Love, and Life

Three hundred and eighty-eight days ago one of my dearest friends died. Today is her birthday; this is for Jennifer. When I think of Jen I see a collage of memories of our lives together, there were so many adventures we shared; we were six women growing up together through acne and high school and first crushes and broken hearts; we were and still are at the core of each others lives. I know that words can never express how I feel about her and how blessed I was to have Jen in my life, for the gifts she has given, and the love and compassion and laughter we all shared. I can never thank her enough for being there during heartbreaks and losses, and for celebrating successes and joys. Jen was loving, kind-hearted, funny, silly, courageous, generous. She was an amazing friend, woman, and mother. We will meet again and it will only take a fleeting glimpse to recognize each other once more. Jen made a difference; what she did was so very important in my life, in our lives, she will always be in my heart, our hearts, always remembered and loved to infinity and beyond.

~ Helen R. Ollerenshaw

*Building resilient lives and teams, **Helen Ollerenshaw** works with individuals and businesses to transform and create success. She is the owner of LifeEthereal.com.au. Her expertise is as a trainer, coach, author, and speaker.*

December 10

The Christmas Dog

I am not a "pet person." My husband grew up in the country and always had pets, but not in the house. When our sons requested a dog for Christmas, we both agreed that our current living situation was not conducive to owning a dog. We told our sons not to expect a dog for Christmas. A pet was not on our list of Christmas presents. But our family returned home on Christmas Eve to find a dog on our doorstep. Nobody claimed the black-and-white Boston Terrier. It appeared God heard the hearts of our sons and sent a Christmas dog. Rascal was named, fed, and loved. She changed our family. This friendly dog rode with my mother to the post office. Rascal loved to accompany my husband on his ranch rounds. She escaped from the backyard to follow the children to school. Jumping upon the cinder tile fence, Rascal walked the perimeter and made her way to recess on a regular basis. With her sanguine personality, Rascal remained our adored pet for many years. A pet changes hearts.

~ Margaret G. Holmes

Margaret G. Holmes *is an education consultant, Christian leader, author, and speaker. Contact her at MHolmes1968@att.net.*

December 11

Quiet Bliss

I'm grateful for moments of quiet bliss with my dog, Rincon. Especially the game of Apple. On summer evenings I pick an apple from the tree in our backyard, bite off a piece, and throw it across the yard. Rincon tears after it. While he's gobbling up that piece, I take a quick bite for myself. Then I throw the next piece to the other side of the yard, and Rincon is a streak of Yellow Labrador lightning flashing in that direction. And so the game goes. I get roughly every other piece while Rincon zigzags his way across the yard, chasing down his share. When the game is over, we are both beaming. In Apple, there is nothing happening but beauty and fun. It's the simple stuff: the apple is juicy, the grass is green, the sky is sunset-y. A running dog is gorgeous and fluid—and a running dog you love is over-the-moon beautiful. Nothing is happening outside the game of Apple and the tiny backyard oasis that is the stadium for it—not even in my head. I am never thinking any further than the next bite. That's bliss—the quiet kind.

~ *Martia Nelson*

Martia Nelson, *life coach and author of* Coming Home: The Return to True Self, *guides professionals into richer, more joyful lives. For a free gift, visit MartiaNelson.com.*

December 12

A Treasured Gift

"Gratitude unlocks the fullness of life. It turns what we have into enough and more."

~ Melodie Beattie

I am grateful for the things I've received from my clients: for their trust in me; for their giving me the awareness I could become more than anything I'd imagined for myself; for their unwavering support; for the opportunity to serve them, and by doing so live in and be fulfilled by my purpose; for the experience of being filled with joy and awe as I watched them take control of their lives and step forward into their own bright, new futures.

I am filled with gratitude for the presence of these people in my life. Because of them, my life has changed immeasurably for the better. They've given me a gift of incalculable value: the gift of discovering I can step beyond any limits I've placed upon myself and move into a life of light and joy and peace and abundance. It's a gift freely given, one I treasure, and one I'll strive to pass on to others for the rest of my life.

~ *Janet Thomasson*

Janet Thomasson *helps people discover how to engineer the transformation they want to see in their lives. Connect with Janet at www.JanetThomasson.com to learn more.*

December 13

Roxy: Remembering with Gratitude

Roxy's routines rolled their way into my heart. I hadn't thought that would happen when two Maine Coon cats came to live with us. Melissa, her half-sister, was the cute one. Roxy would circle the bed to my husband's side and cross the headboard to my pillow, then curl up next to my heart. Her long fur needed daily brushing, so I'd sit on the floor, Roxy circling round until she just plopped. I'd call, "Plop?" each day, and she would come running. When I sat to meditate, she would squeeze into the two or so inches between me and the arm of the couch. Once Roxy must have sensed my nervousness as I meditated before a workshop presentation, and she rested her head on my thigh. Her soulful look spoke volumes. Roxy had a gentle spirit, and when she became very sick, she drew gentleness from me, teaching me about patience and kindness. The neurological symptoms came and went, yet she purred when she could. When Roxy became agitated, I'd sit in our recliner and hold her close. My heart and breath calmed her. Caring for Roxy became my expression of gratitude for her presence in my life.

~ *Edith Jaconsky-Hamersma*

Edith Jaconsky-Hamersma *is also grateful for discovering the labyrinth and mindfulness practice. She runs New England workshops on these. E-mail her at Hamersmae@yahoo.com.*

December 14

Candid Conversations with Cats

Looking into the bright, shiny eyes of my two cuddly kitties is like seeing a reflection of pure love and understanding, speaking to me through their numerous extraordinary expressions. Yes, I'm a self-proclaimed "cat person." I am grateful they're in my life because of their undeniably sweet characteristics, like quick wit, compassion for others, and the insatiable need to create mischief whenever possible, just to name a few.

Some people think it's crazy to have conversations with your pets. Well, experience tells me my cats, Maynard and Sebastian, comprehend everything I say, even if they decide to ignore me, which happens frequently. Maynard is the vocal one. His insistence on getting his way is almost human. His most common tirades are: "I want out now!" "I'm bored," and, his favorite, "I need a massage." Lately, his request to go out really means "I will hunt down a mouse and bring it to you as a peace offering!" Sebastian, on the other hand, enjoys being a stealth kitty, only talking when he really wants attention. "Comb me now" is his favorite expression. My cats have brought great joy and warmth into my life, and for that I am ever grateful.

~ *Sandy Anchondo*

Sandy Anchondo *is a professional interior decorator and home stager whose passion is making your design dreams a reality. You can find her at ReStyleInteriors.net.*

December 15

I'm Beating Diabetes

It's bad enough to contract an incurable disease, but then to be told that you could end up enduring a painful death, with the likelihood of amputations—at least a decade earlier than otherwise—is unbearable. The news of my type 2 diabetes diagnosis sent me into a state of despondent denial, particularly as I was not feeling any symptoms whatsoever.

I can't speak for the millions of people around the world who have received the same bleak news, but I sank into despair at this diagnosis. I felt like a dead man walking. There was so much information, so many new rules, so much to worry about.

And then, the most wonderful thing happened: I was given the news that even though the disease cannot be cured, it can be controlled. Suddenly, I realized I could still live life to fullest and the threat of the dreaded complications of this insidious disease could be averted. That was the moment when my heart filled with unbounded gratitude. Suddenly, I was beating diabetes, and I knew that I had a new mission: to tell others in the world how they can beat it, too.

~ Bill Eykyn

Bill Eykyn *is an author and broadcaster who lives in Spain. His latest book is* I'm Beating Diabetes...So Can You! *Find it at www.Amazon.com or www.ImBeatingDiabetes.com.*

December 16

Bunny Love

I've always wanted a bunny. I realized this the last time I went to visit my parents and looked around my old bedroom—it was full of stuffed and ceramic bunnies. In August 2006, I adopted a bunny that had been dumped in a park. I brought home the bunny, afraid of what I had gotten myself into, thinking that if someone dropped this bunny off in a park, surely it must be a bad bunny! I took it home and named it Stanley. I had two surprises in store: Stanley turned out to be a girl, and Stanley is the bunny by which all other bunnies will be measured. Stanley is a little bossy and doesn't let anyone push her around (not even our 93-pound dog), but she's also very affectionate. She licks my ankles when I'm sitting in the living room, greets me at the front door when I come home, and snuggles on the rug with me in the middle of the night when I can't sleep. Stanley has beautiful pink eyes and soft ears, and her pure white fur sparkles in the sunshine. Actually, there was a third surprise: I found out there is no love like bunny love.

~ *Marjorie Old*

Marjorie Old *lives in Vista, Calif., with her husband, three rescued bunnies, four hens, and a German Shepherd dog.*

December 17

Creating Space for Motherhood

Most couples can do it by themselves. For us, it took a team of 20 people, plenty of our time and money, plus God's intervention to get us pregnant. My biological clock started ticking the minute I turned 30.

Three years later, we still had no baby. We worked with a clinic and progressed to our first IVF. Negative. We were devastated. I got so busy trying to avoid the pain that I crammed hours and hours of work into my days.

Then I heard someone talking on a business teleseminar about creating space for your future dreams. I had an aha moment about our infertility: A baby would not fit into my life as it currently was, so I decided to create space for that baby. I intentionally got less busy, delegated everything except what only I could do, and freed myself up so that I was positioned for a baby.

IVF2 then happened. On Christmas Eve 2008, we found out that we had a positive pregnancy. Apparently I cleared space extremely well, as we were blessed with beautiful twins, a boy and a girl. Yes, our hands are full but, as the saying goes, so are our hearts.

~ *Marcia Francois*

Marcia Francois is a wife, mother of twins, time-management speaker, and coach who inspires overwhelmed women to passionately succeed in life and business at PurposefulTimeManagement.com.

December 18

My Magical Moments Journal

I believe life is made up of strings of moments that are occurring minute by minute. With our busy everyday lives it does take an extra ounce of effort to be present, and to notice and savor the magic and miracles that are happening all around. I am grateful and blessed to have discovered a simple way to capture, prolong, and enjoy these fleeting events. A few years ago I started a "magical moments journal" to capture and record the many amazing, magical moments and experiences that seemed to follow me everywhere. On a regular basis, sometimes daily, I take a few minutes to record in my journal everyday miracles such as: prayers answered, issues sorted, goals achieved, new and sudden insights, personal and client breakthroughs, milestones such as hitting a growth target like student enrollments or income levels, debts cleared, and all sorts of perfect moments and synchronicities. The more I keep track of these amazing experiences, the more I tend to notice how blessed I am. This has helped me to have a more positive outlook in life. Just flipping through and reviewing past entries helps me relive the moments further anchoring them.

~ *James N. Karundu*

James N. Karundu *is a speaker, author, and business mentor. He teaches top achievers and service-based entrepreneurs how to find, get, and keep high-paying clients. Visit www.about.me/JamesKarundu.*

December 19

Thanks for the Sign

"A 12-week, very rough ride," promised the renal specialist. Steroids, chemotherapy, plasmapheresis, and haemodialysis were ordered to counter this rare, aggressive, one-in-a-million, kidney-attacking autoimmune disease, Goodpasture's syndrome. Six weeks later, my wife, Kay, developed a nasty, metallic-taste sensation and almost lost her vision. She uncharacteristically refused her medication. The next day she had four epileptic seizures. She irrationally accused everyone of conspiracy. Goodpasture's was finally whipped. But with a compromised immune system Kay caught the flu, had chicken pox again, then developed a life-threatening infection on two heart valves. Open-heart surgery was imperative. Kay needed nightly peritoneal dialysis. But the inserted tubes became blocked. No surgeon was available on Christmas Eve. Distraught, Kay found comfort in her God. "How many more times will things go wrong?" she asked. "Lord, please send a sign that you have not abandoned me." After lunch, on Christmas Day—a beautiful summer's day—we sat out on the deck overlooking our semi-rural, Perth property. We noticed a large bird overhead. Binoculars confirmed it was an eagle. In 10 years at that residence we had never seen on eagle. This day it circled directly overhead for 20 minutes. "There's the asked-for sign," we agreed.

~ *Vivian G.J. Hill*

Vivian G.J. Hill *is a retired secondary school teacher who enjoys researching and writing. His latest book, not yet finished, details his wife's experiences resulting from her Goodpasture's syndrome ordeal.*

December 20

Dare to Be Joyful

In today's world of instant gratification, cyber-relationships, and virtual reality, happiness is temporary and almost impossible to achieve. Do we dare to seek lasting joy instead?

Webster's Dictionary defines "joy" as "delight." Doesn't that word speak to your soul? Joy is not an ephemeral feeling that disappears as soon as you sense it. It is a state of contentment that triumphs over time and circumstance, inviting you to experience it in every moment of your life. Joy promises much, yet delivers even more; it is delightful!

Delight is the outpouring of gratitude that comes from joy being shared. It is a deep awareness of what is truly valuable in life. When we cultivate intimate, joy-full relationships with God and each other, we will experience gratitude in even the simplest of things, such as the infectious laughter of a child. Now that's an expression of delight!

Joy does not come from abundance; abundance comes from joy. This radical, courageous mindset reveals that we have all we need—right now—to be joyful. All that is required from us are an open heart and a willingness to love in such a way that joy abounds.

Will you dare to be joyful?

~ *Sandra Harlow*

Sandra Harlow, *an attorney for over a decade, witnessed families tearing each other apart. Now, she coaches people all over the world, helping them to experience joy in their lives instead!*

December 21

Gratitude for Extra Time

Today, I am totally grateful to You, Dear God. Thank You for giving me extra time to represent You on Earth. I recognize that my fall on December 21, 2011, was not an accident. When I tripped and broke my ankle instead of my head, You let me know my mission was not finished yet.

Today, I desire to use my extra time wisely. I thank You for all blessings and will listen only to You for guidance. I ask to see Your light in all people on Earth and all creation.

Today, I thank You for giving me more time to practice forgiveness for myself, others, and so-called enemies.

Today, I come to You with an open heart. I accept Your help as I write about what has worked in my life, especially overcoming childhood abuse and post-traumatic stress disorder (PTSD). I desire to encourage all trauma victims to treat their old wounds, to release them, and to fill the empty space in their soul with hope and peace of mind.

Today, I thank You, God, for giving me the opportunity to serve You a little bit longer, and extend your love right here and right now.

~ Bettina Sparkles Obernuefemann

Bettina Sparkles Obernuefemann, *a retired flight attendant, developed a beautiful relationship with her Higher Power while recovering from childhood abuse. She's passing on the hope at BettinaSparkles.com.*

December 22

I Believe in You

What would life be without people? People are what give life joy, meaning, and purpose. I am grateful for the many people in my life.

At the top of my gratitude list is my mother. I am grateful for her unconditional love, and the values and lessons I learned from her.

I admire her courage, ambition, and determination. I am grateful that she instilled in me the values of love, honesty, and integrity.

My mother said, "You can be whatever you want. I believe in you."

She taught by example. When I was 8 years old we were living in a partly finished house. There were no steps to the front door. My father was away at work. Because we lived in the country, there were no service people available for hire. My mom said, "If I was a man I would build the steps myself," and then she did it. If she didn't know how to do something she would learn how by doing.

I am grateful for that lesson. Whenever I feel stuck, no matter what the problem, her words came back to me. It always makes me smile, and I do it anyway.

~ Barbara Macdonald

Barbara Macdonald is family person first. Professionally she is a teacher, life coach, and writer. Her passions are travel and connecting with people.

December 23

Gingerbread Houses

For the last 13 years my nieces (and now nephews) have come to my house to decorate a gingerbread house. It started with Danielle (now 15), and then her sister, Samantha (13 today!), was born and joined in. Then a few years later came Alexandria (now 7). Now we have her brothers, Dylan (5) and Jackson (3), too. Each child gets his or her own house, which my husband helps me put together the night before so that they are ready when the kids arrive. That way there is no waiting while the "glue" (frosting) dries. (They are simply too excited to wait; we learned that one the hard way the first couple years!) I put all the decorations in the center of the table, along with a couple plates of Christmas cookies to munch on while they decorate. The kids go home the next morning with a decorated gingerbread house, and I have memories of their laughter and creativity in my house until the next time. Danielle asked if we'll make gingerbread houses forever. I would love if they want to make gingerbread houses forever and ever! I could not be more grateful for this annual tradition.

~ *Jodi L. Brandon*

Jodi Brandon *is a book editor and writer living in the Philadelphia suburbs with her husband and their pup. Connect with her on Twitter and Facebook.*

December 24

Follow Your Heart

I have learned that starting my day with a prayer of gratitude before even opening my eyes helps my day go better. Some days it's a challenge.

The other morning was that challenge. I awoke on that hamster wheel of "poor me" thinking, when I received a call from my daughter sharing that she used me as an example recently to a friend. Her friend was struggling with a career choice, as she has young kids, and she felt torn, as some mothers do, when it comes to taking care of her children's needs and her own wants and needs.

My daughter shared that I had been an inspiration to her by going back to school while raising two daughters and that showed her that she could do it, too. She shared that she watched me follow my heart in my career path, which gave her the strength and courage to do what she loves. She told her friend that by following her heart, which may seem risky, she is giving her children a beautiful gift, as I had given to her, of being able to feel safe and loved as they follow the music of their own heart.

~ *Brenda Strong*

Brenda Strong lives in Washington. She enjoys spending time with her daughters and grandchildren, and helping people reach a higher state of being through forgiveness, joy and love.

December 25

Unconditional Self-Love

I am recognizing that the relationship I have with myself is the most important relationship of my life. I choose taking care of myself as priority moment by moment. Until recently I hadn't given much thought that love was something I had to choose for myself. I've lived my life by doing the best I can, unaware that the relationship with myself affects everything else. I am conscious that I am having a relationship with myself being my own best friend. As a woman I have been socialized to accept, admire, and express love by giving my energy, time, and companionship with little thought for myself. I've experienced a great deal of discomfort in giving to myself first. I was taught to love others more than myself and to look outside of myself for love. This has made it difficult for me to love myself unconditionally. I am grateful for the opportunity to feel what it means to truly grow, change, and provide unconditional love to family, friends, and most importantly myself. I find a deep, quiet place within myself and I practice getting still in relationship with this part of me. I feel the richness and abundance of me and my life by recognizing everything as a gift appreciating its value. To realize something is to give myself the potential to shift it, or at least to shift my relationship to it.

~ Melissa Rowe

Melissa Rowe *inspires/motivates women in their transitional process. She provides opportunities to reclaim their greatness and personal power and take action. She enables clients in recognizing their power from within. Email her at MRowe45@hotmail.com.*

December 26

3dB: God's Blessing

C an you imagine a mate who is a constant friend—a partner in the truest sense—someone who, in oneness, shares the adventure and excitement of life? For me, her name is Ella. It's not just the romantic that feeds life. Marriage involves two less-than-perfect people coming from separate backgrounds and living in a less-than-perfect world. Good marriages don't just happen. They take resolve.

Ella makes it seem simple. She shows me that individual strengths provide opportunity for mutual mentorship. Ella is the most beautiful and generous person I have ever known. Her heart and mind inspire me.

Ella has made our home one of love, understanding, and patience—never to remain the same, but growing better and stronger with the passing of time, and through the love we share. Her love defines "accepting you the way you are, respecting you as a whole person with your own interests, desires, and needs." My wife gives me encouragement, strength, and trust, on our walk together, throughout all our tomorrows—in our times of joy and of sorrow.

I don't have to imagine! My wife, Ella, has given this to me.

~ *Warren L. Henderson, Jr.*

Warren L. Henderson, Jr. *is the owner of Bridges 2 Empowerment life coaching and author of* 3dB of Life: Transformational Lessons in Cycles of Success. *Email him at WarrenHCL@gmail.com.*

December 27

The Goddess Within Me

"At times our own light goes out and is rekindled by a spark from another person. Each of us has cause to think with deep gratitude of those who have lighted the flame within us."

~ Albert Schweitzer

With deepest gratitude to the Lady of the Lake who blessed me by healing my broken spirit and lighting my inner flame. She set me back on the path to my calling and purpose with grace and gentleness. When I stumbled she extended her hand to lift me up and see the light that was before me. As I stumbled through the darkness that was within me, she held the torch high above so I could see the pathway that was before me. As I faced my inner demons, she stood by my side to support me and encourage me. Her divine blessings assisted me to put my pieces back together again, stronger than before. Here I now stand, humbled and vulnerable with a deep inner strength and knowingness that my flame burns true, That I Am the Goddess Within.

Blessings to all those still searching for the Goddess Within and to all those who have found her.

Thank you.

~ Carol Watson

Carol Watson, *after the devastation of burnout, reconnected with her own divine power. She blends practical knowledge and intuitive abilities to assist individuals to manifest their greatness. Contact her at www.CarolWatson.ca or ArianMor@gmail.com.*

December 28

An Ear, a Smile!

I am happy and grateful I am able to bring a smile to a tired, anxious, exhausted, and sometimes-tearful face.

I work as a naturopath. Each day I sit beside my clients and hear their stories. I hear joy, and I hear despair. I hear of giving up, and more often than not I hear that I am a last try. I take no offense! I am grateful they end up at my door.

There is nothing better than having tears turn into a smile. Nothing better than hearing the words "I feel better just having spoken with you!"

Sometimes a health concern is not about the body. It may be about relationships, personalities, or money. Together, let's get started on a fix. Sometimes people just need to have someone to hear them—to know they have value, and that their opinions and feelings matter.

I can talk—a lot! But I can also listen. And for that skill, I am ever grateful.

~ *Jeanette Shipston*

Jeanette Shipston of Laidley, Queensland, a naturopath, nutritional medicine specialist, and owner of HealthNette—Health & Wellness Clinics. More health! More wealth! More happiness! Whatever that means for you! Learn more at www.HealthNette.com.au.

December 29

Weather or Not

I am grateful for intolerable climates. Really. When I lived in Minnesota, the best day of the year was the first seriously warm spring day when I felt safe to go out without a coat, confident that I could not be chilled. I loved feeling the sun on my cheekbones and seeing the new lime-green leaves. The early bit of moisture helped my skin revive after a desperately dry winter.

Now I live in Louisiana and everything is reversed. The best day of the year is in late October when I feel the first hint of coolness after a sauna-like summer. Fall air in my lungs for the first time is dry enough to allow me, finally, to breathe deeply without choking. A few leaves might even turn orange, chrysanthemums proliferate, and my skin never cracks or flakes.

It's not that I crave cold, hot, wet, or dry in itself. What I love and am grateful for is the simple reality of change that restores balance. Growing up in California, I never understood that weather is related to my soul. Without contrast, no joys like these exist. Only true discomfort can make comfort so sweet, and for that I am grateful.

~ *Patricia Drury Sidman*

Patricia Drury Sidman is a Louisiana-based writer, actor, spiritual advisor, and life coach who explores the many ways humans flounder, change, and sometimes thrive. Reach her at Facebook.com/Patricia. Drury.Sidman.Personal.

December 30

Career Do-Over

I am grateful for a career do-over and a husband who is with me every step of the way—even when he might have doubts.

It would have been so nice to have a crystal ball when I was 20 and in college! I chose a great life in most aspects, but the jobs always lacked, especially as I grew older. Increasingly I longed to be on my own—an entrepreneur to follow my own dreams and not a captive to someone else's whims.

But finally the stars aligned and I listened to my heart. I was able to seize the opportunity to quit my job outright and leave that world behind—literally! We moved 2,000 miles across the country toward the outdoor lifestyle we craved, and I started a business to serve other women business owners and aspiring entrepreneurs.

As difficult as being an entrepreneur can be, I wake each day excited by the prospect of working on my business, helping other women learn to market their businesses for success. My husband is by my side, as a sounding board, assistant, cheerleader, and whatever else I need him to be—a true gem.

The word "grateful" seems so inadequate.

~ Joan F. Muschamp

Joan F. Muschamp *of LemonZest Marketing takes her 35+ years' experience and teaches you how to Zest Your Marketing™. A skilled marketing strategist, speaker, author, and trainer, find her at www.LemonZestMarketing.com.*

December 31

Each Day an Amazing Opportunity

"You can have everything in life that you want if you will just help enough other people get what they want."

~ Zig Ziglar

Daily, I journey to my office for the opportunity as a CPA to have businesses owners pay me for my advice and counsel. I experience my clients' life work, their joys and sorrows, their family's tribulations almost like extended family.

My position as their CPA allows me to develop a trusted, significant relationship that I hold dear with these clients. As their most trusted business advisor, I get the amazing opportunity to watch as their businesses thrive—businesses that are the lifeblood of a community, giving a better life to the owners, their family, and the employees and their families.

It is an unimaginable joy and privilege to see these companies prosper, knowing I have had a part in making this happen. It is an absolute favor from God that I have the daily good fortune to have a career that affords me this unbelievable opportunity.

~ *Samantha Plank*

Samantha Plank *is a CPA and business coach who helps small business owners and their businesses thrive. Get in touch with her at www. SamanthaPlank.com or www.MyCPAPlus.com.*

The Gratitude Book Project®

is proud to donate its net proceeds
from retail sales to the following organizations:

Women for Women International

who supports women in war-torn regions with financial and
emotional aid, job-skills training, rights education,
and small business assistance so they can rebuild their lives

Feeding America

whose mission is to feed America's hungry
through a nationwide network of member food banks
and engage our country in the fight to end hunger

American Society for the Prevention of Cruelty to Animals (A.S.P.C.A.)

providing effective means for the prevention of cruelty to animals

The Gratitude Book Project® team
thanks you for being a part of supporting these
worthwhile charities.

For more information please contact
Support@TheGratitudeBookProject.com.

Want to be a published author?

Book writing, publishing and consulting services we provide include:

Write Your Book

Write a Book in a Weekend® is an online, virtual course that guides you in writing a "short and powerful" book in two days with pre-formatted templates, how-to information, and expert guidance. Find out more at WriteWithDonna.com.

Publish Your Book

Done for You™ Publishing Services offers everything from editing, proofreading, interior formatting, and cover design, while providing personal connection and top-rate customer service. Find out more at DoneForYouPublishing.com.

Get Answers to Your Book Writing and Publishing Questions

If you're struggling with what to write about or organizing your material, or if you're frustrated because you can't find answers about how the book publishing process works, get a "Big Breakthrough Session" with two-time award-winning author and publishing expert Donna Kozik. More at MyBigBreakthroughSession.com.

Get Started Now

Download your free book planner at
www.FreeBookPlanner.com

Acknowledgments

Thank you to the following for making The Gratitude Book Project® possible:

- Members of The Gratitude Book Project® Team: Jodi Brandon, Becky Cohen, Donna Kozik, Deanna McAdams and Susan Veach.

- Non-profit organizations Women for Women International, Feeding America, and the ASPCA.

- Print on demand specialists Lightning Source, an Ingram Content Group company.

- Amazon.com

- All the co-authors of this 2014 edition—we are grateful for you!

Get Your
FREE
Gratitude
Journal!

Get your journal at
www.TheGratitudeBookProject.com.